Love and Thunder:
A Spirituality
of the Old Testament

John F. Craghan, C.SS.R.

The Liturgical Press   Collegeville, Minnesota

ACKNOWLEDGMENTS

Scripture texts used in this work are taken from the NEW AMERICAN BIBLE, copyright © 1970, by the Confraternity of Christian Doctrine, Washington, D.C., and are used by license of copyright owner. All rights reserved.

Chapter 8 of this book was originally published in *Emmanuel* 86 (1980) 39–50 and is reprinted by permission in substantially the same form. Chapter 19 of this book was originally published in *Biblical Theology Bulletin* 12 (1982) 11–19 and is reprinted by permission in substantially the same form. Chapters 9 and 11 were originally published in somewhat different form in *Emmanuel* 86 (1980) 639–648 and 87 (1981) 611–616 respectively.

Library of Congress Cataloging in Publication Data

Craghan, John F.
    Love and thunder, a spirituality of the Old Testament.

    Includes bibliographical references and indexes.
    1. Bible. O.T.—Criticism, interpretation, etc.
2. Spirituality.   I. Title.
BS1171.2.C7 1983   230′.2   82-25903
ISBN 0-8146-1279-2 (pbk.)

To
BARBARA LYNNE
in
deep gratitude and affection
for
having learned much
about
response to the Word of God in community

CONTENTS

PREFACE

Spirituality, and especially biblical spirituality, is a subject that continues to claim a wide audience. Many experience the need to be nourished by the Word of God in their daily lives. They seek the challenge of the text, that is, the opportunity to reflect on the biblical text and then express that reflection in communal living. The Word of God is as necessary and as vital today as ever.

The God of the Old Testament is also the God of the New Testament, a God who continues to manifest loving concern. That God is also one who jealously insists on our faithful response. The title *Love and Thunder* attempts to capture both dimensions of God's involvement. At the same time love and thunder affect us as members of the believing community. We are exhorted to receive divine love and then translate it into loving concern for others. We are urged to hear divine thunder and respond in fidelity to the covenant. Our response to the Word of God in community is thus touched by both love and thunder.

This book is the result of courses I have given at Fordham University, Bronx, New York, at St. Norbert College, De Pere, Wisconsin, and at St. Joseph College, West Hartford, Connecticut. I have attempted to make the text contagious by suggesting how it may relate to the key questions we pose about ourselves and our communities. This book, therefore, is but a modest effort to let the Word of God have an impact on the various dimensions of our lives. It presupposes that we can read ancient texts in a new setting and be enriched in the process.

The text is the thing! At the start of each chapter I indicate the biblical passages to be read. There is absolutely no substitute for knowing the text. Hence the reader is urged to study these passages before proceeding to the exposition of the material.

In general, at the beginning of each chapter I seek to state our apprehensions, fears, and reactions to different aspects of life. In some respects this is a brief survey of common human experiences. I then present the Old Testament material which I judge to be applicable to the difficulties and questions raised in the survey. Finally I attempt to reflect on how the Old Testament traditions can be employed in our everyday living. Not infrequently this includes an appreciation of the person and work of Jesus as found in the New Testament.

This book is not intended for the biblicist but rather for all those non-specialists who wish to be enriched by the advances in biblical studies. Rather than distract the reader with long verbatim quotes, I have chosen to list bibliographical suggestions at the end of each chapter. These suggestions will indicate my great debt to many authors. At the same time I have tried to present the results of a critical study of the Old Testament in such a way that a solid spirituality is linked to a scientific analysis of these ancient texts. This implies that spirituality and exegesis are remarkably compatible.

I wish to express my gratitude to the Rev. Paul J. Bernier, S.S.S., editor of *Emmanuel,* for the copyrights to several articles that appeared in that magazine. I am also indebted to the Rev. David M. Bossman, O.F.M., editor of *Biblical Theology Bulletin,* for the copyright to a paper which was published in that journal. In a very special way I am grateful to the Rev. Daniel Durken, O.S.B., director of The Liturgical Press, for his suggestions in developing an Old Testament spirituality.

Finally I have the pleasant task of acknowledging my profound appreciation and gratitude to Barbara L. Wenzel. Her encouragement, good humor, and constructive criticisms provided the enthusiasm to see this work through to completion. This effort, therefore, is a testimony to her indomitable spirit.

John F. Craghan, C.SS.R.

Tulsa, Oklahoma
Easter, 1982

INTRODUCTION

The Old Testament, or the first half of the Christian Bible, is not a manual of spirituality. It is, rather, a collection of various responses to the God of Israel. Over a period exceeding a millennium Israel encountered its God in moments of hope and despair, in periods of unusual prosperity and national catastrophe. Israel's response—or lack of response—provides the inspiration and the norms from which a biblical spirituality can develop.

The term "spirituality" is misleading. It seems to evoke a unilinear pattern of response. However, since spirituality is rooted in actual life, there must necessarily emerge a variety of responses. The individual writers as well as the particular circumstances of their writing combine to offer a possibility of different spiritualities.

CREATION THEOLOGY

In salvation theology we tend to exalt God and put down humans. God appears as the great intervenor who supplies panaceas for a sinful people. Creation theology emphasizes humans as actors and actresses in an ongoing plan. The arena of activity is God's world—our world. Creation theology is a theology of trust, not a retreat into utilitarianism. In creation theology our task is to make our world a more human world. By the same token, when God does "save," that saving or redemption is subsumed under ongoing creation. Redemption, therefore, has to do with creation and the element of trust.

THE FEMININITY OF GOD

Although the Hebrew Bible lacks a word for "goddess" and consistently uses masculine pronouns for Yahweh, the imagery, however, is not only masculine but also feminine. Thus God is the pregnant woman, mother, midwife, and mistress. A solely masculine understanding of Yahweh is a distortion. Only an appropriate blend of male and female imagery offers the basis for a sound hermeneutic and hence a sound spirituality.

COVENANT: THE CALL TO COMMUNITY

Covenant grounds humans in Another who initiates personhood and remains bound to those humans in an unrelenting loyalty. Covenant implies that Yahweh takes the covenant partner seriously. However, since covenant is never a one-to-one relationship, covenant insists that true community emerges only when other humans receive our loyalty. Hence, we mature only insofar as we contribute to the community. The autonomous Israelite is a contradiction in terms.

Law is part of the covenant experience. Israel's contribution in its legal formulations was to insist on an I-Thou relationship. Law could never become an objective fulfillment of a positive command or the avoidance of a prohibition. Rather, law was response to the God of the covenant and hence to the community. Israel's history, however, teaches us the aberration of law whereby obligation becomes an end in itself and not something constitutive for God and the community. In this way we can fathom the predicament of Paul and at the same time learn that legal response must be a response to Another and others in community. To fulfill obligations merely because they are commanded and to avoid things/persons merely because they are commanded are a caricature of responsibility and human freedom. Israel's legal history is an important chapter in spirituality.

PROPHECY

People can become numb to the evil around them. People can be manipulated to adopt the "normal" pattern. When people cease being people and God is reduced to a caricature, Israel's prophets emerge as the great critics. A sound spirituality calls for a proper evaluation of one's world and one's reaction to that world. A sound spirituality beckons for God's outlook on reality. It is as prophet that the Christian responds to such challenges. Not to accept the challenge is to be a dropout from history.

The prophetic task must also be energizing. Where despair sets in and national catastrophe is a reality, prophets such as Jeremiah, Ezekiel, and Second Isaiah undertake a program of reconstruction. Such a program is calculated to offer hope and assurance to God's people that catastrophe is a means, not an end. In turn, a sound spirituality seeks to be positive and constructive. Disaster is not meant to be God's final word.

PSALMS

In its laments Israel did not have to fake it. Israel boldly communicated its pain to Yahweh and expected Yahweh to be more than an interested bystander. Covenant implies response to pain and frustration. The individual and communal laments show how suffering can be redemptive, hence creative. In the laments of Jeremiah (the "Confessions") we learn of the demands of prophetic ministry but also of the possibilities of spiritual transformation. The lament, whether in the Psalter or the Book of Jeremiah, continues to be a source of renewal.

Because creation is an ongoing reality and our lives are part of that reality, the hymns of the Psalter must not be overlooked. To praise God is to break out of one's hell of isolation into the world of communal response. The hymns are a challenge, not only to uncover the beauty of God in the world of nature, but more importantly to discover that very God in the gifts and talents of others. To uncover such gifts and to make them known is to say with the Priestly Writer: "It is good, very good!" A spirituality without praise is no spirituality.

WISDOM

Wisdom is a biblical category which is a corollary of creation theology. Wisdom asserts that the meaning of life is not survival or security but healthy community. People are to be both free and responsible in communication with others. Wisdom maintains that we can rely on our own experience, that we must look at the world with discerning eyes and try to uncover the order that is there or should be there. Wisdom holds that God trusts people and grants them primary responsibility for their own destiny and the destiny of their community. Wisdom believes that people are to enjoy, celebrate, and appreciate life and recognize that culture is a gift of God. Finally, wisdom confesses that people are the highpoint of God's creative activity and so they can and must face head-on the challenges of life.

In the Book of Job, JIP (Job the Impatient), unlike the conventional pious man of antiquity, will claim a communications leak from on high whereby God does not distinguish between the righteous and the unrighteous. JIP will be reprimanded but he must also be congratulated for noting the inadequacy of the equation: righteousness = success. Job is also instructive on the meaning of friendship. A friend is one who is loyal, not only when a person loses faith in the Almighty, but also when taking a stand with such a friend against the onslaughts of the Almighty.

HUMAN LOVE

The Song of Songs is a collection of love poems. The Song implies that believers must accept their sexuality openly and without guilt or fear. The Song also teaches that believers must incorporate their sexuality into a vision of faith. It must be a vision of faith that acknowledges that God is the author of human love, of human sexual love, of human sexual erotic love.

The human love in the Song is a force which compels one to go out of oneself, flee the world of isolation, and join in the hymn of creation in Genesis 1. It is the world of community where eros is person-oriented, not thing-oriented. Eros is union with another, not mere pleasure acquired through another.

Ultimately the Bible is the distillation of personal religious experience. The reaction of the Yahwist, the laments of Jeremiah, and the seeming iconoclasm of Job are not filtered through a "conform to the deity" norm. In the Bible God chooses to communicate, not simply through a people, but through a sinful people. Frequently the "wrong" religious experience of Israel's heroes and heroines is more telling for our modern world than a Procrustean conformity. The judgment of both the synagogue and the church in canonizing these texts is at least a clue that they have enduring human value because they are typically human experiences of the divine.

ABBREVIATIONS OF BOOKS OF THE BIBLE

Acts	Acts of the Apostles	2 Kgs	Second Kings
Am	Amos	Lam	Lamentations
Bar	Baruch	Lk	Luke
1 Chr	First Chronicles	Lv	Leviticus
2 Chr	Second Chronicles	Mal	Malachi
Col	Colossians	1 Mc	First Maccabees
1 Cor	First Corinthians	2 Mc	Second Maccabees
2 Cor	Second Corinthians	Mi	Micah
Dn	Daniel	Mk	Mark
Dt	Deuteronomy	Mt	Matthew
Eccl	Ecclesiastes	Na	Nahum
Eph	Ephesians	Neh	Nehemiah
Est	Esther	Nm	Numbers
Ex	Exodus	Ob	Obadiah
Ez	Ezekiel	Phil	Philippians
Ezr	Ezra	Phlm	Philemon
Gal	Galatians	Prv	Proverbs
Gn	Genesis	Ps(s)	Psalm(s)
Hb	Habakkuk	1 Pt	First Peter
Heb	Hebrews	2 Pt	Second Peter
Hg	Haggai	Qoh	Qoheleth
Hos	Hosea	Rom	Romans
Is	Isaiah	Ru	Ruth
Jas	James	Rv	Revelation
Jb	Job	Sg	Song of Songs
Jdt	Judith	Sir	Sirach
Jer	Jeremiah	1 Sm	First Samuel
Jgs	Judges	2 Sm	Second Samuel
Jl	Joel	Tb	Tobit
Jn	John	1 Thes	First Thessalonians
1 Jn	First John	2 Thes	Second Thessalonians
2 Jn	Second John	Ti	Titus
3 Jn	Third John	1 Tm	First Timothy
Jon	Jonah	2 Tm	Second Timothy
Jos	Joshua	Wis	Wisdom
Jude	Jude	Zec	Zechariah
1 Kgs	First Kings	Zep	Zephaniah

ABBREVIATIONS OF JOURNALS, SERIES, ETC.

AB	Anchor Bible
AnBib	Analecta Biblica
ANQ	*Andover Newton Quarterly*
BA	*Biblical Archaeologist*
Bib	*Biblica*
BJRL	*Bulletin of the John Rylands University Library of Manchester*
BZAW	Beihefte zur *ZAW*
CBQ	*Catholic Biblical Quarterly*
HeyJ	*Heythrop Journal*
HomPastR	*Homiletic and Pastoral Review*
HTR	*Harvard Theological Review*
HUCA	*Hebrew Union College Annual*
IB	*Interpreter's Bible*
IDBSup	Supplementary Volume to *Interpreter's Dictionary of the Bible*
Int	*Interpretation*
JAAR	*Journal of the American Academy of Religion*
JBC	*Jerome Biblical Commentary*
JBL	*Journal of Biblical Literature*
JSOT	*Journal for the Study of the Old Testament*
NAB	*New American Bible*
OTL	Old Testament Library
OTS	*Oudtestamentische Studien*
SBLDS	Society of Biblical Literature Dissertation Series
SBLMS	Society of Biblical Literature Monograph Series
SBT	Studies in Biblical Theology
ScrB	*Scripture Bulletin*
TD	*Theology Digest*
TS	*Theological Studies*
TToday	*Theology Today*
VT	*Vetus Testamentum*
VTS	Supplements to *Vetus Testamentum*
ZAW	*Zeitschrift fur die alttestamentliche Wissenschaft*

CHAPTER 1

The Invitation to Biblical Spirituality

A WORKING DESCRIPTION

For many of us the word "spirituality" too often connotes the esoteric, the unique, the more than ordinary. It thus becomes the flight from earthly concerns into a world where we least-common-denominator mortals dare not tread. The word seems to conjure up visions and revelations where only a few initiates are selected to commune with God. In such a world the relationship is one-on-one.

From a theological perspective, however, spirituality means response to the Word of God. In Hebrew the word for "word" (*dābār*) includes event, deed, happening. In this sense the Exodus and the Incarnation are "words" of God. Spirituality implies letting these events, deeds, happenings have an impact on our total humanity. Since such "words" look to the common good, the relationship is never one-on-one—it is always community oriented.

As J. N. Wijngaards has observed, biblical spirituality is the communitarian response to the Word contained in the Scriptures. From a negative viewpoint we are not engaged in drawing up a list of virtues or a catalogue of the qualities of prayer. From a positive viewpoint we are involved in a multiplicity of responses which possess all the flavor of real life. The Scriptures deal with real people caught up in typically human situations. It is precisely such situations which become the raw material of biblical spirituality.

A biblical spirituality of the Old Testament narrows the field of concentration to the first half of the Christian Bible. In the division of the Hebrew Bible this field embraces: (1) the Torah or Pentateuch (Genesis through Deuteronomy); (2) the Prophets, both Former (Joshua through Second Kings) and Latter (Isaiah through Malachi); and (3) the Writings (a generic term including Job, Psalms, Daniel, Chronicles, etc.). In the literature of the ancient Near East

1

the Old Testament is unique in that Israel knew Yahweh in a way which was not true of the pagans vis-à-vis their gods. The God of Israel is uniquely personal, alive, and involved in the world of his/ her people. The Old Testament preserves the record of Israel's response or, more often than not, the lack of response to such a vibrant God. A biblical spirituality of the Old Testament is thus bound up with a real God interacting with real people in real situations.

The Old Testament dimension of spirituality is fundamentally an expression of trust in our community since that community offers the Old (as well as the New) Testament as model for a variety of responses. While reacting to the Word of God in community, we are at the same time acknowledging our link with the past—here the experience of Israel. Spirituality thus becomes a present reflection of a past record in view of future needs. A consoling aspect of this past record is that God chooses to be revealed not simply through a people but through a sinful people. We ordinary mortals, therefore, do not find it exceedingly difficult to identify with this God.

THE ROLE OF CANON

By speaking of the community which offers us the biblical experience, we are necessarily speaking of the role of canon in our lives. As applied to the Bible, canon means that authoritative and definitive list of books which are regarded not only as words of humans but also as the Word of God. Out of a larger body of literature the Jewish community selected certain works which it recognized as significant for the history and welfare of that community. (The Roman Catholic canon has added to that selection.) When compared with the extant literature of the ancient Near East, the Old Testament writings possess something extra, a certain plus-value. While the Old Testament has much in common with these ancient works in terms of language, thought patterns, and basic human needs, it parts company with its neighbors by reason of the plus-value. Biblical spirituality is necessarily a study in the significance of canon and hence the plus-value.

J. A. Sanders has made notable contributions to our understanding of canon. For him stability and adaptability characterize canon. Thus the canonical story is one which can and must be repeated. Canon seeks to be remembered, to be contemporized. By its very nature canon seeks to provide answers to these questions: (1) who am I? and (2) what should I do? Canon presupposes that an event, deed, happening—a "word"—has transpired and that it must continue to exercise an impact on the believing community. Ultimately canon offers answers to the question of identity.

When we reflect on our own experience, we realize that certain past events have the power to energize us, to give us hope, to supply

2

us with the courage to continue coping. These events may capture the experience of happiness when everything fell perfectly into place and we were able to see the maze of life against the background of a meaningful pattern. These events may recall the experience of catastrophe when the bottom fell out of life and we sought in vain to pull the pieces together. These experiences serve as our own canon. At the same time they challenge us to pool our experiences with the experiences of the larger community.

In drawing up the canon of the Old Testament the Jewish community chose experiences that related to most of the people. They were experiences that had the radical capacity to empower the people. Hence they were experiences that met a common need. Canon possesses resiliency and suitability—it is able to span and interlock centuries. The experiences of the monarchy in Jerusalem could apply to times when God's people were no longer politically independent. Time is not able to impoverish the ability of the canonical experiences to speak to the needs and desires of later generations. Canon is resolutely opposed to any and every form of generation gap.

EXAMPLES OF CANONICAL EXPERIENCES

According to J. A. Sanders the Pentateuch itself is a parade example of the canonical experience. Although it is likely that the early authors of the Genesis stories concluded with Israel's possession of the Promised Land (now found in the Book of Joshua), the Pentateuch recites the account of God's people outside the land of Canaan. Deuteronomy 34 reveals Israel in the plains of Moab—hence outside the Promised Land. In this way the Pentateuch serves as a primer for coping. Deprived of political autonomy, Israel must learn to deal with the new situation. The Pentateuch is calculated to proffer courage and hope. It is a stimulus to have continuity within discontinuity.

Religious communities share the canonical experience of the founder or foundress. Language, customs, and circumstances—to name only a few—separate the modern religious community from the pioneer days. Yet the religious community continues to recite the initial experiences as well as the ongoing experiences. Though there may be drastic changes, the community seeks to link itself with the past. The canonical experience thus offers both identity and hope.

Families share canonical experiences. There may be the hard times of immigration and the subsequent struggle to survive both religiously and economically in new surroundings. The experiences are a weave of great successes and colossal failures. The skeletons in the closet cannot remain there! The family canonical experiences seek to elicit courage when times are hard and to promote identity when times are easy and the danger of forgetting is rampant. A

3

biblical spirituality, therefore, is heir to our human need to know ourselves, to prod ourselves, to share ourselves.

HERMENEUTICS

How does one deal concretely with canon or the canonical experience? Is it sufficient to respond to the following questions? (1) in what circumstances did the original author work? and (2) what message did the original author communicate? While the answers to these questions are necessary for assessing and understanding the texts, by themselves they are inadequate. Scripture is more than the neutral, painstaking study of ancient texts. Scripture goes beyond the penetrating search for the original meaning of classical literature. Interpretation must also mean that the text speaks to us today. To isolate the thought of Isaiah of Jerusalem will not do. To have Isaiah of Jerusalem speak to us today is also demanded.

Hermeneutics is the delicate science that endeavors, for example, to have an eighth century B.C. prophet speak to a rather disparate twentieth century A.D. audience. Hermeneutics is the science of determining how the thought or event in one cultural context may be understood in another and different cultural context. Among others S. M. Schneiders has insisted on the nature of a text. A text is more than the aggregate of meaning from the distant past. A text not only contains meaning, it also mediates meaning. This implies that a text in some way exceeds the meaning of the human author. Disengaged from its ancient setting, a text is capable of bearing a new meaning, although one related in some manner to the ancient audience.

S. M. Schneiders suggests that the task implied in hermeneutics is to engage the question behind a text. This presupposes questions larger than those addressed by the original author. For example, Genesis 3 seems to focus on the larger question of coping with limitations and thereby resisting the temptation to infinity, viz., to become the biggest and the best. Hermeneutics seeks to bring the ancient and modern audiences together. The legacy of the past must bear on the needs of the present.

The legacy is rich. The beauty of the canon, among other things, is its richness of models and forms. When we are tempted to say, "Well, that's the only way to go!" the canon reminds us—and reminds us forcefully—that there are often other possibilities. Thus, when we are prone to insist on God's assuming direct control of all human events, the wisdom literature insists that humans can and do make a difference. When we are liable to favor the exuberance of hymns (psalms of descriptive praise) in the Psalter, the entire collection suggests that we must also proffer our pain and frustration in the timely expression of lamentation. Which model to choose, which

4

form to follow or adapt will always remain a problem. However, canon is the ongoing challenge never to be satisfied with only one possible model or form.

This book is basically an exercise in the pluralism and multiformity of the canon. It attempts to reflect on dimensions of spirituality that we may prefer to put aside. It tries to uncover patterns and models that do not fit neatly into our response to the Word of God in community.

ANTHROPOLOGY

When speaking of spirituality, we are apt to think of a head trip, a cerebral undertaking that relates only to our thinking powers and nothing else. For the biblical authors, however, humans are not the sum of their parts. They are not compartmentalized into higher and lower faculties. They are not departmentalized into body and soul. In the Old Testament (as well as the New Testament) the entire person comes under the impact of God's Word. To heed that Word is to let God involve our total humanity. To disregard that Word is to refuse to let God involve our total humanity. Hence response to the Word of God in community is always the response of the entire person.

The biblical authors, however, view the entire person from different perspectives. For example, "flesh" often implies the person with a history of sin and weakness (see Gn 6:3). Consequently the total person must experience God's redemption (note Jn 1:14: "The Word became flesh . . ."). "Spirit" frequently means the person as open to the sphere of God's activity (see Is 31:3; Ez 3:24). Hence the whole person makes himself/herself the recipient of God's power. "Heart" is the organ of volition or willing. When the human heart is warped, the person is warped (see Gn 6:5). The word usually translated "soul" often means the entire person viewed as the thinking, conscious self. When the psalmist states in Ps 6:4, "My soul, too, is utterly terrified . . . ," he is stating he is totally frightened. A sound biblical spirituality demands the response of our whole person.

BIBLIOGRAPHICAL SUGGESTIONS

Brown, Raymond E. "The Meaning of the Bible," *TD* 28 (1980) 305–320.

Cherian, C. M. " 'Now My Eye Sees Thee': The Bible as a Record of Religious Experience," *Review for Religious* 32 (1973) 1002–1011.

Coats, George W. & Long, Burke O. (eds.). *Canon and Authority: Essays in Old Testament Religion and Theology.* Philadelphia: Fortress, 1977.

Croix, P. - M. de la. *Spirituality of the Old Testament.* New York: Herder & Herder, 1966.

Crossan, John D. "Waking the Bible: Biblical Hermeneutic and Literary Imagination," *Int* 32 (1978) 269–285.

Fiorenza, Elisabeth S. "'For the Sake of Our Salvation. . . .' Biblical Interpretation as Theological Task," *Sin, Salvation, and the Spirit.* Edited by D. Durken. Collegeville: The Liturgical Press, 1979, 21-39.

MacKenzie, Roderick A. F. "The Self-Understanding of the Exegete," *Concilium* 70 (1971) 11-19.

McEvenue, Sean E. "The Old Testament, Scripture or Theology?" *Int* 35 (1981) 229-242.

Montague, George T. "Hermeneutics and the Teaching of Scripture," *CBQ* 41 (1979) 1-17.

Ricoeur, Paul. "Biblical Hermeneutics," *Semeia* 4 (1975) 108-135.

Robinson, John A. T. *The Body. A Study in Pauline Theology.* SBT. London: SCM, 1952.

Sanders, James A. *Torah and Canon.* 2nd edition. Philadelphia: Fortress, 1974.

_____ . "Reopening the Old Questions about Scripture," *Int* 28 (1974) 321-330.

_____ . "Torah and Christ," *Int* 29 (1975) 372-390.

_____ . "Hermeneutics," *IDBSup,* 402-408.

_____ . "Adaptable for Life: The Nature and Function of Canon," *Magnalia Dei. The Mighty Acts of God. Essays on the Bible and Archaeology in Memory of G. Ernest Wright.* Edited by F. M. Cross, Jr. et al. Garden City: Doubleday, 1976, 531-560.

_____ . "Text and Canon," *JBL* 98 (1979) 5-29.

Schneiders, Sandra M. "Faith, Hermeneutics, and the Literal Sense of Scripture," *TS* 39 (1978) 719-736.

_____ . "From Exegesis to Hermeneutics: The Problem of the Contemporary Meaning of Scripture," *Horizons* 8 (1981) 23-39.

Wijngaards, Joanne N. "Biblical Spirituality," *ScrB* 9, #1 (Summer, 1978) 9-14; #3 (Winter, 1979) 32-36.

Wolff, Hans W. *Anthropology of the Old Testament.* Philadelphia: Fortress, 1974.

CHAPTER 2

The Invitation to Image God

Biblical passages to be read: Gn 1:1-2:4a; 3:21; 5:1-2; 43:24-34;
Ex 16:4-36; 17:1-7; 34:1-9; Nm 11:1-15, 31-35; 20:2-13; Dt 8:1-5;
32:15-29; 2 Kgs 16; Neh 9:16-22; Ps 103; Is 1:2-3; 30:1-5; 42:
10-25; 49:8-26; 66:7-16; Jer 3; 31:15-22; Hos 1-3; 11.

STATE OF THE QUESTION

In responding to the Word of God in community, in being challenged by its wealth of traditions, we are responding to the person
of our God. Spirituality is never the relentless search for a thing, it
is always the unending pursuit of the person of our God (and of people
as they related to God and ourselves). The questions that spontaneously suggest themselves are: who is this God? is this God perfectly
neuter? is this God somehow not only masculine but also feminine?
what does it really mean to image this God? how can divine qualities
become human qualities?

The canon constitutes a challenge. In relating to our God, we
are naturally conditioned by our culture and religious heritage. We
certainly know God as father. Many of us feel content to stop there,
reasoning that to adopt a feminist stance towards our God is both
unsavory and misguided. On the other hand, the canon forces us
to pause, to investigate new insights, to raise more questions, and
hopefully to gain in the process. To evade the implications of the
canon is to avoid appreciating and loving our God. Ultimately we
must be as big and as tolerant as the canon.

YAHWEH'S UNIQUENESS AND HUMAN THEOLOGIZING

The religion of the ancient Near East was nature religion. The
fertility of crops, animals, and humans was thought to depend on

7

the relationship which obtained between the god of fertility and his consort. By practicing the so-called "sacred marriage" rite, i.e., by having intercourse with the devotees of the gods, humans sought to emulate the god and the goddess and thus provoke the blessings of fertility on themselves as well as on their crops and animals. The Old Testament witnesses to the fact that over the centuries Israel never found it easy to relinquish its attachment to the Canaanite fertility religion. While some would argue that the inherent danger was one of morality, the more obvious risk was one of role confusion. The temptation was to reduce Yahweh to the status of a fertility deity and so deprive Yahweh of the radical capacity to give. To force Yahweh to grant the blessings of fertility was, in the final analysis, to practice idolatry of one form or another.

For Israel Yahweh is not a nature deity like the Canaanite Baal. However, the Old Testament does picture Yahweh as the bestower of fertility after the manner of Baal—see Ps 68:5 where Yahweh, like Baal, is the rider of the rain-producing clouds. Throughout the Old Testament the authors consistently employ masculine pronouns when speaking of Yahweh. At the same time these authors adamantly refuse to require a female consort for their God. For Israel Yahweh is always unique.

Hos 11:8-9 reveals Yahweh in all the trappings of human emotions. Yahweh is torn between abiding love for Israel and the compulsion to punish Israel. The prophet concludes that Yahweh will not give way to unbridled passion and so utterly destroy Israel. "For I am God and not man (male), the Holy One present among you; I will not let the flames consume you" (Hos 11:9). Similarly in the Balaam episode in the Book of Numbers God does not yield to the human proclivity to say one thing and then do another. "God is not man [male] that he would speak falsely, nor human [a son of humankind], that he should change his mind" (Nm 23:19). Yahweh continues to be Yahweh.

In the other direction the writers of the Old Testament are not practitioners of abstract thought. While they could never match the speculative genius of Greek philosophy in conceiving of God as pure act, they nonetheless surpassed such thinkers by their awareness of the person of their God. In order to show their God reacting to human concerns and human needs, they had to employ both male and female images. By nature Yahweh is not a divine architect content to create and then equally content to let creation carry on by itself. By nature Yahweh must relate to creation and such a relationship calls for representing Yahweh as both male and female.

GN 1:26-28 AND THE IMAGE OF GOD

Gn 1:1-2:4a is part of the work of the Priestly Writer who works

8

during the time of the exile (586–539 B.C.). In his plan of reconstruction for God's people he speaks of a God who takes that people seriously. Gn 1:26 speaks of God's intent to make humankind "'in our image, after our likeness.'" Gn 1:27 specifies the extent of God's image: "in the divine image he created him (humankind), male and female he created them." When it is a question of implementing that image by taking charge in Gn 1:26 ("'Let them have dominion over the fish of the sea . . .'"), both male and female are addressed (see Gn 1:28). In Gn 5:1-2 the Priestly Writer again extends the likeness of God to male and female: "When God created man (humankind), he made him in the likeness of God; he created them male and female."

This seemingly harmless passage from the opening chapter of Genesis must nevertheless appeal to our imagination. The image of God is not only male, it is also female. While the author clearly establishes the distance separating God from humans, he also invites us to begin to perceive the richness of the person of our God. To attempt to appreciate the depth of God's person demands that we speak not only of God male but also of God female. The clarity of the text compels us to put aside our prejudices and search out the implications of God male/female. What does it mean to say that Yahweh is both father and mother, man and woman?

Our first reaction is to limit the terms to the sexual relations of male and female. The procreative powers are thus the dimensions that strike us immediately. However, as P. Trible has shown, Yahweh as father/mother opens up new avenues and new possibilities. Once we refuse to limit ourselves to the procreative dimension, we begin to realize that father/mother implies much more—it connotes protection. It also carries over into sustaining life and exercising care for others. Father/mother is richer than our first indications would seem to allow.

In attempting to respond to the Word of God in community, we are not interested in males becoming females or females becoming males. Ultimately we are interested in becoming better images of our God, hence interested in implementing the qualities suggested by Yahweh father/male and Yahweh mother/female. The question that really confronts us is the following: do we dare to become more human? are we willing to run the risk of demonstrating the world of concern and interaction implied by these ostensibly sexual terms? To speak of father/mother automatically implies others. The person who incorporates the values inherent in father/mother is the one who embarks upon the perennial task of providing for others. Hence the one who meets the needs of other members of the community unequivocally exhibits the qualities of father/mother.

9

The quest of God's image is the quest of human liberation. We are challenged to be free *for* others, hence to react to human problems in a human way. We are challenged to reject being free *from* others, hence being free only *for* purely personal pursuits. Response to the Word of God in community evokes the crisis of human liberty and provokes our decision to implement the varied images of our God.

FATHER/HUSBAND IMAGE IN COVENANTAL CONTEXTS

The biblical writers did not hesitate to borrow from the literature of their neighbors. The language of international treaties is a case in point. In such treaties a vassal king would often consider his overlord his father and regard himself as his son. The very heart of the relationship was the son's unswerving obedience to the overlord. However, the "father" status of the overlord implied protection and care. In the second half of the eighth century B.C., King Ahaz of Jerusalem welcomed such protection and care from the neo-Assyrian king, Tiglath-pileser III. His request bespoke the political meaning of fatherhood: "'I am your servant and your son. Come up and rescue me from the clutches of the king of Aram and the king of Israel . . .'" (2 Kgs 16:7).

According to Deuteronomy, Yahweh is a father who does not spare the rod. Although the prophet Hosea speaks of Yahweh's tender love in the wilderness experience (see Hos 2:16-17), Deuteronomy speaks of Yahweh as a father who disciplines his son (see Dt 8:5). To describe Yahweh as father means to see him as the one to whom reverence, loyalty, and obedience are owed (see Is 1:2-3; 30:1-5). As W. Brueggemann notes in his remarks on Jeremiah, the sexual language of fatherhood is employed to demonstrate Yahweh's overwhelming desire to bless his children, hence to show concern: "I had thought: How I should like to treat you as sons, and give you a pleasant land, a heritage most beautiful among the nations! You would call me, 'My Father,' I thought, and never cease following me" (Jer 3:19). By using the father image, these biblical writers insist on the covenantal understanding of the person of Yahweh. The sexual language carries the message of concern and care for Israel.

The father image is the precise opposite of aloofness, coldness, or indifference. Instead, it emphasizes Yahweh's abiding desire to enter the human world of pain and frustration and transform the divine-human relationship. While it does not exclude tenderness, it accentuates the ongoing need to correct, discipline, and provide. The masculine term is calculated to encourage human qualities which both men and women are to exhibit in their interacting in community.

Hosea was the first biblical writer to use the marriage relationship as a model for the relationship between Yahweh and Israel. Preaching in the second half of the eighth century B.C. against the background of religious syncretism, Hosea pictured renewal as a return to the site of the honeymoon (the desert) where estranged lovers could be reconciled. "On that day, says the Lord, she shall call me 'My husband,' and never again 'My baal.' . . . I will espouse you to me forever: I will espouse you in right and in justice, in love and in mercy . . ." (Hos 2:18, 21). According to H. W. Wolff, by using "my husband," the prophet is implying a deep personal relationship with Israel, Yahweh's wife. On the other hand, by excluding "my baal," the prophet seeks to avoid the legal prerogative of the husband as owner of the wife (see Ex 21:22; Dt 22:22). The husband image is clearly masculine. However, it transcends the boundaries of masculinity by underlining the dimension of faithfulness. By being a faithful lover, Yahweh has the best interests of his wife at heart. By reflecting the husband quality of Yahweh, all humans are bent upon exercising forgiveness and the subsequent willingness to begin anew. The masculine imagery serves to elicit human qualities.

WOMB IMAGERY OF MOTHER YAHWEH

In a very provocative study P. Trible investigates the Hebrew word for "womb" (*reḥem*), indicating that it is the basic root for such words as "mercy" and "merciful." This obviously female imagery is employed to express God's maternal compassion and feeling. One of Israel's ancient creedal formulas is the following: "'The Lord, the Lord, a *merciful* and gracious God, slow to anger . . .'" (Ex 34:6; see also Ex 20:5-6; Dt 5:9-10). The imagery speaks of a mother who provides for the child in her womb. In the context of Exodus 34 Yahweh demonstrates her maternal compassion by renewing the covenant with Israel after the incident of the Golden Calf (Ex 32). Hence covenant renewal is one manner of exemplifying Yahweh's motherly feelings for her child Israel.

Jer 31:15-22 is a poem of consolation that Jeremiah originally addressed to his compatriots in the northern kingdom of Israel. It is the summons to return to Yahweh, to begin to live the covenant once more. Rachel, the ancestress of the principal tribe of Ephraim, refuses to be consoled until Mother Yahweh intervenes with the prohibition to weep (Jer 31:16) and reveals the contortions of maternal love in these words: "Is Ephraim not my favored son, the child in whom I delight? Often as I threaten him, I still remember him with favor; my heart stirs for him, I must show him *mercy,* says the Lord" (Jer 31:20).

With this imagery Yahweh's concern is not based on a legal obligation. No external force is required to remind Yahweh that compassion and understanding are now the order of the day. Rather,

11

Yahweh as mother spontaneously reacts to the misfortunes of her family. To imitate Mother Yahweh is to reach out to the members of the family.

Significantly the Old Testament employs the womb imagery for males as well. Ps 103:13 establishes the compassion of a father for his family as the basis for appreciating Yahweh's compassion for all who fear him/her: "As a father has *compassion* on his children, so the Lord has *compassion* on those who fear him . . ." In the Joseph Story the author paints a moving picture of Joseph when the latter recognizes his brother Benjamin. "With that, Joseph had to hurry out, for he was so overcome with *affection* for his brother that he was on the verge of tears" (Gn 43:30). This is an instructive example of how the literal becomes figurative and the concrete becomes abstract. The imagery is clearly feminine but the quality is decidedly human.

OTHER IMAGES OF YAHWEH MOTHER/WIFE

The covenantal poem of Deuteronomy 32 describes Israel's tendency to wander away from that intimate relationship with Yahweh. Employing the vocabulary of forgetting as a personal affront to a very personal God, the author makes this telling statement: "You were unmindful of the Rock that begot you, you forgot the God who gave you birth" (Dt 32:18). While the verb "to beget" is used for both males and females, the verb "to give birth" is applied only to females. It expresses the travail experienced by the mother in the act of giving birth. Against this imagery Israel has ceased to remember the birth pangs of Mother Yahweh.

In Second Isaiah (Is 40-55) Yahweh is pictured as a warrior who has held back too long, refusing to become involved in the plight of Israel. But the Divine Warrior resolves to end this period of silence and to intervene by defeating Israel's enemies. The masculine imagery of warrior is followed by the feminine imagery of an expectant mother writhing in pain: "But now, I cry out as a woman in labor, gasping and panting. I will lay waste mountains and hills, all their herbage I will dry up" (Is 42:14-15).

Both Second and Third Isaiah (Is 56-66), prophets of the exilic and postexilic periods respectively, were deeply moved by the despair and depression of God's people. Among other images they resorted to that of a nursing mother who is determined to comfort her children and thus ward off any impression of not caring. "Oh, that you may suck fully of the milk of her comfort, that you may nurse with delight at her abundant breasts! . . . As nurselings, you shall be carried in her arms, and fondled in her lap; as a mother comforts her son, so will I comfort you; in Jerusalem you shall find your comfort" (Is 66:11, 12-13). The human tendency is to forget, the human temptation is to be unconcerned. Ordinarily mothers are not like that toward their children. But even if a mother should "forget her infant, be without tenderness towards the child of her womb, even should she forget, I will never forget you" (Is 49:15).

In one of the murmuring traditions from the wilderness experience Israel again complains about God's intent in initiating the Exodus. To the bewildered in the desert, Egypt, the despised place of bondage, seems like the land flowing with milk and honey to which they should return. At this point Moses complains about the helplessness of the whole situation. His argument is that the one who began this whole endeavor should see it through to completion by providing for the needs of the people. "'Was it I who conceived all this people? or was it I who gave them birth that you tell me to carry them at my bosom . . .?'" (Nm 11:12). To conceive and give birth means to continue to respond to the problems of the family. Mother Yahweh identifies in terms of her child Israel.

The household chores of providing food and drink fall to the mother and wife. In the wilderness experience Yahweh as mother/wife sees to it that the family has sufficient food. The quail and the manna indicate that Yahweh has not failed her household (see Ex 16:4-36; Nm 11:31-35). Similarly the finding of water at Massah and Meribah (see Ex 17:1-7; Nm 20:2-13) shows that Yahweh has looked after the needs of her family.

A final image exemplifying Yahweh's unrelenting devotion to Israel as mother/wife is that of seamstress. According to the Book of Nehemiah the garments of the Israelites did not become worn during the time of the forty years' wandering. Mother/wife Yahweh did the sewing and the darning (see Neh 9:21). Towards the end of the scene in Eden Yahweh remembers the condition of the man and his wife and goes on to demonstrate motherly concern. "For the man and his wife, the Lord God made leather garments, with which he clothed them" (Gn 3:21). To make the needs of the family one's personal needs is to imitate Yahweh mother/wife and thus demonstrate genuinely human qualities.

ASEXUAL YAHWEH AND SEXUAL HUMANS

While the Old Testament develops the imagery of Yahweh male and female and beckons to its audience to incorporate the imagery in exhibiting the decidedly human qualities of care and concern, we are still left with an asexual Yahweh. This becomes a pressing question when we attempt to offer a prototype for human sexual erotic love. Since Yahweh is not Baal, we are forced to look elsewhere for such a prototype. Our final chapter on the Song of Songs and human sexuality will take up this question. We can anticipate its conclusions

13

by saying that God chooses to make the human couple the paradigm of such love.

HUMAN QUALITIES

Do we dare to become truly human? A. Y. Collins has pointed out that we have need of an inclusive biblical anthropology. This is an anthropology that emphasizes human qualities, not exclusively masculine or feminine qualities. The danger to polarize is ever present. Yet a genuine response to the Word of God in community will note that Yahweh father/husband and Yahweh mother/wife capture qualities that both sexes must emulate. We are challenged to incorporate the sense of community that Yahweh male and Yahweh female express. Whenever we meet the needs of others, we demonstrate decidedly human qualities which are rooted in God as Father and God as Mother. It is never a question of losing our sexual identity but of finding our covenantal identity.

BIBLIOGRAPHICAL SUGGESTIONS

Barr, James. "The Image of God in the Book of Genesis," *BJRL* 51 (1968-1969) 11–26.

Boer, Pieter A. H. de. *Fatherhood and Motherhood in Israelite and Judean Piety.* Leiden: Brill, 1974.

Brueggemann, Walter. "Israel's Social Criticism and Yahweh's Sexuality," *JAAR* 45 (1977) 739-772.

Bruns, J. Edgar. *God as Woman, Woman as God.* New York: Paulist, 1973.

Collins, Adela Y. "An Inclusive Biblical Anthropology," *TToday* 34 (1978) 358-369.

Engelsman, Joan C. *The Feminine Dimension of the Divine.* Philadelphia: Westminster, 1979.

Fensham, F. Charles. "Father and Son as Terminology for Treaty and Covenant," *Near Eastern Studies in Honor of William Foxwell Albright.* Edited by H. Goedicke. Baltimore: The Johns Hopkins University Press, 1971, 121-135.

Fischer, James A. *God Said: Let There Be Woman.* New York: Alba House, 1979, 75-105.

Hanson, Paul D. "Masculine Metaphors for God and Sex-Discrimination in the Old Testament," *Ecumenical Review* 27 (1975) 316-324.

Horowitz, Maryanne C. "The Image of God in Man: Is Woman Included?" *HTR* 72 (1979) 175-206.

McCarthy, Dennis J. "Notes on the Love of God in Deuteronomy and the Father-Son Relationship between Yahweh and Israel," *CBQ* 27 (1965) 144-147.

Mollenkott, Virginia. *Women, Men, & the Bible.* Nashville: Abingdon, 1977, 51-71.

Swidler, Leonard. *Biblical Affirmations of Woman.* Philadelphia: Westminster, 1979, 21-73.

Trible, Phyllis. "Depatriarchalizing in Biblical Interpretation," *JAAR* 41 (1973) 30-48.

_____ . "Good Tidings of Great Joy: Biblical Faith Without Sexism," *Christianity and Crisis* 34 (1974-1975) 12-16.

Trible, Phyllis. "God, Nature of, in the OT," *IDBSup,* 368-369.

——————— . *God and the Rhetoric of Sexuality.* Overtures to Biblical Theology. Philadelphia: Fortress, 1978, 1-71.

Williams, Jay G. "Yahweh, Women, and the Trinity," *TToday* 32 (1975-1976) 234-242.

Wolff, Hans W. *Hosea.* Hermeneia. Philadelphia: Fortress, 1974, 3-64.

sion. The words of a contemporary prophet sum up their malaise: "'Our crimes and our sins weigh us down; we are rotting away because of them. How can we survive?'" (Ez 33:10). Again: "'Our bones are dried up, our hope is lost, and we are cut off'" (Ez 37:11). To offset this malaise, God chooses to breathe and with that, chaos begins to cede to cosmos.

In this first chapter of Genesis the highpoint is the simultaneous creation of male and female. The setting is the heavenly council where God seeks advice from the assembly of courtiers and deliberates with them on plans and programs (see 1 Kgs 22:17-23; Jb 1-2; Ps 82:1). The council's resolution, viz., "'Let us make man (humankind) in our image, after our likeness'" (Gn 1:26), is an unequivocal vote of confidence in humanity. As B. W. Anderson notes, "in our image" may also be translated "as our image." It thus endorses the inherent goodness of humans and, at the same time, offers the challenge to be human by exercising responsibility. Although the Priestly Writer tends to play down the regal stature of man and woman, he cannot conceal it completely. For this author man and woman are the ones through whom God will manifest himself/herself to the world. Depression yields to the expression of human dignity.

Because humans image God, they are called upon to have dominion. The Hebrew verb "to have dominion" (*rādāh*) is used elsewhere in the Bible for the ruling of kings. At his investiture the Davidic prince is instructed, "'Rule in the midst of your enemies'" (Ps 110: 2; see also Ps 72:8). The invitation inherent in the Priestly Writer's creation account is to take one's rightful place in society by exercising responsibility. To be a dropout from society, hence to refuse to contribute flies in the face of God's bold move to put humans in charge of creation. The God who spoke to the despairing exiles of the sixth century B.C. speaks the same message to the timid dropouts of the twentieth century A.D. "You can and will make a difference!" Only human collaboration keeps cosmos from slipping back into chaos.

PSALM 8 AND GN 2:4b-3:24

Psalm 8 is a hymn praising God's sovereignty. The hymn opens and closes with: "O Lord, our Lord, how glorious is your name over all the earth!" While awestruck by God's transcendent sovereignty, the psalmist must nevertheless pause and reflect on that sovereignty vis-à-vis the apparent insignificance of humans: "What is man that you should be mindful of him, or the son of man that you should care for him?" (Ps 8:5). However, the author then moves on to show that God, far from disparaging humans, actually exalts them. Whereas humanity in Gn 1:27 is in/as the image of God (*'ĕlōhîm*), humanity in Ps 8:6 is slightly inferior to the members of the heavenly council (also *'ĕlōhîm*—but see Heb 2:9). Notwithstanding, God does not hesitate to elevate humans to the position of royalty: "... and crowned him with glory and honor" (Ps 8:6). The terms "glory and honor" belong to the language of royal investiture (see Pss 45:4-5; 110: 3). Humans exercise their royal office by ruling over the works of God's hands (Ps 8:7). According to the psalmist humans do not merely occupy a position slightly above the animals. On the contrary, they participate in God's kingly rule. In this view humans can and do make a difference.

The Yahwist, the brilliant writer of the David-Solomonic period (tenth century B.C.) who is the author of Gn 2:4b-3:24, calls for some special mention at this point. His story reads so smoothly that we assume it is not a combination of two separate accounts. C. Westermann, however, has suggested that the text masterfully brings together two originally different accounts. The first tells how God puts humanity in the garden and issues the prohibition regarding the tree and how humanity reacts by disobeying the prohibition and suffering expulsion as a result. The second deals with the creation of humanity. Thus God creates the earth creature but then recognizes that the earth creature is incomplete. This leads to the creation of the animals and finally to the creation of the woman. It is only the creation of the woman that overcomes the initial incompleteness.

What complicates matters is the translation of the Hebrew word 'ādām. In the first account it is always a collective singular meaning humanity in general. Because of the link with the earth/ground (in Hebrew 'ādāmâ) 'ādām may also be translated "earth creature." In the second account 'ādām is initially humanity in general or earth creature, i.e., until the creation of the woman. Thus from Gn 2:22 to 3:8 'ādām means, not the personal name "Adam," but the masculine collective personality. For example, Gn 3:8 speaks of "the man and his wife." For clarity's sake we will translate the collective singular as "humanity" or "earth creature" and the masculine collective personality as "man" or (more frequently) "the man."

The Yahwist also shares the optimism of Psalm 8. In Gn 2:7 the Lord God forms humanity from the dust of the ground. Taken by itself, this may seem to imply humanity's lowly origins. However, biblical usage elsewhere suggests that the author is envisioning much more than humble beginnings.

In 1 Kgs 16:2-3 the Lord directs this attack against King Baasha of Israel: "'Inasmuch as I lifted you from the dust and made you ruler of my people Israel, but you have imitated the conduct of Jeroboam ... I will destroy you, Baasha, and your house'" (see also 1 Sm 2:6-8 Ps 113:7). As W. Brueggemann remarks, the language is that of royal enthronement. "To be taken from the earth" means to be made a king and hence to exercise royal prerogatives. God's action in Gn 2:7 establishes humanity as king. This God is not jealous of another's royal status. This God willingly shares such status so that a more human world will result. At the same time royal status is not absolute. Failure to abide by the terms of royal status results in dethronement, viz., the return to the dust: "'For you are dirt (dust), and to dirt (dust) you shall return'" (Gn 3:19).

Gn 2:7 seems to contain another expression of royal enthronement. According to this text God also breathes into humanity's nostrils the breath of life. W. Wifall has made a good case for showing that in the language and art of the ancient Near East the deity's breathing into the nostrils can constitute the person a king. The Book of Lamentations bewails the plight that overcame God's people in the aftermath of the siege and destruction of Jerusalem in 586 B.C. The king was not exempt from the enemy's clutches: "The anointed one of the Lord, our breath of life, was caught in their snares . . ." (Lam 4:20). Gn 2:7 sings in effect: "Long live humanity—the king!"

CONCLUSIONS, COMPARISONS, CONSEQUENCES

In view of the texts just studied we may draw certain conclusions. Humans are subjects, not objects. Humans are participants, not spectators. Humans are serious co-workers with God, not flattered lackeys. Humans are invited to undertake the human task of making a more human world. "Humans" means both men and women. The God of the Old Testament is not one who will go it alone. This God freely chooses to depend on the free acceptance of the invitation inherent in creation.

It is worth noting that such a view of human dignity was at odds with Israel's environment. In the Enuma Elish, the Babylonian account of creation which serves as background for the Priestly Writer's account, the creation of humans is subsequent to a rebellion that broke out among the gods. Once the rebellion is crushed, a problem ensues with regard to providing for the needs of the Babylonian pantheon. To resolve this problem, humanity is made from the blood of the rebellious god Kingu. The task of humans is to serve as waiters, waitresses, and bus persons for the gods. There is no sharing of royal prerogatives. There is only the daily subservience involved in feeding the host of Babylonian deities.

Noblesse oblige. With status there go corresponding obligations and relationships. As we shall see shortly under covenant, a triangular relationship always emerges in Israel's theology. Thus the individual is related to both God and other humans. Here we may also add that the relationship to both God and other humans likewise entails responsibility towards the created world. In the invitation to be human the following values result: (1) humans have a relationship

20

to God; (2) humans have a relationship to each other; and (3) humans have a relationship to the created world. (In developing the first two we will focus on the Yahwist's creation account.)

HUMANS HAVE A RELATIONSHIP TO GOD

According to the Yahwist, God trusts the man and the woman to run their world. At the same time, without disparaging human autonomy, this writer clearly insists that there is a relationship of dependence on God. To entrust with responsibilities does not mean the divine retreat to the world of laissez faire. The man and the woman are not absolute monarchs, they are coresponsible partners with God. The inobtrusive manner of this God does not mean fleeing the scene and abdicating power. To create also means to enter into an ongoing exchange with the created.

As H. Kenik notes, the Yahwist paints a clear picture of God's intimacy with humans—an intimacy that is bound up with dependence. It is important to observe that this intimacy on the part of God does not obtain only prior to the fall. Rather, this intimacy continues in the more crucial situation after the fall. God's actions demonstrate such intimacy. In Genesis 2 the Lord God fashions (v 7), breathes (v 7), plants (v 8), sees (v 19), and builds (v 21). In Genesis 3 this God walks (v 8), calls (v 9), dialogues and passes sentence (vv 9-19), and clothes (v 21). We may tend to label these chapters a very naive story about the beginning. However, further reflection will bear out the truth that a writer of profound psychological insight has captured the essence of what goes right and what goes wrong in the relationship between God and humans. It is not simply a story about the beginning. It is a story about incidents in the tenth century B.C. which also reflect our situation today.

Hand in hand with dependence goes limitation. It is likely that the Yahwist drew his inspiration for the violation of trust from the life and exploits of King David. David was truly God's trusted creature, endowed with great talents and charged with ruling the united kingdom of Judah and Israel. As Second Samuel shows, David attempted to throw off the burden of limitations. Among other things he resorted to murder to cover up his adultery (see 2 Sm 11). David found it exceedingly difficult to cope with limitations. (We will treat this at greater length in a later chapter.) A solid spirituality demands recognition of both human dignity and human frailty.

The prohibition regarding the tree of the knowledge of good and evil in Gn 2:16-17 (distinguished from the tree of life in Gn 2: 9, but see also Gn 3:3) demonstrates not only limitation but also intimacy. It is formulated in the second person ("from that tree you shall not eat"). It is not an imposition from without. God chooses to deal with people as subjects, not objects. Commands and pro-

21

hibitions must somehow be tied in with the person of our God. Otherwise we run the risk of reacting to an impersonal will.

The sexual and omniscient interpretations of the sin in the garden have their defenders. Thus some would regard the sin as some sexual aberration while others would see in the sin the attempt to acquire knowledge of everything that is proper to God alone. However, there is no indication of any special sexual sin for the married couple. (There is a Hebrew play on words involved in the words "cunning" [Gn 3:1] and "naked" [Gn 2:25; 3:7]. Hence the irony of the whole situation wherein the man and the woman merely learn that they are naked [Gn 3:7]!) With regard to omniscience the knowledge involved is the knowledge of good and evil. What the context suggests nonetheless is the violation of some divine prerogative.

The expression "to know good and evil" or its equivalent appears elsewhere in the Old Testament as a divine prerogative. The wise woman of Tekoa in Second Samuel 14 lauds David's sagacity in these terms: "'. . . indeed, my lord the king is like an angel of God, evaluating good and evil'" (2 Sm 14:17—see also v 20). After Solomon's judgment in the case of the two prostitutes the author concludes: ". . . they saw that the king had in him the wisdom of God for giving judgment" (1 Kgs 3:28—see also v 9). In the light of such texts W. M. Clark concludes that the ability to discern good and evil is a divine prerogative. What this involves is that humans attempt to determine on their own what is good and what is evil. Thus to eat of the tree is good, not evil. (This is also the view of St. Thomas Aquinas in *Summa Theologiae*, II-II, q. 163, a. 2, c.).

S. Terrien remarks that the man and the woman violate the implications of humanity, which the Creator imposes on them, in their attack on the tree of knowledge. Hence they adamantly refuse to accept the crucial limitations of their regal yet creaturely status. He calls their sin one of theological lust.

In the view of L. Alonso Schökel the story in the garden is ultimately a paradigmatic wisdom story. (Note the subtlety of the serpent and the sapiential character of the tree—see Ez 28:2-19.) It is the human temptation to pursue infinity. We still want to be the biggest and the best. If we cannot achieve that fame by accomplishing great feats, we choose to pursue infinity in our sinning. Response to the Word of God in community demands that we resist the temptation to infinity by acknowledging the creaturely dimension of our regal status. We are called upon to accept who and what we are. This does not entail renouncing our royalty. It does entail pursuing our call to covenant, viz., to provide for others.

HUMANS HAVE A RELATIONSHIP TO EACH OTHER

Whereas the Priestly Writer offers the simultaneous creation of male and female, the Yahwist elects to separate the creations. It is worth observing that the Yahwist's account is the only one in the literature of the ancient Near East that has a separate creation of the woman.

The Lord God's remark in 2:18 that it is not good for the earth creature to be alone is the first indication that the work of creation is not yet complete. Humanity means community. To meet this need, the author pictures the earth creature playing a game called "What's My Name?" In giving names to the animals in Gn 2:19-20, the earth creature must painfully conclude a suitable helper/partner is wanting. ("Helper" should not be limited to help in procreating. It means help in the entire gamut of man-woman relations.) The text implies two things: (1) there is no one similar to the earth creature; and (2) there is no one who complements the earth creature. As S. Terrien remarks, the earth creature without the woman is still incomplete. It is only the woman who can bring wholeness.

The deep sleep which God casts on the earth creature should not evoke an anesthesia that would aid in surviving the divine removal of the notorious rib. (The rib is probably borrowed from a Sumerian myth where "the lady of the rib" is also "the lady who makes live"— a pun that is lost in Hebrew where the words for "rib" [Gn 2:21-22] and "Eve, mother of all the *living*" [Gn 3:20] are different.) Rather, the deep sleep is a divine revelation induced during the state of unconsciousness. The man thus realizes a violent disruption which, as S. Terrien notes, is at the core of sexual differentiation.

The man's reaction in Gn 2:23 ("'This one, at last, is bone of my bones and flesh of my flesh'") attests that God has finally succeeded in proving a complementary-supplementary partner. Whereas the game of "What's My Name?" failed, God's delicate creation of the woman has admirably succeeded. However, besides communicating the man's ecstasy, this verse also implies the mutuality of a covenant commitment. W. Brueggemann has examined the "bone-flesh" imagery. While flesh connotes weakness, bone connotes strength. In 2 Sm 5:1 the tribes of the north come to David and acknowledge that they are his bone and flesh. In 2 Sm 5:3 these tribes accept David as king and enter into covenant with him (see also 2 Sm 19:13-14). "Bone-flesh" is a statement of abiding covenantal loyalty. The human couple thereby assumes the obligation of being faithful to each other through thick and thin. They share in a common cause that envisions mutual concern in all circumstances, i.e., both of strength and of weakness.

The author's remark in Gn 2:24 ("That is why a man leaves his father and mother and *clings* to his wife, and the two of them become one flesh" ["body" in *NAB*]) also has covenantal overtones in the view of W. Brueggemann. For example, in Dt 11:22 (Deuteronomy is the covenant book par excellence) the Israelites are bidden to observe all the commandments, love Yahweh, and *cling* to him. As M. Gilbert points out, the Hebrew word for "flesh" (*bāśār*) is never used for the sexual union of man and woman. On the contrary, "one flesh" captures the unity of these two people in the entire dimension of the man-woman relationship (see Jgs 8:7, 17; Mal 2:14).

According to the Yahwist the response of husband and wife to the Word of God in community is based on observance of mutual obligations. To be faithful through thick and thin is to sing anew the hymn of creation. The spirituality of the married couple is founded on the delicate work of the Creator.

HUMANS HAVE A RELATIONSHIP TO THE CREATED WORLD

The problem of the relationship of humans to the created world is not a new one. The Gilgamesh epic, the story of the Beowulf of the ancient Near East which serves as a partial inspiration for the Yahwist, deals with this concern. In this epic Enkidu, later Gilgamesh's friend, originally lives in total harmony with the animals. He neither attacks them nor is attacked by them. Food and drink are items that all share in common. After his first sexual experience with a prostitute Enkidu is radically changed. He now requires human food and beer. Moreover, he departs from his former way of life by hunting the animals. The former harmony between humans and animals no longer exists. C. Westermann maintains that the Enkidu story and the account of the naming of the animals in Gn 2:19-20 reflect a very early tradition in which humans and animals had a closer relationship. This tradition suggests harmony should prevail in that relationship.

The Priestly Writer establishes a link between cattle/creeping things/wild animals and humans by having all of them created on the sixth day. Although some have derived divine permission to abuse the created world from the verbs "to have dominion" and "to subdue" in Gn 1:26, 28, the case is not a solid one. While the verb "to have dominion" (*rādāh*) is used for the treading of grapes (see Jl 4:13), it is used in Genesis 1:26, 28 for royal dominion. Thus humans function as kings and queens, imaging their God by the faithful discharge of their office. While the verb "to subdue" (*kābaš*) can mean "to rape" (see Est 7:8), it is never employed for the environment. Rather, for the Priestly Writer the subdued earth represents God's presence in the midst of Israel after the exile by a non-Joshua type of conquest (see Jos 18:1; 19:51).

For the Priestly Writer humans are to exercise their royal prerogative of dominion by avoiding all killing. Thus in Gn 1:29-30 animals, birds, etc., share the same food as humans, viz., plants and trees. It is only after the flood (hence in view of human sinfulness) that humans are permitted to kill animals (see Gn 9:3). A final significant point for this author is that God's covenant with Noah embraces not only humans but all other creatures: "'As the bow appears in the clouds, I will see it and recall the everlasting covenant that I have established between God and all living beings—all mortal creatures that are on the earth'" (Gn 9:16).

In the Yahwist's account of creation the earth creature identifies in terms of the earth/ground (see Gn 2:6-7). In the Greek translation of the Hebrew Bible known as the Septuagint, the Hebrew word for "garden" is rendered *paradeisos,* hence "paradise." However, this is a Persian loanword meaning "fenced orchard." As a result, the garden is not a utopia, it is not our kind of paradise. Indeed it is a land that calls for tilling and care. According to the Yahwist, work is an essential ingredient of human existence. In Gn 2:15 God places the earth creature in the garden "to cultivate and care for it."

The naming of the animals in Gn 2:19-20, besides pointing up the absence of a complementary-supplementary partner for the earth creature, also demonstrates the exercise of responsibility. "To name" means to take one's rightful place in the ongoing ordering of nature. Because of sin, however, the relationship of humans to the created world is warped: "'Cursed be the ground because of you . . . Thorns and thistles shall it bring forth to you . . . By the sweat of your face shall you get bread to eat . . .'" (Gn 3:17-19). In dealing with the created world human autonomy is insufficient. It is only an exercise of genuine freedom, i.e., concern for God and others, that will realize the blessing of the land. The human task is to seek to integrate oneself with God, other humans, and nature itself.

SPIRITUALITY AND COSMIC REDEMPTION

As S. Lyonnet describes it, cosmic redemption is the transformation of the material universe whereby it attains its goal (hence no more frustration) by sharing in the total redemption of humans who in turn share in the total redemption experience of Jesus (see Rom 8:20-21). Creation is not merely a means, an instrument of redemption. It is also an object of redemption. Just as breach of covenant isolates Israel and the created world (see Hos 4:1-3), so too covenantal harmony unites humans with the created world. "I will make a covenant for them on that day, with the beasts of the field, the birds of the air, and with the things that crawl on the ground" (Hos 2:20).

For Paul the redemption of the universe is based on the redemption of humans that in turn is based on the resurrection of Jesus (see Rom 8:11, 20-21). The groaning of nature (Rom 8:22) is tied up with human groaning and with the hope of our groaning, viz., the glory of the resurrection. For Paul nothing in the universe is excluded from the redemption. Just as the Spirit is the transforming agent in the resurrection of humans, that same Spirit is the transforming agent in the restoration of the material universe. All human efforts, all human labors have a great value since they are part of this transforming process. In the matter of the sacraments, e.g., bread and wine, the material world has already been transformed.

This dimension of spirituality may be called either ecological theology or theological ecology. Negatively this spirituality does not allow for the raping of nature. Positively this spirituality calls for a respect for the created world, a respect which flows from the presence of the Creator and the responsibility inherent in the human task to provide for a more human world.

BIBLIOGRAPHICAL SUGGESTIONS

Alonso Schökel, Luis. "Sapiential and Covenant Themes in Genesis 2-3," *TD* 13 (1965) 3-10.

Anderson, Bernhard W. "Human Dominion over Nature," *Biblical Studies in Contemporary Thought*. Edited by M. Ward. Somerville: Green, Hadden, 1975, 27-45.

Barr, James. "Man and Nature—The Ecological Controversy and the Old Testament," *BJRL* 55 (1972-73) 9-32.

Brueggemann, Walter. "King in the Kingdom of Things," *The Christian Century* 86 (1969) 1165-1166.

—————. "From Dust to Kingship," *ZAW* 84 (1970) 1-18.

—————. "'Of the Same Flesh and Bone' (Gen. 2, 23a)," *CBQ* 32 (1970) 532-542.

—————. *In Man We Trust. The Neglected Side of Biblical Faith*. Richmond: John Knox, 1972.

Clark, W. Malcolm. "A Legal Background of the Yahwist's Use of 'Good and Evil' in Genesis 2-3," *JBL* 88 (1969) 266-278.

Coats, George W. "The God of Death," *Int* 29 (1975) 227-239.

Fretheim, Terence E. *Creation, Fall, and Flood. Studies in Genesis 1-11*. Minneapolis: Augsburg, 1969.

Gilbert, Maurice. "'One Only Flesh,'" *TD* 26 (1978) 206-209.

Hartman, Louis F. "Sin in Paradise," *CBQ* 20 (1958) 26-40.

Hendry, George S. *Theology of Nature*. Philadelphia: Westminster, 1980.

Jobling, David. "Dominion over Creation," *IDBSup*, 247-248.

Kenik, Helen. "Toward a Biblical Basis for Creation Theology," *Western Spirituality: Historical Roots, Ecumenical Routes*. Edited by M. Fox. Notre Dame: Fides/Claretian, 1979, 27-75.

Lyonnet, Stanislas. "La rédemption de l'univers," *Lumière et Vie* 48 (1960) 43-62.

Sakenfeld, Katharine D. "The Bible and Women: Bane or Blessing?" *TToday* 32 (1975-1976) 222-233.

Steck, Odil Hannes. *World and Environment*. Biblical Encounter Series. New York: Abingdon, 1978.

Terrien, Samuel. "Towards a Biblical Theology of Womanhood," *Religion in Life* 42 (1973) 322–333.

Trible, Phyllis. "Ancient Priests and Modern Polluters," *ANQ* 12 (1971) 74–79.

_____ . "Eve and Adam, Genesis 2–3 Reread," *ANQ* 14 (1973) 251–258.

_____ . "A Love Story Gone Awry," *God and the Rhetoric of Sexuality*. Overtures to Biblical Theology. Philadelphia: Fortress, 1978, 72–143.

Vogels, Walter. " 'It Is Not Good That the Mensch Should Be Alone: I Will Make Him/Her a Helper Fit for Him/Her' (Gen 2:18)," *Église et Théologie* 9 (1978) 9–35.

Westermann, Claus. *The Genesis Accounts of Creation*. Facet Books—Biblical Series. Philadelphia: Fortress, 1964.

_____ . *Creation*. Philadelphia: Fortress, 1974.

Wifall, Walter. "The Breath of His Nostrils: Gen 2, 7b," *CBQ* 36 (1974) 237–240.

CHAPTER 4

The Invitation to Covenant

Biblical passages to be read: Gn 31:25-54; Ex 6:2-8; 19; 24:1-11; 1 Chr 2; Mk 14:22-26; 1 Cor 11:17-34.

THE EMPIRIC SITUATION

We are always concerned about our identity. We are ever anxious to know who we are and what we are about. Whether we articulate it or not, we seek to establish our niche in the world. We want to be assured that we have really made it to the top. The crucial questions are: (1) have I really made it so that I am a somebody? and (2) have I actually failed to make it so that I am a nobody?

In raising these questions we must note that we have set up certain presuppositions. We seem to think that only those who make it to the top have identity. Thus only those who break into print, only those who leave their names on monuments, only those with yearly salaries in six figures have really succeeded. Identity equals success. Anything less than this equation means the limbo of anonymity.

Unwittingly perhaps we act upon certain pre-presuppositions in our quest. We choose to live in a hell of isolationism. We enact a "hands off" policy, thus keeping humanity at a respectable distance and resisting every opportunity to interact with others in a truly human society. Certain criteria become the driving force in our lives, viz., "through myself, with myself, in myself." To this we can certainly add "by myself." We are rooted in ourselves, we cling to ourselves (the very opposite of Gn 2:24 and Dt 11:22!), we publish ourselves.

In this empiric situation society is anonymous. It is, at best, an artificial aggregate of quasi-rational animals. In this aggregate laws are artificial impositions from without that are calculated to impede our drive for self-fulfillment. Laws like society itself do not bear *in se* on our quest.

Everything noted in the preceding paragraphs is diametrically opposed to the response to the Word of God in community. Even when we can perceive that Word at work, our response is often not in community. Given the above parameters, our response is necessarily an egotistical reaction to a God who must operate on our terms, viz., one-on-one. Triangular vision, i.e., God, others, and ourselves, disappears. Ours is thereby the myopic vision of the egotist who shuns the challenge of creation, eschews the needs of society, and excludes the very notion of sisters and brothers. Perhaps the saddest comment of all is that all too many people prefer this less demanding notion of isolationism to the more exigent view of community.

THE CONCEPT OF COMMUNITY

As D. J. McCarthy observes, covenant in its widest sense is a form of relationship. More specifically, it is a relationship in which a moral connection between parties is defined and affirmed. Hence it overlaps with contracts. Since human beings must deal with each other, covenants of one sort or another belong to the very fiber of human existence—we must define and affirm our relationships with other people. Covenant, however, goes beyond our understanding of contract by introducing a more personal, intimate dimension. In covenant we divorce ourselves from the "party of the first part" language. Covenant demands that its partners view themselves as persons relating to persons, not third person objects reacting to other third person objects. As M. Buber phrased it, in covenant we are dealing with "I and Thou."

The relationship between Laban and Jacob is an early biblical example of covenant. Both Laban and Jacob are concerned about mutual safety, property, and the welfare of the women and children (see Gn 31:43-44). They agree to set up a heap of stones that will witness to their agreement. They also swear an oath: "'May the God of Abraham and the god of Nahor maintain justice between us!'" (Gn 31:53). Finally a ritual meal seals the covenantal relationship: "He (Jacob) then offered a sacrifice on the mountain and invited his kinsmen to share in the meal. When they had eaten, they passed the night on the mountain" (Gn 31:54).

OTHER EXAMPLES OF THE COVENANT RELATIONSHIP

Ex 6:2-8 is part of the Priestly Writer's account of the call of Moses (see Ex 3:7-4:17 for two earlier accounts). For this writer it is essential to establish continuity in covenant. Consequently God states that he appeared to the patriarchs, not under the name of "Yahweh," but under the name of "El Shaddai" (meaning either

"God the Almighty" or "God of the Mountain"). This covenant God is not subject to amnesia. This God recalls that the promise to the patriarchs entails fulfillment at a given point in time. The text recalls the affliction of the Israelites: "'And now that I have heard the *groaning* of the Israelites whom the Egyptians are treating as slaves, I am mindful of my covenant'" (Ex 6:5). The expression "my covenant" is also telling. It speaks of a God committed to a people, of a God who has determined to honor the terms of the covenant.

Ex 6:6-8 is an oracle of salvation: "'I am the Lord. I will free you . . . I will rescue you . . . You will know that I, the Lord, am your God when I free you from the labor of the Egyptians.'" It states in forthright terms God's determination to intervene on behalf of Israel. T. M. Raitt has shown how this unique literary form responds admirably to the needs of Israel in the confusion and despair of exile.

According to T. M. Raitt the oracle of salvation manifests that the covenant of God is bent upon providing hope for Israel and building a new basis for her religious faith. The oracle of salvation shows that this God of judgment is also a God of mercy. It also indicates that God is not bound by the parameters of human logic. Hence God is able to raise up a renewed people from the experience of failure. Israel's political reverses do not defeat the God of Israel.

For the Priestly Writer covenant implies that one must regard the events of history as the setting for the revelation of the God of Israel. Covenant means that the deliverance of Israel is an insight into the nature of Yahweh. Covenant means that people must react to the person of their God: "'You will know that I, the Lord, am your God when I free you from the labor of the Egyptians and bring you into the land which I swore to give to Abraham, Isaac, and Jacob'" (Ex 6:7-8). The defeat of the Egyptians (the overthrowing of exilic despair) is not a neutral event in a purely profane history. It is the dramatic intervention of a covenant God who demands recognition ("you will know") from the covenant partners. To be part of a covenant is to be part of a history.

Is 43:1-7 is another example of the oracle of salvation which speaks to the same situation as Ex 6:2-8. Second Isaiah's poem divides into two parts: (vv 1-4, 5-7), each one containing the phrase "Fear not." The basis for not fearing is Yahweh's covenantal love/concern for Israel. Here covenant is not the cold language of legal documents. It is the warm expression of mutual concern: "Fear not, for I have redeemed you; I have called you by name: you are mine." No matter what the obstacles, whether overwhelming floods or consuming fires (v 2), the God of the covenant will be present. In v 4 Israel is precious in Yahweh's eyes, Israel is glorious, Israel is the object of Yahweh's love. Both the beginning of the oracle (v 1) and

31

the end (v 7) are replete with the vocabulary of creation: "who created you, O Jacob, and formed you, O Israel . . . whom I created . . . whom I formed." As we will see later, the deliverance of Israel is part of God's ongoing creation. For Second Isaiah, therefore, the God who spoke in the beginning is the God who continues to speak, especially in Israel's experience of need and frustration.

Genealogies often strike us as an exercise in boredom. "And so and so begot so and so" seems so utterly removed from our real world and its drive for "Let's get on with today's business now." We tend to flip the pages of our Bible more quickly and resolutely since we have already determined to find nothing of lasting value in such tedious tabulations.

Hopefully A. Haley's "Roots" has taught us a more healthy respect for our origins. For the biblical audience, as for many audiences, genealogies serve several purposes. They are a form of survival. By being included in the membership, e.g., of a tribe, an individual knows that the tribe assumes the obligation of caring for him/her. Secondly, genealogies provide identity. They tell us something about our present situation and also our idiosyncrasies. Thus Matthew goes through forty-two generations to identify Jesus as "son of David, son of Abraham" (Mt 1:1). Thirdly, genealogies provide status. Thus a king seeks to align himself with his predecessors and hence with their prerogatives. Fourthly, genealogies structure history, i.e., they divide history into convenient periods. Significantly genealogies are founded on the need for community. Genealogies presuppose that by nature we are covenant people, that we must be part of an ongoing history, that we must interact with sisters and brothers.

1 Chr 2, the work of the final editor of the Chronicler's History (the books of First and Second Chronicles, Ezra, and Nehemiah), deals with the genealogy of the tribe of Judah. It seeks to remind the audience of ca. 400 B.C. that they are part of a great history, that they still have a future, that they are somebodies. Whereas for us this passage may be fifty-five verses of odd sounding names, for the original audience it was a vital listing—it engendered the will to live. Genealogies correspond to our own experience whereby we resent being left out of the catalogue or being omitted from the directory.

THE COVENANT AT SINAI

The above examples focus largely on Yahweh's determination to honor the demands of covenant. To appreciate covenant fully, however, we must also look to the roles of both covenant partners, i.e., not only Yahweh but also Israel. Moreover, the covenant at Sinai, besides insisting on Israel's commitment, contains the theological reflection of God's people over a long period of time. Sinai becomes the depository of texts interpreting the ongoing relationship of the covenant partners. It thus exemplifies the unrelenting response—not a simple stereotyped reply—to the Word of God in community.

Ex 19:24:11 is ample proof that Israel could never be satisfied with one least-common-denominator view of Yahweh. While the variety of opinions and traditions does not always lend itself to easy reading, it does reveal that an oversimplified view of the covenant partners will never do. Fortunately there is an overall pattern that brings the material together in a somewhat manageable form. There is, first of all, the encounter with God. We will see below that the traditions interpreted that meeting in several ways. Secondly, there is the manifestation of the divine will. Since the divine presence will overawe the people, a covenant mediator will be required for this manifestation. Specifically, Moses performs this task as he receives the will of the sovereign. Thirdly, Moses repeats to the people what he has heard from God. Fourthly, the people accept the terms of the covenant.

The Priestly Writer provides most of the information in Ex 19: 1-2. This is the geographical setting for the covenant making: "In the third month after their departure from the land of Egypt, on its first day, the Israelites came to the desert of Sinai. After the journey from Rephidim to the desert of Sinai, they pitched camp" (Ex 19: 1-2). There next follows in Ex 19:3-8 a tradition that in D. J. McCarthy's view is a piece of liturgical poetry. It is not one of the standard Pentateuchal traditions, such as the Yahwist or the Priestly Writer. It is, rather, a separate tradition appealing for a particular way of thinking and acting vis-à-vis the covenant Lord, not one establishing detailed norms of conduct. These verses are especially rich in describing many of the basic elements of covenant living.

"'Thus shall you say to the house of Jacob: tell the Israelites: You have seen for yourselves how I treated the Egyptians and how I bore you up on eagle wings and brought you here to myself'" (Ex 19:4-5). As J. Muilenburg has pointed out, the tradition insists on God's relating to the Israelites in terms of direct address—it is once again an "I and Thou." At the same time there is the unmistakable mark of proclamation. This is clearly a solemn occasion. In offering Israel the possibility of covenant, Yahweh cites the dramatic intervention against the Egyptians in the Exodus. Thus covenant is grounded in the solid credentials of this saving God. Hand in hand with the omnipotence and awesomeness of this God goes intimacy. In this covenant-making scene Yahweh does not merely bring Israel to a given geographical location in the Sinai—rather, "'I brought you here to *myself*" (Ex 19:4). Israel has to do with a person, not with an impersonal power at work in the desert. Moreover, Yahweh speaks of this covenant as "'my covenant'" (Ex 19:5). Far from being an arid list of do's and don't's, this covenant is an expression of an exceedingly personal God. "'My special possession'" (Ex 19:5) is not all that clear. The best explanation is that in covenant Israel becomes the personal private possession of the king.

Obedience, liberty, and holiness are also key elements in the covenant relationship. According to Ex 19:5 Israel is to hearken to Yahweh's voice. It is clear from the start that this is a covenant between unequals, not equals. In covenant Israel must acquiesce to the will of this generous yet demanding God. At the same time Israel is not coerced into this relationship. Israel is bound, only if Israel so chooses: "'Therefore, *if* you hearken to my voice . . .'" (Ex 19:5). Obedience to the terms of the covenant means holiness: "'You shall be to me a kingdom of priests, a holy nation'" (Ex 19:6). This phrase is somewhat perplexing. To be sure, only certain people were priests in Israel. The phrase seems best interpreted as referring to the totality of Israel, i.e., the royalty of the priests and the rest of the nation. By accepting covenant, Israel takes upon herself the obligation of demonstrating holiness, i.e., her separation from the sphere of the profane.

COVENANT MAKING AND ISRAEL'S TRADITIONS

The Yahwist's tradition of God's presence and its demands probably consists of the following verses in Exodus 19:

"The Lord added, 'Go to the people and have them sanctify themselves today and tomorrow. Make them wash their garments and be ready for the third day'" (vv 10-11a). "'Set limits for the people all around the mountain, and tell them: Take care not to go up the mountain, or even to touch its base. If anyone touches the mountain he must be put to death. No hand shall touch him; he must be stoned to death or killed with arrows. Such a one, man or beast, must not be allowed to live'" (vv 12-13a). "Then Moses came down from the mountain to the people and had them sanctify themselves and wash their garments. He warned them, 'Be ready for the third day. Have no intercourse with any woman'" (vv 14-15). "On the morning of the third day (v 16aA) . . . Mount Sinai was all wrapped in smoke, for the Lord came down upon it in fire. The smoke rose from it as though from a furnace, and the whole mountain trembled violently" (v 18). "When the Lord came down to the top of Mount Sinai, he summoned Moses to the top of the mountain, and Moses went up to him" (v 20).

According to the Yahwist the manner of God's presence—theophany—is that of a volcanic eruption. Moses is God's chosen mediator who hears the divine revelation and communicates it to the people.

34

In view of covenant making the people purify themselves (washing of clothes, continence, readiness for the third day). The people are overcome by awe, not fear. Yahweh manifests power and majesty by descending upon the mountain. As D. J. McCarthy notes, it is this presence that founds the covenant. It is interesting to observe "the third day" in vv 11, 15. "The third day" is the day for covenant making, a tradition that is of significance for the resurrection of Jesus (see Hos 6:1-3; 1 Cor 15:4). (For the Yahwist the stipulations of the covenant are now found in Ex 34:10-26.)

The Elohist (so called because he uses only the generic name of "God" [ʾĕlōhîm] rather than Yahweh when speaking of Israel's God in Genesis and the beginning of Exodus [see Ex 3:14-15]) probably wrote in either the ninth or eighth century B.C. In D. J. McCarthy's analysis the Elohist's tradition of God's presence and its demands probably consist of the following verses from Exodus 19:

> ". . . 'for on the third day the Lord will come down on Mount Sinai before the eyes of all the people'" (v 11b). "'Only when the ram's horn resounds may they go up to the mountain'" (v 13b). "There were peals of thunder and lightning, and a heavy cloud over the mountain, and a very loud trumpet blast, so that all the people in the camp trembled" (v 16aBb). "But Moses led the people out of the camp to meet God, and they stationed themselves at the foot of the mountain" (v 17). "The trumpet blast grew louder and louder, while Moses was speaking and God answering him with thunder" (v 19).

According to the Elohist the manner of God's presence is that of a storm, indeed a storm that frightens the people (God responds in the peals of thunder). Unlike the Yahwist who has God choose Moses as mediator, the Elohist has the people do so (see Ex 20:19). Indeed it is the terror produced by the storm that makes the people willing to acquiesce to the demands of the covenant God. Finally the mention of lightning flashes (= torches—see Jgs 7:16), the trumpet blast, and the camp suggests that the people regard themselves as God's militia engaged in a holy war. They position themselves in battle array, prepared to carry out the will of the Divine Warrior. (For the Elohist the stipulations of the covenant are found in Ex 20:1-23:19.)

Although both the Yahwist and the Elohist present complete pictures of the covenant making on Sinai, those responsible for the final form of the text added two other scenes of covenant making where ritual actions symbolize Israel's acceptance of the covenant. These scenes are found in Ex 24:1-2, 9-11 and Ex 24:3-8. Our reaction is perhaps to label them excess biblical baggage. However, the judgment of those responsible for the present arrangement should prevail.

In D. J. McCarthy's study Ex 24:1-2, 9-11 is basically a covenant meal. Israel's leaders ascend the mountain, see God, and then eat and drink in the divine presence. The simplicity of the scene strikes us as a healthy corrective of the awesome display of Yahweh's power in both the volcanic eruption and the storm. God's awesome attributes must now be put aside and yield to the security of a communal meal. This God is thus perceived as one who will bring life, not destruction. In terms of background this tradition seems to stem from a nomadic setting. Here Yahweh is the tribal leader, the father who accepts Israel, represented by Moses and the clan leaders, into the family. As a result, this tribal leader obliges himself to provide protection for the newly accepted members. In turn, Israel is now under the obligation of total commitment to this tribal leader. The covenant meal symbolizes these mutual obligations.

The tradition of Ex 24:3-8 reflects a somewhat later period in Israel than the tradition of Ex 24:1-2, 9-11. It is now no longer a meal celebrated in a holy place and, therefore, in the presence of God. It is a more elaborate ceremony involving communion sacrifices and blood rites. What is especially significant is the acceptance of God's will (see Ex 24:3, 7). The communion sacrifices (Ex 24:5) signify the union between God and the people—the sacrifices actually effect the covenant.

The blood rite is particularly meaningful—for one reason, it is never found again in the entire Old Testament. It is important to note that the rite is interrupted by the reading of the stipulations of the covenant in Ex 24:7. Since blood signifies life, Israel assumes the obligation of obedience to the stipulations as the basis for enjoying life with Yahweh. The reading of the stipulations and the sprinkling of the blood (Ex 24:8) thus form a unity that is more sophisticated than the communal meal of Ex 24:1-2, 9-11. Life hinges on obedience to the terms of the covenant.

VALUE OF THE TRADITIONS

We may tend to label the Yahwist's tradition of volcanic eruption/divine peals of thunder and the Elohist's tradition of storm theophany/divine warfare as rather naive understandings of God's presence. We thus welcome the communal meal of Ex 24:1-2, 9-11 and the blood rite/formal reading of Ex 24:3-8 as an improvement over the grotesque features of the Yahwist and the Elohist. While this may be partially true, we may yet miss the community dimensions of the so-called more primitive traditions.

In both the Yahwist and the Elohist God speaks through a mediator, Moses, to Israel. It is the community that responds to this personal God who is present in seemingly bizarre ways. It is the community that resolves to accept the terms of this awesome and terrifying

God. It is the community that chooses to live precisely as Israel, i.e., God's community. In these apparently primitive traditions all notion of isolationism is absent. One must react to this God of Israel as a member of the people of Israel. Indeed Moses only makes it to the top and thereby achieves notoriety because he identifies in terms of the people. Ultimately the apparent naivete of these scenes is a healthy corrective of our pursuit of anonymity and our flight from community. These scenes, therefore, demonstrate par excellence response to the Word of God in community.

COVENANT AND OUR IDENTITY

W. Brueggemann has written persuasively about covenanting as human vocation. He notes, first of all, that identity means being grounded in Another, viz., Yahweh, God of Israel. Thus the process of identity does not begin within the human person. It begins, rather, outside the human person—it is the work of a God who is capable of calling forth the potential and drive within the person. At the same time covenant making presupposes the fundamental capacity to accept gifts. It is not a question of "Now, Yahweh, I owe you one" or "You scratch my back, Yahweh, and I'll scratch yours." Covenant means evoking that quality that is perhaps the most difficult for the isolated human, viz., the ability to say "thank you." For both the Priestly Writer and Second Isaiah the gift beckoning for gratitude is the overcoming of exile with its concomitant despair.

Covenant making in this setting of gratitude is the basis of hope. It is the painfully wrenched admission that we do not dispose of our own lives all by ourselves. There is Another who longs to fulfill promises and provide continuity in fidelity to the pledged word. As W. Brueggemann has perceived, this act of covenant making does not transpire in splendid silence. It is linked with "Let it be" of creation. God freely chooses to set aside human chaos and confusion by speaking. In turn, the human partner must be willing to let it happen and acknowledge it as "good, very good." Covenant binds us in the ongoingness of creation in our daily living. Covenant binds us to Another.

However, the challenge of genuine identity does not end with the recognition of Yahweh as Lord of the covenant and ourselves as individuals committed to the faithful response of obedience. It is much more demanding than that. W. Brueggemann further notes that person means belonging with, belonging to, and belonging for. While most of us can eventually acknowledge belonging with God, belonging to God, and belonging for God, we find it much more difficult and demanding to belong with, to belong to, and to belong for the God of *Israel*. Covenant means that by being bound up with our God, we are necessarily bound up with the people of God. The traditions of Exodus 19 supply ample proof that it is the people who react to the covenant God—it is not a gathering of otherwise isolated individuals. To react to and to interact with this God means to react to and to interact with the entire people. Covenant implies the annihilation of all purely one-on-one relationships to God. Yahweh is only "my" God on the condition that I am linked to the people of God.

NEW TESTAMENT COVENANT MAKING AND ITS IMPLICATIONS

The Last Supper tradition of the New Testament is rooted in the covenant-making traditions of the Old Testament, viz., the meal and the blood rite. Jesus chose to relate to his community by means of a meal. The bread and the wine which they shared symbolized their covenant relationship to one another. To share the bread and the wine meant to share the destiny and fate of Jesus. It was the solemn pledge to be part and parcel of the life-style of Jesus, which was best reflected in his self-giving, viz., his death-style. "'My blood, the blood of the covenant, to be poured out on behalf of many'" (Mk 14:24) clearly alludes to the blood rite of Ex 24:6-8. For the biblical audience blood symbolizes life. Their concern and their future are thereby interlocked.

Paul was the one who saw most realistically the community dimensions of Eucharist. In 1 Cor 11:17-34 he responds to the divisive practices of the Corinthian community. Their celebration of the Lord's Supper involved: (1) a fraternal meal in which the members of the community were to share their food and drink; and (2) the actual Eucharist itself. Paul is forced to discipline the Corinthians for their lack of charity in the first part that clashes with the very notion of Eucharist. The refusal to share led to drunkenness in one case and hunger in another. Paul then goes on to quote the words of institution. To share the Lord's body and blood means to share as a community on all levels. Eucharist is not intended to generate a multiplicity of factions. As J. Murphy-O'Connor writes, for Paul Eucharist without concern for the body of Christ, i.e., the community, is nothing less than a sham.

BIBLIOGRAPHICAL SUGGESTIONS

Baltzer, Klaus. *The Covenant Formulary.* Philadelphia: Fortress, 1971.

Brueggemann, Walter. "The Formfulness of Grief," *Int* 31 (1977) 263–275.

_____ . "The Covenanted Family: A Zone for Humanness," *Journal of Current Social Issues* 14 (1977) 18–23.

_____ . "Covenanting as Human Vocation," *Int* 33 (1979) 115–129.

Craghan, John F. *This Is the Word of the Lord.* Liguori: Liguori Publications, 1972.

Craghan, John F. "The Elohist in Recent Literature," *BTB* 7 (1977) 23-35.

Freedman, David N. "Divine Commitment and Human Obligation," *Int* 18 (1964) 419-431.

Hillers, Dilbert R. *Covenant: The History of a Biblical Idea.* Baltimore: The Johns Hopkins University Press, 1969.

McCarthy, Dennis J. "The Symbolism of Blood and Sacrifice," *JBL* 88 (1969) 166-176.

_____ . *Old Testament Covenant.* Growing Points in Theology. Richmond: John Knox, 1972.

_____ . "Further Notes on the Symbolism of Blood and Sacrifice," *JBL* 92 (1973) 205-210.

_____ . *Treaty and Covenant.* AnBib. 2nd edition. Rome: Biblical Institute Press, 1978.

Mendenhall, George E. "Law and Covenant in Israel and the Ancient Near East," *BA* 17 (1954) 2-50 = *Law and Covenant in Israel and the Ancient Near East.* Pittsburgh: Biblical Colloquium, 1955.

Muilenburg, James. "The Form and Structure of the Covenantal Formulations," *VT* 9 (1959) 347-365.

Murphy-O'Connor, Jerome. "Eucharist and Community in First Corinthians," *Worship* 50 (1976) 370-385, 51 (1977) 56-69.

Newman, Murray. *The People of the Covenant.* New York: Abingdon, 1962.

Raitt, Thomas M. *A Theology of Exile: Judgment/Deliverance in Jeremiah and Ezekiel.* Philadelphia: Fortress, 1977.

Vaux, Roland de. *The Early History of Israel.* Philadelphia: Westminster, 1978, 441-447.

Vawter, Bruce. "The God of Hebrew Scriptures," *BTB* 12 (1982) 3-7.

Weinfeld, Moshe. "Berit—Covenant vs. Obligation," *Bib* 56 (1975) 120-128.

Wilson, Robert R. "The Old Testament Genealogies in Recent Research," *JBL* 94 (1975) 169-189.

_____ . *Genealogies and History in the Biblical World.* New Haven: Yale University Press, 1977.

CHAPTER 5

The Invitation to Law
As Response to Covenant

Biblical passages to be read: Ex 19-23; Lv 18; Dt 5-11; Tb 4; Pss 15, 24; Jer 35; Hos 4:1-3; Mt 22:34-40; Mk 12:28-34; Lk 10:25-28; Rom 7-8.

THE EMPIRICAL SITUATION

For most of us laws are distasteful realities. We often view them as limitations on our freedom. Laws prevent us from doing or omitting something since we are reasonably assured that punishment will follow in the wake of non-observance. We often see laws as impersonal extrinsic impositions. We often sense that they are dictated by anonymous bodies or persons. We realize that we cannot genuinely identify the lawgiver(s), and we feel we are doomed to react to impersonal forces that restrict our otherwise regular behavior. Our distaste becomes most evident in the very formulations of the laws. Laws, as we know them in the Church and society at large, are generally cast in third person constructions. Thus the lawgiver does not meet us on the personal plane of "I and Thou." We are reduced to coping with minutiae of technical language where law-keeping is as far removed from people-keeping as possible.

We are the product of our own age and previous ages. We try to get around the laws as much as possible. We devote no little time and energy to studying the statutes and regulations with the fond hope that we will not be obligated. Even when we knowingly violate the law, we are apt to employ the most eloquent mouthpiece or the most convincing advocate "to get us off the hook." Ultimately law is an unhappy fact of life. We grimly accept the penalty for violation, although we often have no purpose of amendment in avoiding future violations.

Both the Ten Commandments and the Covenant Code of Israel are a challenge to regain some of our rich biblical heritage. They warn us that frustration and desperation will only result if we view legislation as an impersonal curtailing force. On the other hand, they assure us that the ability to cope and the capacity to live will emerge if we see legislation in terms of a person or persons who have a claim on our covenantal response. Laws are an instructive area for assessing our genuine response to the Word of God in community.

THE TEN COMMANDMENTS

At the end of Exodus 19 Moses once again undertakes his mediatorial task of descending the mountain and communicating the results of his meeting with Yahweh to the people. However, the next verse, Ex 20:1, begins rather abruptly: "Then God delivered all these commandments (the Ten Commandments)." But Ex 20:19 is even more abrupt when the people ask Moses to speak to them, under the plea that a direct communication from God would only result in their untimely death. This text presumes that the Decalogue has not yet been given. To confound matters, Yahweh speaks directly to Moses alone (see Ex 20:22) in compliance with the people's wishes.

We begin with the expectation that to explain the present state of the text is a plus. We start by noting that both the Ten Commandments (Ex 20:2-17) and the Covenant Code (Ex 20:22-23:19) are generally allotted to the Elohist tradition. However, they are not Elohist traditions after the manner of Moses' call in Exodus 3-4 or the storm theophany in Exodus 19. Rather, they are independent traditions which the Elohist has inserted into his text. Originally the great fear of the people expressed in Ex 20:18 ("When the people witnessed the thunder and lightning, the trumpet blast and the mountain smoking, they all feared and trembled") followed upon the storm theophany in Exodus 19. At this stage Moses complies with the people's request and hears the entire revelation from Yahweh. At a later stage, however, the people had to listen to the fundamental revealed law, viz., the Ten Commandments. On this level only Moses receives the rest of the legislation because of the people's fear now arising from direct communication with God.

We may be inclined to conceive of this shuttling between levels as subtle biblical maneuvering. However, it would be wrong to yield to this inclination. According to the covenant pattern some form of commands/prohibitions is demanded. It would be only too natural to link the presence at Sinai with the basic formulation of the divine will in such a way that Yahweh confronts the people directly. What

42

is of the utmost importance here is that Israel establishes her commands/prohibitions in the very person of Yahweh. Sinai thus becomes the primer for seeing legislation as bound up with a person whom Israel has freely chosen to follow.

APODICTIC LAWS AND THE ORIGIN OF MOST OF THE DECALOGUE

The Decalogue is a series of apodictic laws. Such laws impose a command directly on a person. They oblige that person to perform (or refrain from performing) some particular action that the lawgiver judges to be desirable (or harmful). "Honor your father and your mother" (Ex 20:12) and "You shall not kill" (Ex 20:13) are clear examples of apodictic laws. Although the famous scholar A. Alt thought that apodictic laws were unique to Israel, subsequent study has shown that, while they are not unique to Israel, they are characteristic of Israel and are found only exceptionally in the ancient Near East at large.

R. A. F. MacKenzie has contributed notably to our appreciation of the apodictic laws and thereby to their significance for response to the Word of God in community. He notes that only in Israel is the god conceived of as actually drafting and dictating legislation. (On the stela of the Code of Hammurabi the Babylonian god Marduk is pictured as merely handing the code to the king.) Although the Israelite receives these apodictic laws as a member of the believing community, he/she cannot hide in the group and thus escape being involved. The apodictic form directly challenges the believer's conscience. Earlier laws of the ancient Near East forbade such abuses as adultery and theft. However, the direct style and formulation of "You shall not commit adultery" (Ex 20:14) and "You shall not steal" (Ex 20:15) make them new laws. Here a superhuman authority has spoken to the Israelite and confronted that Israelite in the most absolute manner.

Initially there probably were separate series of succinct commands that were rhythmic and hence relatively easy to learn. (For example, Hos 4:2: "False swearing, lying, murder, stealing, and adultery!") These separate series eventually became part of a larger composition. E. Gerstenberger and J.-P. Audet have convincingly shown that most of the Ten Commandments (the first three commandments are obviously not included) were originally tribal wisdom, hence they are older than Moses and Sinai. The young learned these principles of human conduct and later passed them on to the next generation. Tribal elders and parents were authorized to watch over, transmit, and develop these prime principles.

Tribal wisdom is simply the human observation that certain actions make for good order while other actions jeopardize the community. Leviticus 18 is an example of such tribal wisdom: "'You

43

shall not have intercourse with your son's daughter or with your daughter's daughter, for that would be a disgrace to your own family. You shall not have intercourse with the daughter whom your father's wife bore to him, since she, too, is your sister'" (vv 11-12). Incest harms the common good, especially in the small tribal setting.

Jeremiah 35 is also an example. During the reign of the faithless King Jehoiakim, Jeremiah is presented as offering an example of people who have been faithful to the traditions of their ancestors, viz., the Rechabites. They lived on the border between the settled land and the desert, observing the traditions of the desert community by not drinking wine or building houses: "'We do not drink wine,' they said to me (Jeremiah): 'Jonadab, Rechab's son, our father, forbade us in these words: "Neither you nor your children shall ever drink wine. Build no house and sow no seed; neither plant nor own a vineyard ...""" (vv 6-7). (For another instructive example see Tobit's advice to his son Tobiah in Tb 4:3-19.)

YAHWEH'S POSITION

The opening of the Ten Commandments (Ex 20:2—the NAB may also be rendered: "'I am the Lord, your God'") uses the self-presentation formula that was common in royal inscriptions. It later made its way into liturgy. In Ex 20:2 Yahweh is seen as one who has intervened on Israel's behalf—the liberated slaves are now Yahweh's people ("'who brought you out of the land of Egypt, that place of slavery'"). With regard to most of the Ten Commandments Yahweh assumes the position of the tribal elders and parents. But there is a new and significant dimension. Israel is called upon to obey, not only because these regulations are for the good of the tribe, but also because Yahweh has acted decisively in their lives. The foundation of commands/prohibitions is a person who has a claim on Israel owing to a love clearly demonstrated and established.

Israel's later liturgy adapted the recitation of commands/prohibitions as the condition for taking part in the ceremonies of the temple. For example, Ps 15:1 asks the question: "O Lord, who shall sojourn in your tent? Who shall dwell on your holy mountain?" Ps 15:2-5 then recites the commands/prohibitions whose observance makes participation in liturgy possible, e.g., "slanders not with his tongue, who harms not his fellow man, . . . who lends not his money at usury and accepts no bribe against the innocent" (vv 3, 5). It is significant that this liturgy emphasizes the demands of social justice (see also Ps 24), not merely cultic obligations.

THE BOOK OF THE COVENANT

The Book of the Covenant is the content of God's deliberations with Moses after the latter is instructed by the people to approach

44

God and receive the message directly (see Ex 20:18-21). The material includes Ex 20:22-23:19. It is called the Book of the Covenant because of Ex 24:7: "Taking the book of the covenant, he read it aloud to the people . . ."

Most of us probably experience some disgust as we pore over the legal material in the Book of the Covenant. We may think that the Decalogue is sufficient and that we should not be plagued by the legal niceties of this section. Once again, however, we should be guided by Israel's tradition. That tradition presumes that there are values yet to be discovered. This section discusses how theological and ethical principles apart from the Decalogue work out in practice. At the same time the Book of the Covenant shows how Israel adopted and adapted the legal traditions of the ancient Near East.

Ex 21:2-22:16 may be called the casuistic or case law section of the Book of the Covenant. For example, "when an ox gores a man or a woman to death, the ox must be stoned; its flesh may not be eaten. The owner of the ox, however, shall go unpunished. But if the ox was previously in the habit of goring people and its owner, though warned, would not keep it in; should it then kill a man or a woman, not only must the ox be stoned, but its owner also must be put to death" (Ex 21:28-29). Casuistic or case law is typical of the ancient Near East—hence an indication that Israel has borrowed from the environment. Such law is purely pragmatic. It does not contain any formal obligation on the individual. As R. A. F. MacKenzie observes, such an individual is merely warned of the unpleasant results of a given action. Instead, the obligation falls on the judge who must carry out the solution contained in the legislation. We are dealing *per se* with third person impersonal laws.

However, two points are noteworthy. First of all, the economic and political background of such legislation points to a time after the occupation of the Promised Land—hence after the experience at Sinai. This implies that later obligations could be linked with the divine presence in the desert. Secondly, although these are *per se* third person impersonal laws, they take on a personal character because they are the will of the God of Israel. Hence by their inclusion in the Book of the Covenant they are removed from their former arid legal setting and become the demand of the God who intervened in the Exodus.

Ex 20:22-26; 22:17-23:19 is the apodictic section of the Book of the Covenant. This section demonstrates another feature of Israel's legal system, i.e., paraenesis or exhortation. It is rather typical of Israel to suggest motives or reasons for fulfilling an obligation. For example, "'Never take a bribe, for a bribe blinds even the most clear-sighted and twists the words even of the just'" (Ex 23:8). Similarly

45

"'You shall not molest or oppress an alien, for you were once aliens yourselves in the land of Egypt'" (Ex 22:20). Israel's jurisprudence advocates learning from one's history and experience. Hence the experience of oppression should serve to counteract any unjust treatment of a resident alien. For Israel law means response to the covenant God.

THE GREAT COMMANDMENT AND SPECIFIC STIPULATIONS

Not too long ago a considerable number of biblicists believed that Israel's covenant with Yahweh in Exodus 19-24 was modelled on the suzerain (Yahweh)–vassal (Israel) treaties. These biblicists pointed to the Hittite (the Hittites were a main power in the ancient Near East from ca. 1400 to 1250 B.C.) treaties with their vassal states. The prevailing view today is that Exodus 19-24 cannot be cut to fit the Procrustean bed of these treaties. However, the discovery of a possible analogy has proved to be extremely valuable elsewhere.

There is a reasonable consensus that the Book of Deuteronomy follows the format of these suzerain-vassal treaties. (Here the neo-Assyrian treaties of the seventh century B.C. are significant.) The treaty format includes the following elements: (1) a preamble introducing the suzerain; (2) an historical prologue narrating the previous relationship between the two parties with an implicit exhortation to obey (see Dt 1-3; also 29:1-7); (3) stipulations, both general (see Dt 5-11; also 29:16-21) and specific (see Dt 12-26); (4) a clause for preservation and regular reading (see Dt 31:9-13, 26); (5) a list of gods as witnesses to the treaty (see Dt 30:19 where heaven and earth function as witnesses); and (6) curses for disobedience and blessings for obedience (see Dt 28; also 4:25-31; 29:22-27; 30:1-10). Once again Israel makes use of foreign models in order to express her unique relationship with her covenant lord.

To appreciate Israel's personalistic jurisprudence further, we must take note of the relationship between the general stipulation and the specific stipulations. This general stipulation is known as the Great Commandment. Its requirement of loyalty is much more than the first or most important commandment. As K. O'Connell explains it, it is the very soul of all the specific commandments. It provides the proper spirit that is to be found in the individual commandments. It points to the intention that should, in turn, control the observance of all commands/prohibitions. This is the one commandment that sets up the proper moral attitude. The Great Commandment, therefore, is the key to the ethical dimension of Israel's legislation.

The creativity of Israel is evident from the fact that she was never satisfied with merely a once and for all Great Commandment. Israel looked with discerning eyes at her own status as covenant people and the subsequent demands of her covenant lord. Her writers were able to choose the proper formulation for the proper time.

N. Lohfink has made an exhaustive study of the exhortatory passages that comprise Deuteronomy 5-11. He has shown, first of all, that Israel formulated versions of the Great Commandment by borrowing from the political treaty language of the ancient Near East. In the treaties the suzerain has exclusive rights to the vassal's loyalty. This automatically presupposes the elimination of all others as claimants to the vassal's loyalty. This political language is evident in Dt 6:14: "'You shall not follow *other* gods . . .'"

Yahweh's exclusive right to Israel's wholehearted obedience is also expressed in the language of love. Extrabiblical documents attest to the fact that "to love" means "to obey" (see 2 Sm 19:7; 1 Kgs 5:15). Far from implying mere sentiment, Dt 6:5 calls for the complete dedication of Israel to the Lord of the covenant: "'Therefore, you shall love the Lord, your God, with all your heart, and with all your soul, and with all your strength.'" It is such loyalty that provides the proper incentive and motivation for responding to all the specific stipulations. It is interesting to note that the New Testament has preserved the connection between the commandment of love and legal observance: "'He who obeys the commandments he has from me is the man who loves me'" (Jn 14:21; see also 1 Jn 2:3-5).

N. Lohfink has also uncovered other formulations of the Great Commandment in Deuteronomy 5-11 that do not derive from the political sphere but from Israel's own religious perception. Dt 6:12-15 reformulates the Great Commandment in terms of fear of God: "'The Lord, your God, shall you fear; him shall you serve and by his name shall you swear'" (Dt 6:13). The accent is now on religious respect which is to characterize all the specific commandments. The author links this fear with Israel's trembling before Yahweh at Sinai (see Dt 5:5) and with Israel's suggestion that only Moses approach Yahweh because of this experience (see Dt 5:24-27).

Humans are always prone to forget when times are prosperous. It is against such a background that Deuteronomy 8 offers a fresh interpretation of the Great Commandment: "'But when you have eaten your fill, you must bless the Lord, your God, for the good country he has given you. Be careful not to forget the Lord, your God, by neglecting his commandments . . .'" (vv 10-11). In carrying out the specific commands/prohibitions the Israelite is thereby urged to be mindful of the gifts received. To remember the gifts is, therefore, not to forget the Giver implied in the specific legislation.

Not human righteousness but divine gratuitousness! When Israel is tempted to see her own righteousness as the basis for possession of the land, she needs to be reminded of her record of sinfulness. In this situation she must recall God's graciousness and make divine gift-giving the motivation for observance: "'After the Lord, your God, has thrust them out of your way, do not say to yourselves, "It is because of my merits that the Lord has brought me in to possess this land"; for it is really because of the wickedness of these nations that the Lord is driving them out before you'" (Dt 9:4). In the temptation to haughtiness Israel should recall her history of rebellion (see Dt 9:23-24). This recollection should evoke God's generosity which, in turn, should inform her response to Yahweh's will.

The Synoptics present Jesus' understanding of the Great Commandment in their own ways (see Mt 22:34-40; Mk 12:28-34; Lk 10:25-28). (Because of his audience Luke does not use the expression "great" or "first" commandment. Instead, he answers the question of everlasting life with the parable of the Good Samaritan.) In all of them, however, Jesus combines love of God (Dt 6:5) with love of neighbor (Lv 19:18). For the Synoptics Jesus seeks to find the heart of Israel's legislation that then serves to give meaning to the entire corpus of commands/prohibitions. Hence Jesus is faithful to his Old Testament roots. In the New Testament it is also interesting to observe the reformulation of the Great Commandment à la Deuteronomy. It is reduced to "Follow me." Legislation is, therefore, rooted in a person. To acknowledge Jesus as the mediator of the new covenant is to see all laws as somehow linked to his person.

LEGISLATION AND CHRISTIAN MATURITY/LIBERTY

Why do we obey laws? In the Judeo-Christian tradition most of us obey because we know that obedience will bring its own reward in the hereafter. While such observance is a value, it may also suggest that we are unfaithful to the Old Testament tradition. According to the common view, belief in an afterlife did not emerge in Israel until the second century B.C. As a result, the Israelites who obeyed the Ten Commandments prior to this time did not anticipate eternal bliss because of obedience. Rather, they accepted the Decalogue because they accepted the person of Yahweh. They obeyed because obedience was the right response. This must make us pause and ask if we are not overly reward-oriented. Is doing the right thing because it is the right thing sufficient for us?

The Old Testament provides ample evidence of several attempts at reform. In the second half of the seventh century B.C. King Josiah initiated a sweeping reform when a copy of the core part of Deuteronomy was discovered in the temple (see 2 Kgs 22:8-23:25). The reform, however, was shallow so that, when the king died suddenly some years later, the reform movement collapsed. In the second half of the fifth century B.C. the scribe Ezra also introduced a sweeping reform (see Ezr 7-10; Neh 8-10) which was based on a brand new edition of the Torah or Pentateuch. Like the reform of Josiah, the reform of Ezra lacked that dynamic element of open-ended response which is the Great Commandment. Such response gave way to fixed legal codifications that the people had to observe without complaint. As K. O'Connell remarks, person-oriented legal observance now degenerated into thing-oriented legal observance. There were no longer any attempts at reformulation of the Great Commandment. Such truncated legal observance led the Jews to disregard God's help and to find their own righteousness in fulfillment of the law. In the first century A.D. the meticulous observance of the Law became *the* practice of religion.

Paul is the best example, on the one hand, of the viciousness of depersonalized legal exactitude and, on the other hand, of the liberating experience of putting a person at the heart of all legal requirements. Basically Paul rediscovered his roots. He rejected casuistry and recovered covenant. Religion was no longer the exact execution of legal requirements, no longer the precise fulfillment of unending do's and don't's. Religion was now the needing of the Spirit of Jesus in meeting the needs and demands of the community. For Paul this was really "old time religion." The person of Jesus in the death-resurrection experience had overcome the impersonalism of legal formalism: "The law of the spirit, the spirit of life in Christ Jesus, has freed you from the law of sin and death" (Rom 8:2).

It is obvious to most that living in society by its very nature calls for legislation. A biblical spirituality, however, requires that we ferret out the values inherent in laws. According to Paul, the Christian is freed from all laws (see Rom 8:14-16; Gal 5:18). According to Paul, also, the Christian is redeemed, yet not totally redeemed. The Christian can always fall back into that egotistical, self-serving caricature of living known as "the flesh." Because of that possibility the Christian must ask whether he or she has perhaps lost a value that the positive law seeks to preserve. The genuine Christian senses the need to worship God in community. Such a Christian is not obliged, for example, by the precept requiring attendance at Sunday Mass. If, however, the Christian's dispositions change so that the need to worship in community is no longer felt, then the positive law fulfills an important function. By commanding attendance at worship, the positive law informs such a Christian that he or she has lost a value and should attempt to regain it.

Both S. Lyonnet and J. Murphy-O'Connor point out that in his commentary on 2 Cor 3:17 St. Thomas Aquinas speaks succinctly yet eloquently about the tension between human liberty and legal enforcement. He writes that only a person who acts of his or her own accord really acts freely. On the other hand, a person who must

49

be impelled by another to do or to refrain from doing something is not really free. Thus the person who avoids evil, not because it is evil but because the law forbids it, is not free. Only the person who avoids evil precisely because it is evil is really free.

The covenant tradition of the Old Testament must be ever rediscovered and reapplied in the multitude of both civil and ecclesiastical laws. It must force us to appreciate the personalism of its legal formulation. Israel's penchant for apodictic laws should teach us that only third person impersonal formulation is dehumanizing and demeaning. Above all, Israel's quest for ever newer formulations of the Great Commandment should remind us—and remind us forcefully—that we must always preserve a hierarchy of values and that ultimately our values must reside in a Person. The response to the Word of God in community demands the rediscovery of our biblical legal tradition. We may legitimately ask if this rich biblical tradition will have an impact, e.g., on the revision of the Code of Canon Law. If the Church rightly borrows from Roman law, should she neglect Israel's contributions to adopting and adapting borrowed material?

BIBLIOGRAPHICAL SUGGESTIONS

Alt, Albrecht. "The Origins of Israelite Law," *Old Testament History and Religion*. Garden City: Doubleday, 1968, 101-171.

Audet, Jean-Paul. "Origines comparées de la double tradition de la Loi et de la Sagesse dans le Proche-Orient ancien," *Orientalists' Congress*. Moscow: 1962. I, 352-357.

Benoit, Pierre. "The Law and the Cross according to St. Paul," *Jesus and the Gospel*. New York: Seabury, 1974. II, 11-39.

Botterweck, G. Johannes. "The Form and Growth of the Decalogue," *Concilium* 5 (1965) 58-79.

Fensham, F. Charles. "The Role of the Lord in the Legal Sections of the Covenant Code," *VT* 26 (1976) 262-274.

Fitzmyer, Joseph A. "Saint Paul and the Law," *The Jurist* 27 (1967) 18-36.

Gerstenberger, Erhard. "Covenant and Commandment," *JBL* 84 (1965) 38-51.

Lohfink, Norbert. "The Great Commandment," *The Christian Meaning of the Old Testament*. Milwaukee: Bruce, 1968, 87-102.

Lyonnet, Stanislas. "St. Paul: Liberty and Law," *The Bridge* 4 (1962) 229-251.

MacKenzie, Roderick A. F. *Two Forms of Israelite Law*. Toronto: 1961.

—————. "The Formal Aspect of Ancient Near Eastern Law," *The Seed of Wisdom. Essays in Honour of T. J. Meek*. Edited by W. S. McCullough. Toronto: University of Toronto Press, 1964, 31-44.

McCarthy, Dennis J. *Old Testament Covenant*. Growing Points in Theology. Richmond: John Knox, 1972.

—————. *Treaty and Covenant*. AnBib. 2nd edition. Rome: Biblical Institute Press, 1978.

Moran, William L. "The Ancient Near Eastern Background of the Love of God in Deuteronomy," *CBQ* 25 (1963) 77-87.

Murphy-O'Connor, Jerome. *Becoming Human Together.* Wilmington: Michael Glazier, 1977.

Nicholson, Ernest W. *Exodus and Sinai in History and Tradition.* Growing Points in Theology. Richmond: John Knox, 1973.

Nielsen, Eduard. *The Ten Commandments in New Perspective.* SBT. Naperville: Allenson, 1968.

Noth, Martin, "The Laws in the Pentateuch," *The Laws in the Pentateuch and Other Essays.* Edinburgh: Oliver & Boyd, 1966, 1-107.

O'Connell, Kevin G. "Obedience to the Word," *The Word in the World. Essays in Honor of Frederick L. Moriarty, S. J.* Edited by R. J. Clifford and G. W. MacRae. Cambridge: Weston College Press, 1973, 47-57.

Phillips, Anthony. *Ancient Israel's Criminal Law.* Oxford: Blackwell, 1970.

Stamm, Johann J. & Andrew, Maurice E. *The Ten Commandments in Recent Research.* SBT. Naperville: Allenson, 1967.

Wright, Christopher J. H. "The Israelite Household and the Decalogue: The Social Background and Significance of Some Commandments," *Tyndale Bulletin* 30 (1979) 101-124.

CHAPTER 6

The Invitation to Redemption

Biblical passages to be read: Ex 7-13; 15:1-18; 32-34; Jos 3-4.

THE REDEMPTION AND ENNUI

For many of us the pawnshop is the setting for our understanding of redemption. Because of circumstances we have to surrender an item, receive a low price for it, and in improved circumstances buy it back or "redeem" it. As a result, redemption is merely so much buying and selling. We find it difficult to see a person at work in this tedious task of redemption. As a result, the term "redemption" seems condemned to a meaningless existence at the edge of our spiritual existence. Thus it cannot affect our response to the Word of God in community.

We are tempted to regard redemption as a *fait accompli*. Something occurred somewhere in the distant past and that something somehow continues to have an impact on us now. For many of us redemption is an open and closed case—we cannot imagine how it can be open-ended. As a result, we are content to move along, undisturbed by the shocks in our world and untroubled by our own lack of reaction to those shocks.

Given our own sinfulness, we may be content to put ourselves down and dismiss any possibility of renewing our covenantal allegiance. Thus, even though we can conceive of redemption as open-ended, our history of sin impinges on our will to begin anew. In our theology sinfulness always means failure—hence we cannot conceive of success arising out of failure. In this view to know failure is to persist in failure.

Granted the ongoingness of redemption and granted the possi-

53

bility of renewal, we may conclude that we must reinstate ourselves personally. We exclude the possibility of a mediator or mediators. We insist that we are duly prepared to work out our own reinstatement. In this model spirituality is always a one-on-one relationship.

The central event in Israel's relationship with Yahweh is the Exodus, and the central reflection on that event is the Book of Exodus. Surprisingly perhaps that collection of stories, laws, and song addresses our questions about redemption. It is that book especially that can provide a variety of insights into our God and ourselves since Exodus regards redemption as a many-splendored thing because the redeemer is a many-splendored person. In our dissatisfaction and ennui regarding redemption Exodus can yet empower us to respond to the Word of God in community.

YAHWEH, A MANY-SPLENDORED REDEEMER

Yahweh has an exclusive claim on human life. Our first biblical story demonstrating Yahweh's right is the legend of Abraham's sacrifice of Isaac (see Gn 22). As a legend, it is a narrative intended to edify later generations by emphasizing the virtues of the main figure. Although Israel's neighbors sacrificed their first-born, Israel abhorred this practice. In Israel, therefore, one did not kill the first-born; instead, one "redeemed" the first-born both of humans and animals.

In the Book of the Covenant there is the bald statement: "'You shall give me the first-born of your sons; you must do the same with your oxen and your sheep'" (Ex 22:28-29). Ex 13:1-2, 11-16, however, interprets the legal requirement. It situates the practice of redemption in the account of the deaths of the first-born of the Egyptians. In place of the first-born of humans Israel is to offer a substitute. The reason is given: "'When Pharaoh stubbornly refused to let us go, the Lord killed every first-born in the land of Egypt . . . That is why I sacrifice to the Lord everything of the male sex that opens the womb, and why I redeem every first-born of my sons'" (Ex 13:15). While this does refer to a buying back from Yahweh, it is also a statement about human life. Yahweh values the lives of the Israelites because they are his sons, sons whom he protected in the harrowing experience of the going forth from Egypt. This redemption is person-oriented.

Yahweh is the caring liberator. The Hebrew verb "to go/come out" (*yāṣā'*) is a common verb in the biblical story of the "going out." However, it is also a legal term that describes a slave's acquisition of freedom. The Book of the Covenant lays down this regulation regarding slaves: "'When you purchase a Hebrew slave, he is to serve you for six years, but in the seventh year he shall be given his freedom (literally: he shall *go out* free without cost)'" (Ex 21:2). In the setting of Exodus redemption means that the nomads regain their freedom. On the feast of Unleavened Bread the following rubric is to be observed: "'On this day you shall explain to your son, "This is because of what the Lord did for me when I came out of Egypt"'" (Ex 13:8). To be redeemed is to be liberated.

The corresponding action of the slave owner is "to dismiss, to let go" (*šillaḥ*). Once again the Book of the Covenant is instructive for legal usage: "'When a man strikes his male or female slave in the eye and destroys the use of the eye, he shall *let the slave go* free in compensation for the eye'" (Ex 21:26). In Exodus Pharaoh is pictured as a slave owner who will not emancipate his slaves. He rejects God's command through Moses: "'Let my people go'" (Ex 5:1). Redemption for the Israelites means being removed from the caprice of Pharaoh and thus regaining their integrity. As redeemer, Yahweh is the one who checks Pharaoh's stubbornness and wins freedom for the slaves: "'When Pharaoh stubbornly refused to *let us go,* the Lord killed every first-born in the land of Egypt . . .'" (Ex 13:15).

Redemption is not only the legal exercise of manumission, it is also the dramatic intervention on Yahweh's part whereby the oppressed gain the upper hand and defeat their enemies. The Hebrew text uses the causative of the verb "to go out" (*hôṣî'*), meaning "to bring out." Thus "'It was with a strong hand that the Lord *brought* you *away'*" (Ex 13:3). This dramatic intervention looks to Yahweh's overpowering deliverance at the Sea of Reeds. As we shall see shortly, redemption means the presence of the commander-in-chief who brooks no opposition from Israel's enemies. To be redeemed means to experience the power and might of the God of Israel.

For Israel redemption includes more than the acquisition of freedom or the experience of liberation. There is a goal in God's activities, viz., the entrance into the Promised Land. The text speaks about Yahweh as the one who "causes to go up" (*he'ĕlāh*). Ex 3:8 speaks about a movement that originates in Egypt (see Gn 46:3-4) but concludes in Canaan: "'Therefore I have come down to rescue them from the hands of the Egyptians and lead them out (literally: cause to go up) of that land into a good and spacious land, a land flowing with milk and honey . . .'" Redemption thus acquires geographical contours: presence in the land is the sacrament of God's redemption. Whereas those who participated in the Exodus experienced it as a "going out," later generations saw it as the acquisition of a homeland. Redemption means having a future.

Yahweh is also the defender of those treated unjustly. The word that we blithely translate as "salvation" (the Hebrew verb *hôšîa'* and its substantives) is associated with Israel's legal system where the "savior" is an advocate or a witness for the defense (see Dt 22: 27). On two occasions Yahweh's dramatic intervention at the Reed Sea is described as "salvation." Yahweh's role as savior is here linked with his role of Divine Warrior whereby he battles on behalf of Israel. "But Moses answered the people, 'Fear not! Stand your ground, and you will see the victory ($t^e\check{s}\hat{u}'\hat{a}$) the Lord will win for you today . . . The Lord himself will fight for you . . .'" (Ex 14:13-14). Similarly in the Song of the Sea Yahweh's military exploits are the concrete demonstration of "salvation": ". . . he has been my savior ($t^e\check{s}\hat{u}'\hat{a}$) . . . The Lord is a warrior . . ." (Ex 15:2, 3). In this context redemption means salvation in the form of active military intervention for those treated unjustly.

Yahweh is also one who takes the situation of the family very seriously. Yahweh is a $g\bar{o}'\bar{e}l$—a term that is usually translated "redeemer." This is the function of the head of the family who is responsible for the family's integrity. If family property is in danger of going to an outsider, the $g\bar{o}'\bar{e}l$ keeps it in the family like Jeremiah in Jeremiah 32 or Boaz in Ruth 4. In a vendetta the $g\bar{o}'\bar{e}l$ exacts a life for the life taken from his clan or group (see Nm 35:12; Dt 19: 6, 12; Jos 20:3, 5, 9). Ex 15:13 speaks of Yahweh as one who "redeemed" Israel and guided her: "In your mercy you led the people you redeemed; in your strength you guided them to your holy dwelling." The sociological background suggests that in the Exodus Yahweh stepped in at a crucial moment of family existence and identified with the needs of the family by guiding her. Redemption here means ongoing interest in family members and family affairs.

The best known form of redemption in Exodus is undoubtedly the Passover. This was originally an offering made by nomadic shepherds for the welfare of the flocks when the tribe would set out for new pasture grounds in the spring. (It is older than the Exodus experience and was only subsequently linked with the Feast of Unleavened Bread, a feast of farmers.) It was a critical time in the life of the tribe, i.e., a time when the young of the sheep and the goats would be born. This pastoral background is evident, for example, in the attire (sandals, staff, loins girt—see Ex 12:11), unleavened bread (ordinary bread used by Bedouin shepherds—see Ex 12:8), and bitter herbs (desert plants used as spices—see Ex 12:8). To ward off all dangers to humans and animals (the enemy is personified as the $ma\check{s}\hat{p}\hat{i}t$ or "destroyer"—see Ex 12:23), blood was smeared on the tent poles (see Ex 12:7). In this setting redemption means that Yahweh will "pass over," i.e., protect the dwellings smeared with the blood (see Ex 12:13, 23, 27). For Israel the old feast of nomadic shepherds is reinterpreted so that the quest is now for the final pasture grounds, viz., the land of Canaan. Redemption means involvement, participation, and protection at the time of transition, viz., the Exodus.

YAHWEH DEFEATS PHARAOH

Redemption means the overcoming of the most obstinate forces and the defeat of the most unyielding powers. The writers of the Book of Exodus did not hesitate to conceive of Yahweh's victory as the undoing of Pharaoh. Since in Egyptian theology Pharaoh is a god from the moment of his birth, Yahweh's victory over Pharaoh is a victory over all those, gods included, who do not respect the rights of the weak and oppressed. In a very perceptive article D. J. McCarthy prefers to speak of "Moses' dealings with Pharaoh" rather than plagues. He shows how the final editors of Exodus arranged the material in such a way that Pharaoh had to bend to Yahweh's will. In this "redemptive" process Yahweh gets the upper hand.

A good example of this redemptive process is Pharaoh's recognition of Yahweh. In Ex 7:17 (the first plague) Pharaoh is instructed: "'This is how you shall know that I am the Lord.'" In Ex 8:6 (the second plague) Pharaoh must acknowledge that there is none like Yahweh. In Ex 8:18 (the fourth plague) Pharaoh must do more, viz., realize that Yahweh is in the midst of the land of Egypt. Finally in the seventh plague Pharaoh must make two more admissions: (1) that there is none like Yahweh in the whole world; and (2) that the earth belongs to Yahweh (see Ex 9:14, 29). The redemptive process means the humbling of the opponent.

Another example of this process is Pharaoh's willingness to grant concessions. In Ex 8:21 (the fourth plague) Pharaoh allows the Hebrews to sacrifice to their God but only within the limits of Egypt. A little later in the same plague he grants them permission to sacrifice in the wilderness provided they do not wander too far (see Ex 8:24). In Ex 9:27-28 (the seventh plague) Pharaoh concedes that he and his subjects are wrong and that Yahweh is right. He thus promises to let Israel go. Finally in Ex 10:16 (the eighth plague) the mighty divine king acknowledges: "'I have sinned against the Lord.'" The redemptive process means giving in to Yahweh.

REDEMPTION IS OPEN-ENDED

The earliest tradition (ca. 1100 B.C.) for the crossing of the Reed Sea is the Song of the Sea in Ex 15:1-18. This is an adaptation of a Canaanite poem some three centuries older which speaks of a battle between Baal, the god of fertility, and Yamm, the god of the sea. In this adaptation Yahweh-Baal defeats Pharaoh-Yamm. The opening words of the poem introduce Yahweh as the commander-in-chief of Israel's armies: "I will sing to the Lord, for he is gloriously triumphant; horse and chariot he has cast into the sea" (Ex 15:1).

The following verses develop Yahweh's military posture: "The Lord is a warrior, Lord is his name! Pharaoh's chariots and army he hurled into the sea . . ." (Ex 15:3-4). In this tradition the Egyptians drown in a storm sent by Yahweh (there is only an allusion to the safe passage of the Israelites). The poem then goes on to speak of Yahweh's victories over Philistia, Edom, Moab, and Canaan (see Ex 15:14-16). The action then concludes at Yahweh's palace/sanctuary: "And you brought them in and planted them on the mountain of your inheritance—the place where you made your seat, O Lord, the sanctuary, O Lord, which your hands established" (Ex 15:17).

There is an obvious connection between the crossing of the Reed Sea and the crossing of the Jordan River in Joshua 3-4. While authorities dispute which tradition (Exodus or Joshua) influenced the other, the link between the crossing and the entrance into the land is apparent. In the light of Israel's history, therefore, the happening in Egypt at the Reed Sea was never in and for itself. That event was open-ended. Consequently it looked to the conquest-settlement. To celebrate the Exodus meant to celebrate the start of a divine action which necessarily included other divine actions. To celebrate the Exodus was to celebrate the open-endedness of God's activities. Redemption is never one single action, although we may single out one aspect. By its very nature redemption is a succession of events in which God challenges the community to ongoing involvement. Living in Jerusalem is thereby linked to coming out of Egypt.

COVENANT RENEWAL

Exodus 32-34 is, in one sense, one of the most difficult passages in all of the Old Testament. It is only too clear that several traditions have sought to interpret the incident and in so doing have left their mark on what thus appears to be a rather confusing text. In another sense, however, there is a general overall structure that has emerged from the work of the final editors. In interweaving their sources, they have provided a rather coherent picture of the whole event. It is this final picture that we shall examine. At the same time our examination is a vote of confidence in the final form of the account.

By admitting the confusing interplay of traditions, we are also admitting our inability to offer a satisfactory answer to the question: "Well, what really happened in the first place?" We cannot give a satisfactory answer since the sources available to us were not interested in relating "the cold facts." The overlay of traditions suggests that their interests lay elsewhere. Reading between the lines, however, R. de Vaux has suggested that it is possible to see the Golden Calf story as linked to an event that occurred during the wilderness experience. Possibly a rival group of dissidents abandoned Moses' leadership. Instead of accepting the Mosaic ark of the covenant as the symbol for the divine presence, they set up a bull image. In any event, it is likely that the calf/bull tradition was an ancient one since Jeroboam I, king of Israel, reintroduced this symbol at his sanctuaries in the northern kingdom in the late tenth century B.C. (see 1 Kgs 12: 26-32).

In its final form Exodus 32-34 is basically an account of covenant renewal. It contains all the elements of the cycle of sin found elsewhere in the Bible (see Jgs 3:7-11). The first element is *sin*, generally apostasy. In Jgs 3:7 the Israelites forget Yahweh and serve the Canaanite deities. The sin leads to the second element, *punishment*. In Jgs 3:8 the Israelites are subjugated by a foreign power. Punishment is then followed by the third element, *repentance*. In Jgs 3:8 the Israelites use the language of lamentation—they cry out to the Lord. The fourth and final element is *restoration*. In Jgs 3:9-11 God answers the plea of the people by sending a judge to rule Israel.

This cycle may strike us as being overly naive, perhaps even overly mechanical. However, it is essentially a description of the human condition. Sin is a fact of life, albeit a rather distressing fact. Yet this sinfulness attests to the fact that God chooses to reveal himself/herself through a sinful people. We know a great deal about our caring God because we know how our God manifests that care in dealing with a very human people. Both the Old and New Testaments lay greater emphasis on God's community as the refuge of sinners rather than the church of the elect. Exodus 32-34 also shows that it is easier to identify with these Golden Calf mavericks than with an idealized Mosaic church of the perfect.

This cycle is basically at the heart of the garden story in Genesis 2-3. As we shall see, it is the depicting of that overly human character David and his experience of sin and forgiveness. Genesis 2-3, Exodus 32-34, and Second Samuel 11-12 are studies in the human condition and, at the same time, studies in the very need for ongoing renewal.

In the Exodus account the *sin* consists of rebellion: "'Come, make us a god who will be our leader; as for the man Moses who brought us out of the land of Egypt, we do not know what has happened to him'" (Ex 32:1). The construction of the Golden Calf is specifically a sin of apostasy: "'They have soon turned aside from the way I pointed out to them asking for themselves a molten calf and worshiping it . . .'" (Ex 32:8). By rejecting the mediator, Moses, the people have rejected Yahweh.

The Canaanite literature from Ugarit helps to explain several features of the Golden Calf. In Ex 32:34 Aaron responds to Moses' question about the construction of the Golden Calf by saying that he threw the gold into the fire and out came the calf. In ancient Canaan the belief was held that cultic objects were self-produced, requiring no human workmanship. In Ex 32:20 Moses dispatches the Golden Calf by mutually exclusive acts: burning, grinding, scattering. In the Canaanite literature when Anat, Baal's consort, kills Mot, the god of death, she seizes him, cleaves him, winnows him, burns him, grinds him, sows him, and scatters him. As P. Watson has indicated, the extrabiblical parallel shows that the Golden Calf is thoroughly destroyed, even to the point of scattering the remains on the water (see Dt 9:21).

The sin of rebellion finds its apt expression in the breaking of the tablets (see Ex 32:19). This should not be construed as only a fitting way in which Moses can communicate his anger. While it is that, it is much more. The tablets represent the covenant relationship—they are the specific stipulations which the people have agreed to accept. Consequently the breaking of the tablets is the breaking of the covenant relationship.

The *punishment* is found in two different traditions. According to the first tradition Moses rallies around himself the Levites who spare no mercy in afflicting the guilty. They slaughter friends and neighbors, reaching no less a figure than three thousand (see Ex 32:25-29). According to the second tradition there is the fact of punishment but not the manner of punishment: "Thus the Lord smote the people for having had Aaron make the calf for them" (Ex 32:35). While this second tradition is ostensibly less violent than the first, it also witnesses to Yahweh's painful reaction to Israel's rebellion.

The text presents Israel's *repentance* in a very symbolic way. In Ex 33:1-3 Moses is informed that, although an angel will accompany Israel on her trek to the Promised Land, Yahweh will not be in her midst. At this point the people react by going into mourning and refusing to wear ornaments (Ex 33:4). After another threat from Yahweh (Ex 33:5) the text adds that the people put aside their ornaments from Sinai onwards (Ex 33:6). The absence of jewelry means the presence of repentance.

Given the manner of expressing the sin, viz., the breaking of the tablets, the manner of expressing the *restoration* is what we would expect—the making of new tablets. According to Ex 34:27-28 Moses spends forty days and forty nights on the mountain, without eating or drinking. During this time he inscribes the new tablets according to God's dictation.

In the light of the Ten Commandments in Ex 20:2-17 it is rewarding to observe the new Ten Commandments (Ex 34:28) in Ex 34:10-26. (Actually there are twelve commandments here—the ten commandment tradition of Ex 34:28 is later.) These commandments should have appeared after the Yahwist's account of the volcanic eruption in Exodus 19. (The Yahwist like the Elohist used a preexisting list of commandments.) However, when pride of place was given to the Elohist's Decalogue and the Book of the Covenant in Exodus 20-23, the Yahwist's commandments were transferred to Exodus 34 where they function as the new covenant stipulations. Although the Yahwist's commandments are often called "ritual" because, e.g., they require celebrating the feast of Weeks (Ex 34:22) or going to the sanctuary three times a year (Ex 34:23), they are as "ethical" as the commandments of Exodus 20. Because they reflect a concern with an agricultural community, they are younger than the desert community. However, they still share in the sense of covenant loyalty, viz., how to remain faithful to Yahweh in the midst of a pagan society. It is understandable, therefore, why this list is often referred to as "Yahweh's privilege law."

MOSES - THE COVENANT MEDIATOR

In relating to Yahweh, Israel insisted on the need for having certain members of the community who would represent the community before the covenant Lord. Israel's awareness of this need goes back to the time of the Exodus experience itself. The traditions are unanimous in attributing the most unique manner of covenant mediation to Moses. However, mediation is not to be construed as a pious mouthing of the will of the deity. As G. W. Coats has noted, Moses appears often as quite the opposite—he functions as Yahweh's loyal opposition. It is his task to dialogue and dispute with God in order to ensure the common good.

In the Golden Calf incident the plan of the rebels is to find a replacement for Moses as leader (see Ex 32:1, 4). However, God's reaction is precisely the opposite. God plans to retain Moses as leader but to start a new group of people (see Ex 32:7-10). Moses begins his mediation by showing Yahweh that there must be continuity in history. To have the people die in the desert would draw only scorn from Yahweh's enemies in Egypt. "'Let your blazing wrath die down; relent in punishing your people. Remember your servants Abraham, Isaac and Israel . . .'" (Ex 32:12-13). Like the rebels Moses opposes the divine will. Unlike the rebels he is not branded an apostate. Moses illustrates that it is possible to change the direction of Yahweh's plan and not incur guilt. Not unsurprisingly the scene concludes: "So the Lord relented in the punishment he had threatened to inflict on his people" (Ex 32:14).

Ex 33:1a, 12-17 is a structural unit that further corroborates Moses' unique role as mediator. In Ex 33:1a Yahweh states that the people are to leave the place. But in Ex 33:12-14 Moses counters by observing that he does not know God's choice of companion for the trip. "'Now, if I have found favor with you, do let me know your ways . . .'" (Ex 33:13). Moses pursues the argument by noting that only the divine presence during the journey will indicate that the people and himself are truly special. The Lord's response is not unexpected: "'This request, too, which you have just made, I will carry out, because you have found favor with me and are my intimate friend'" (Ex 33:17).

In Ex 33:18-23; 34:7-8 Moses receives a special theophany. According to Ex 33:23 Moses will see only God's back, not God's face. The outcome of this encounter is Moses' shining face which is described in Ex 34:29-35. The radiance of his face requires that he wear a veil while conversing with the Israelites. However, when communing intimately with Yahweh, he wears no veil. The glow on the face of Moses is the symbol of the authority that this unique mediator possesses. Significantly that authority is not his own private possession—it is a charism to be exercised for the common good. Moses identifies in terms of Israel. To be mediator means to bring the community's needs before the Lord and to employ one's prerogatives for that community. To be Moses, to be mediator means to be bound up with the struggles and joys of God's people.

REDEMPTION TODAY

In our response to the Word of God in community we are compelled to examine the wealth of theology relating to the experience of Jesus. According to both Jesus and his interpreters redemption is much more than buying and selling. It connotes, among other things, the acquisition of a people and their liberation through the death-resurrection experience of Jesus (see Rom 3:24; Eph 1:14). It is also a Passover that leads to the new pasture grounds of union with the Father (see 1 Cor 5:7). It is the Day of Atonement when the blood of Jesus overcomes the ravages of sin once and for all (see Heb 9:11-28). J. A. Fitzmyer has written that for Paul redemption is basically reconciliation, i.e., at-one-ment, implying that all those forces that separate God from humans are now conquered (see Rom 5:10-11; 11:25; 2 Cor 5:18-20; Eph 2:16; Col 1:20-22). Our response today must acknowledge that redemption is a many-splendored reality because of the many-splendored person of the Redeemer.

Redemption continues to be open-ended. Passion leads to death, death to resurrection, resurrection to exaltation, exaltation to Pentecost, and Pentecost strains forward to the parousia. We are caught up in the tension between the new crossing of the Reed Sea and the new crossing of the Jordan River. This tension calls for our reaction now. New York is still caught up with Calvary and the Upper Room. New York still strains for the final coming. Redemption as open-ended means that New York must reply now.

We are still sinful people, members of a sinful community. Fortunately we can share the Jesus experience which leads from death to life. We can yet be rehabilitated and made contributing members of the community. We can come back from the dead and begin again, enriched by the experience of goodness and the awareness of our weakness. To know failure can still mean to realize success by renewal.

We are still in need of mediators. We share Jesus' unique mediation in a more profound way than the way in which Israel shared Moses' mediation. That mediation means that the plight and trouble, the joy and exuberance of our sisters and brothers become our plight and trouble, our joy and exuberance. Such mediation flows from involvement in covenant. The triangular relationship still obtains!

Reflection on Israel's understanding of redemption, especially in the Book of Exodus, must move us beyond apathy and ennui. Reflection on Jesus' experience of redemption in the light of his Old Testament roots must generate a positive reaction. Such reflection must prove that we are genuinely responding to the Word of God in community.

BIBLIOGRAPHICAL SUGGESTIONS

Coats, George W. "The Traditio-Historical Character of the Reed Sea Motif," *VT* 17 (1967) 253-265.

_____ . "The Song of the Sea," *CBQ* 31 (1969) 1-17.

_____ . "The King's Loyal Opposition: Obedience and Authority in Exodus 32-34," *Canon and Authority: Essays in Old Testament Religion and Theology.* Edited by G. W. Coats & B. O. Long. Philadelphia: Fortress, 1977, 91-109.

Croatto, J. Severino. *Exodus. A Hermeneutics of Freedom.* Maryknoll: Orbis, 1981.

Cross, Frank M., Jr. *Canaanite Myth and Hebrew Epic.* Cambridge: Harvard University Press, 1973, 79-90, 112-144.

Daube, David. *The Exodus Pattern in the Bible.* All Souls Studies. London: Faber & Faber, 1963, 27-35, 39-46.

Fitzmyer, Joseph A. "Pauline Theology," *JBC* 79:80-97 = 814-817.

_____ . "Reconciliation in Pauline Theology," *No Famine in the Land. Studies in Honor of J. L. McKenzie.* Edited by J. W. Flanagan & A. W. Robinson. Missoula: Scholars Press, 1975, 155-177.

Lohfink, Norbert. "The Song of Victory at the Red Sea," *The Christian Meaning of the Old Testament.* Milwaukee: Bruce, 1968, 67-86.

Lyonnet, Stanislas & Sabourin, Leopold. *Sin, Redemption, and Sacrifice.* AnBib. Rome: Biblical Institute Press, 1970, 61-184.

McCarthy, Dennis J. "Moses' Dealings with Pharaoh," *CBQ* 27 (1965) 336-347.

_____ . "Plagues and Sea of Reeds: Exodus 5-15," *JBL* 85 (1966) 137-158.

Miller, Patrick D., Jr. "God the Warrior," *Int* 19 (1965) 39-45.

_____ . *The Divine Warrior in Early Israel.* Harvard Semitic Monographs. Cambridge: Harvard University Press, 1973.

Muilenburg, James. "The 'Office' of the Prophet in Ancient Israel," *The Bible in*

    Modern Scholarship. Edited by J. P. Hyatt. New York: Abingdon, 1965, 74–97, especially 79–88.

Sawyer, John F. A. *Semantics in Biblical Research. New Methods of Defining Hebrew Words for Salvation.* SBT. Naperville: Allenson, 1972.

Stuhlmueller, Carroll. *Creative Redemption in Second Isaiah.* AnBib. Rome: Biblical Institute Press, 1970, 99–131.

Vaux, Roland de. *Ancient Israel.* New York: McGraw-Hill, 1961, 258–267, 484–493.

_____ . *Studies in Old Testament Sacrifice.* Cardiff: University of Wales Press, 1964, 1–26.

_____ . *The Early History of Israel.* Philadelphia: Westminster, 1978, 456–459.

Watson, Paul L. "The Death of 'Death' in the Ugaritic Texts," *Journal of the American Oriental Society* 92 (1972) 60–64.

Wijngaards, Joanne N. *"hwsy'* and *h'lh* - A Twofold Approach to the Exodus," *VT* 15 (1965) 91–102.

CHAPTER 7

The Invitation to Cult

Biblical passages to be read: Gn 1:1-2:4a; Ex 24:12-31:18; 39-40;
Lv 9; Jos 18:1; 19:49-51.

OUR RELUCTANCE TO WORSHIP

On Sunday we put aside our bulky newspapers, interrupt our
bigger than usual breakfast, and drive off to church. We find
ourselves in a group. However, on many occasions we would not
describe it as a community. Other humans converge on the same
geographical location. We move down the pew, search for the missal-
ette, and make sure of the weekly envelope. We begin with a hymn,
become lost in the readings (especially the reading from the Old
Testament), and then more lost perhaps in the homily that may
have nothing to do with the readings anyway. Eventually we hear
the words of institution and at the invitation of the celebrant wish
the other people Christ's peace. We approach to receive the Eucharist.
The single file procession is somehow typical of our worship. We
are individuals lost in a sea of individuals. We feel cut off from the
past and strain for that pleasant release which comes only with: "The
Mass is ended." Worship in such circumstances is definitely an unnatu-
ral act.

Presence of God is elusive. We should find it in the holy place
but are not always successful. We should expect it in the other worshipers but are not infrequently disappointed. We should find it in
ourselves but are often deceived. We must shrug our shoulders and
concede that absence is more evident than presence.

The Upper Room seems so remote. It is difficult enough to identify with the present congregation, let alone a group of Jews in a

Jerusalem setting some nineteen centuries ago. We are even more remote from the "Let it be" of creation. We are adrift, anxious to know about our call to worship and its historical roots, but resigned to keep on drifting.

THE PRIESTLY WRITER AND HIS AUDIENCE

While the Priestly Writer's exilic audience is different in several respects from ourselves, there are significant areas of convergence. He wrote for a community that had lost its sense of community. As the Book of Lamentations describes it, ". . . Jerusalem is defiled; all who esteemed her think her vile now that they see her nakedness; she herself groans and turns away" (Lam 1:7). He wrote for a people that had lost its sense of history. In the words of Ezekiel, the Priestly Writer's contemporary: "He (Yahweh) made me walk among them (the bones) in every direction so that I saw how many they were on the surface of the plain. How dry they were! He asked me: 'Son of man, can these bones come to life?'" (Ez 37:2-3). He wrote for a community that had lost its sense of holiness. In his survey of Israel's relationship with Yahweh, Ezekiel had to lament: "Will you defile yourselves like your fathers? Will you lust after their detestable idols? By offering your gifts, by making your children pass through the fire, you defile yourselves with all your idols even to this day" (Ez 20:30-31).

In order to revive the sense of community, history, and holiness, the Priestly Writer takes advantage of the Sinai tradition in Exodus. From Ex 24:15b to 31:18 this writer has Moses receiving instructions from Yahweh. After the Golden Calf incident (Ex 32-34) this writer then has Moses executing all the instructions received on the mountain, in Exodus 35-40. These chapters, which may strike us, at least initially, as being the most boring in the entire Bible, are basically a political document. By emphasizing such institutions as the tabernacle, priesthood, etc., the Priestly Writer seeks to underline the presence of Yahweh. Unlike the Yahwist and the Elohist, the Priestly Writer does not have any covenant making on Sinai. For him there is only one covenant, viz., the one concluded with Abraham in Genesis 17, which is an ongoing covenant. However, since Sinai focuses on God's presence, the Priestly Writer uses its theophany as the fitting receptacle for the traditions promoting community, history, and holiness.

SINAI, THE TABERNACLE, AND THE FIRST SACRIFICE

Israel's theologians are not always the bluntest of people. Frequently they choose to let the traditions imply their theology rather than articulate it with the utmost clarity. We would prefer to have the Priestly Writer say that Yahweh's manifestation on Sinai is

66

linked to the building of the tabernacle and that both, in turn, are linked to the execution of the first sacrifice, which is thereby the norm for all sacrifices. Instead, this theologian challenges us to read his text and draw the proper conclusions. Although we may experience some incipient difficulty in relating the texts, we may be assured that his audience grasped this relationship immediately and was thus exhorted to recover their sense of community, history, and holiness.

In Ex 24:15b-16a this author describes the divine manifestation on Sinai in the following way: ". . . a cloud covered the mountain and the glory of the Lord settled upon Sinai." "Glory of the Lord" implies all those external trappings that indicate the divine presence (see Jn 1:14). Later on in Ex 40:34 the Priestly Writer states that the divine presence is not limited to Sinai; it is also found in the tabernacle: "Then the cloud covered the meeting tent, and the glory of the Lord filled the Dwelling." This theologian also binds together the divine presence on Sinai with the preparations for offering the first sacrifice. At the same time Yahweh requires human interaction. In Ex 24:16b he writes: "The cloud covered it for six days, and on the seventh day he called to Moses from the midst of the cloud." In Lv 9:1 (the Book of Leviticus, although drawn from various sources, is the work of the Priestly Writer) Yahweh also enlists aid: "On the eighth day Moses summoned Aaron and his sons, together with the elders of Israel . . ."

In Ex 24:17 the Priestly Writer describes the manner of God's presence on the mountain: "To the Israelites the glory of the Lord was seen as a consuming fire on the mountaintop." The mention of fire is significant. It is clearly an element in the Sinai theophany but it is also an essential ingredient in the offering of sacrifice. Thus in Lv 9:23b-24a: "On coming out (i.e., from the tabernacle where God is present) they (Moses and Aaron) again blessed the people. Then the glory of the Lord was revealed to all the people. Fire came forth from the Lord's presence and consumed the holocausts . . ." There is thus a marked parallelism between God's manifestation on Sinai (which is perpetuated in the tabernacle) and the first act of worship after that manifestation. The Priestly Writer has thereby contrived the Sinai experience to make it the model for worship. God's presence in the tabernacle recalls the presence of this same God on Sinai. God's presence in sacrificial liturgies makes one think immediately of Sinai and so link both occasions. Or better, the sacrifice continues the presence of God at Sinai. Whenever sacrifice is offered, the participants are immediately caught up in the central event of Sinai. The seemingly dismal rubrics are charged with a keen pastoral sense.

P. J. Kearney has attempted to show that the work of the Priestly Writer in Exodus 25-31 is actually a reflection of the creation account in Gn 1:1-2:4a. To correspond to the six days of creation, he observes that there are six speeches by Yahweh to Moses (see Ex 25:1; 30:11, 17, 22, 34; 31:1). In each of these speeches he contends that there is some element that overlaps with God's work on the successive days of creation. In Ex 27:20-21, for example, there is mention of the pure olive oil which is to be used for the light—hence a parallel with the overcoming of darkness in Gn 1:2-3. In Ex 30:14 there is reference to the poll tax that must be paid by those twenty and *over*. P. J. Kearney sees this as a possible parallel with the separation of the waters *above* and the waters below the dome on the second day of creation (see Gn 1:6-8). Ex 30:25 speaks of the holy anointing oil. Elsewhere this oil is employed in the anointing of kings (see Ps 89:21). Vv 37-38 of this same psalm sing of David's throne lasting like the sun and the moon—a possible reference to the fourth day of creation, viz., the creation of the sun and the moon (see Gn 1:6). In Ex 31:17 God rests on the seventh day in keeping with the creation account (see Gn 2:2-3).

REACTIONS TO EXODUS 25-31 AND SOME POSSIBLE CONCLUSIONS

The parallels suggested by P. J. Kearney may strike us as being somewhat tenuous, as more than a bit contrived. Our reaction, therefore, is to abandon the quest for the link between creation and liturgy. However, as we shall see shortly, the Priestly Writer has established some telling structures in Exodus 35-40 as well as Gn 1:1-2:4a and parts of the Book of Joshua that provide clearer support for the nexus between creation and liturgy. This should lead us to reevaluate P. J. Kearney's intuitions.

If the structures in the work of the Priestly Writer bear out the connection between creation and liturgy, then we must conclude that for this author the enactment of cult is the experience of God's creative power. Another way of stating this is to assert that creation is ongoing. God did not do something in the beginning and then stop. Rather, God continues to create in and through the covenant people. To take part in worship is to catch up the experience of the initial creation.

The creation-liturgy relationship looks to the Priestly Writer's insistence on the presence of God. In liturgy God continues to be with the covenant people. In turn, this is a reaction to the situation of this theologian's audience, viz., exile. In exile Israel is in chaos. It is God's creative action in Gn 1:1-2:4a that overcomes chaos. The cult, as developed in Exodus and elsewhere, is that perpetual institution by which Israel can overcome chaos. Liturgy is the instrument of reviving and recalling the sense of community, history, and holiness. For this theologian, to know Yahweh as covenant Lord is to know Yahweh as unrelenting Creator.

TWO STRUCTURES IN THE PRIESTLY WRITER AND CONCLUSIONS

J. Blenkinsopp has increased our appreciation of the Priestly Writer's methodology by his study of the structures in that source. This theologian, therefore, cannot be charged with a haphazard arrangement of sterile rubrics. He must be viewed as a serious writer who went about his task meticulously in order to respond to the urgent pastoral needs of his day. These structures reflect a plan behind what might otherwise seem to be a study in confusion.

A first structure, and indeed a very common one, is that of the execution of a command given directly or indirectly to God. For example, in Ex 6:30 Moses replies to Yahweh that he cannot deal with Pharaoh since he is a poor speaker. Yahweh overcomes this objection by making Aaron Moses' prophet (see Ex 7:1). The Priestly Writer concludes this scene by remarking: "Moses and Aaron did as the Lord had commanded them" (Ex 7:6). With regard to the observance of the Passover the people comply with the divine ordinance: "... and the Israelites went and did as the Lord had commanded Moses and Aaron" (Ex 12:28). It is worth noting that this execution of command formula is not limited to the Book of Exodus. It is also in evidence in the Books of Genesis, Leviticus, Numbers, Deuteronomy, and Joshua.

On special occasions the Priestly Writer uses a more solemn statement of execution. For example, at the completion of the tabernacle with all its furnishings, etc., the Priestly Writer observes: (literally) "And all the work of the dwelling of the meeting tent was completed. And the sons of Israel did (it) according to everything which the Lord had commanded Moses. Thus they did (it)" (Ex 39:32; see also 39:43). At the division of the land in the Book of Joshua the Priestly Writer also employs a more solemn statement of execution: (literally) "As Yahweh commanded Moses, thus the sons of Israel did (it) and they divided the land" (Jos 14:5).

A second structure, less frequent but more important than the execution of command formula, is that of successful completion of work. In the work of the Priestly Writer this formula occurs only three times. First of all, towards the end of the creation account: "Thus the heavens and the earth and all their array were completed . . . God was finished with the work he had been doing . . ." (Gn 2:1-2). Secondly, at the conclusion of the tabernacle and all its furnishings: "Thus the entire work of the Dwelling of the meeting tent was completed" (Ex 39:32) and "Finally, he (Moses) set up the court around the Dwelling and the altar and hung the curtain at the entrance of the court. Thus Moses finished all the work" (Ex 40:33). Thirdly, at the completion of the division of the land: (literally) "And they (Eleazar, Joshua, and the heads of the families) finished dividing the land" (Jos 19:51).

The incidence of the successful completion of work formulae and the more solemn execution of command formulae indicates the notoriety that the Priestly Writer attaches to certain events. (Because of the nature of the creation account there cannot be an execution of command formula.) In light of this we must conclude that the Priestly Writer has deliberately chosen to give structural prominence to these events: (1) the creation of the world; (2) the construction of the tabernacle; and (3) the establishment of the tabernacle in the land and the division of the land among the tribes. It must be noted that all three events are concerned with God's abiding presence. The presence in the tabernacle and the presence in the land are linked to creation.

A COMPARISON OF THE CREATION OF THE WORLD AND THE CONSTRUCTION OF THE SANCTUARY

A closer examination of these two events (better, the one ongoing event) shows that the Priestly Writer regards the work of the Creator and the work of Moses as complementary. In Gn 1:31 God looks at all the work of creation and concludes: (literally) "behold, it was very good." Similarly in Ex 39:43 Moses looks approvingly at the construction of the tabernacle and its accouterments and observes: (literally) "Behold, they had done it." At the conclusion of creation God blesses the seventh day (Gn 2:3). In Ex 39:43 at the completion of the tabernacle Moses blesses the Israelites.

An important element in these two passages is the presence of the spirit. In Gn 1:2 God's spirit—or a mighty wind—goes back and forth across the deep. In Exodus the craftsman in charge of executing the tabernacle is Bezalel. In Ex 31:3 God says to Moses: "'. . . and I have filled him with a divine spirit of skill and understanding and knowledge in every craft.'" In Ex 35:31 Moses repeats this statement to the Israelites.

A COMPARISON OF THE CREATION OF THE WORLD AND THE DISTRIBUTION OF THE LAND

We have already noted the Priestly Writer's successful completion of work formula in Gn 2:2 and Jos 19:51. Another recurring formula in the Priestly Writer is Gn 1:28: "'Be fertile and multiply; fill the *earth* and *subdue* it'" (see also Gn 9:1; 17:2, 20; Ex 1:7). As W. Brueggemann has pointed out, the Priestly Writer has employed Holy

War language, but in doing so he does not envision a military take-over. Rather, this theologian anticipates God's abiding presence among the people of Israel. If Israel responds in fidelity, God will continue to be present. Jos 18:1 demonstrates this presence: "After they had *subdued* the land (*earth*), the whole community of the Israelites assembled at Shiloh, where they set up the meeting tent." The presence of the sanctuary in Israel is the presence of the creator God of Israel. Proper cult is one of the responses of fidelity expected from God's people.

The spirit is also manifest in the distribution of the land, just as it was in the construction of the tabernacle. The architect of the takeover and distribution of the land is Joshua. According to the Priestly Writer in Nm 27:18 Yahweh instructs Moses: "'Take Joshua, son of Nun, a man of spirit, and lay your hand upon him.'" Dt 34:9 restates Moses' action: "Now Joshua, son of Nun, was filled with the spirit of wisdom, since Moses had laid his hands upon him . . ."

(The presence of the Priestly Writer in the Book of Joshua creates a problem for those critics who limit this theologian to the Pentateuch. It is likely that Deuteronomy, and not the Priestly Writer, was the last strand in the formation of the Pentateuch—thus a JEPD hypothesis. In any event, an appreciation of the structures in the Priestly Writer should not be dismissed in source criticism of the Book of Joshua.)

THE PRIESTLY WRITER'S DOCTRINE OF CREATION AND CULT

To take part in worship is to continue the refrain of the creation account: "It is good, very good." Cult serves as a meeting place for the sense of community, history, and holiness. The God whom Israel worships is the God who has challenged them to undertake the human task of having a human world. The God whom Israel serves is the God who has acted on their behalf in history—not only in the Exodus and the exile but also in the seemingly insignificant moments of everyday living. The God whom Israel adores is the God who urges a constant realization of the fact of sinfulness and the need for renewal.

In the standard theology of the ancient Near East the Babylonian god Marduk had defeated Yahweh at the time of the fall of Jerusalem in 586 B.C. and subsequent exile. For the Priestly Writer this was unacceptable theology. Indeed Yahweh could appear all the more victorious in the presence of the defeat of Israel. Although there was no temple, although Israel was among the nations, God could yet be present. Reconstruction was a reality contingent upon the response of the people. In his plan of reconstruction the Priestly Writer envisioned the land made holy by the divine presence in the tabernacle. The return would be genuine renewal not only with

71

the occupation of the land but also with the proper covenantal response to Yahweh. Their sacrifices would be genuine if the people's dispositions corresponded to them, viz., an awareness of the all-holy One in their midst.

Rubrics and institutions do not come first, people do! In our casual reading of Exodus we are apt to convict the Priestly Writer of rubricalism and externalism. However, a closer reading of his text suggests the opposite. Rubrics and institutions are expressions of a greater reality, i.e., the complete response of the covenant people to the covenant lord. Specifically, rubrics and institutions are to catch up the dynamism of creation in the beginning and perpetuate that dynamism in the service of Yahweh. If the rubrics and institutions do not communicate the demanding presence of the creator God of Israel, then they cease to lose their reason for being.

THE PRIESTLY WRITER AND MODERN WORSHIP

Christian celebration of the Eucharist is rooted in the Old Testament experience of creation and cult. In Eucharist we once again seek to release the Spirit over the chaos of our world. Thus we ask the Father in the name of Jesus to send the Spirit over our gifts of bread and wine. Hence the Spirit that overshadowed Mary and filled Jesus in the resurrection is again invited to set aside chaos, which is a fact of Christian life. Eucharist means abiding presence, creative presence, challenging presence.

Eucharist sacramentalizes our sense of community. By relating to Jesus, we must relate to his body, the Christian community. Eucharist reminds us that we must respond to the challenge of creation by making a better world for sisters and brothers—in other words, overcoming the chaos in their lives. Eucharist is the rejection of all one-on-one, single file relationships with our God. To celebrate Eucharist is to recommit ourselves to the ongoing work of creation, the rehabilitation of sisters and brothers.

Eucharist sacramentalizes our sense of history. The words of institution link us with the Upper Room, and the language of sacrifice connects us with the creation story. Eucharist urges us to renew our sense of belonging, i.e., of belonging to the covenant people and, by that very fact, of belonging to the human family. Our history is never a quiet study of facts and events that do not touch others. Our history is necessarily an involvement in the family of Jesus and hence the human family. We must be bread and wine for everyone.

Eucharist sacramentalizes our sense of holiness. The very need for bread and wine says that we are weak and must be nourished. The very fact of sharing this bread and wine with the community means that we are challenged to be holy for the community, in the community, and with the community. To profess divine presence within Eucharist means to advertise that same presence outside Eucharist. We are ever a sinful people striving to proclaim our sinless God. Eucharist is the sacrament of our willingness to be renewed. Our rubrics and our institutions are for people.

We must conclude that our Priestly Writer is as timely today as ever. Response to the Word of God in community must imply that his sense of creation, cult, and divine presence is to become viable in us. Ultimately our Priestly Writer is a creative writer.

BIBLIOGRAPHICAL SUGGESTIONS

Ackroyd, Peter R. *Exile and Restoration*. OTL. Philadelphia: Westminster, 1968, 84-102.

Blenkinsopp, Joseph. "The Structure of P," *CBQ* 38 (1976) 275-292.

——— . *Prophecy and Canon*. Notre Dame: Notre Dame University Press, 1977, 54-79.

Boorer, Sue. "The Kerygmatic Intention of the Priestly Document," *Australian Biblical Review* 25 (1977) 12-20.

Brueggemann, Walter. "The Kerygma of the Priestly Writers," *ZAW* 84 (1972) 397-414 = (with H. W. Wolff) *The Vitality of Old Testament Traditions*. Atlanta: John Knox, 1975, 101-113, 143-151.

Clements, Ronald E. *God and Temple*. Oxford: Blackwell, 1965, 109-122.

Clifford, Richard J. "The Tent of El and the Israelite Tent of Meeting," *CBQ* 33 (1971) 221-227.

Cross, Frank M., Jr. *Canaanite Myth and Hebrew Epic*. Cambridge: Harvard University Press, 1973, 293-325.

Haran, Menahem. "The Divine Presence in Israelite Cult and Israelite Institutions," *Bib* 50 (1969) 251-267.

Kearney, Peter J. "Creation and Liturgy: The P Redaction of Ex 25-40," *ZAW* 89 (1977) 375-387.

McEvenue, Sean. "Word and Fulfilment: A Stylistic Feature of the Priestly Writer," *Semitics* 1 (1970) 104-110.

——— . *The Narrative Style of the Priestly Writer*. AnBib. Rome: Biblical Institute Press, 1971.

——— . "The Style of a Building Instruction," *Semitics* 4 (1974) 1-9.

Otto, Rudolf. *The Idea of the Holy*. 2nd edition. New York: Oxford University Press, 1950.

Terrien, Samuel. *The Elusive Presence. Towards a New Biblical Theology*. Religious Perspectives. New York: Harper & Row, 1978, 161-226.

Vaux, Roland de. *Ancient Israel*. New York: McGraw-Hill, 1961, 271-517.

CHAPTER 8

The Invitation to David's Story/Our Story

Biblical passages to be read: Gn 2:4b-3:24; 1 Sm 21:2-8; 2 Sm 7; 11-12; 23:13-17.

IMPLICATIONS OF THE TERM "STORY"

As a literary genre, story is a narrative that seeks to arouse tension and resolve it. This classification is especially true for certain biblical stories about David. However, our concern with the term "story" is at a deeper level. As J. Shea observes, our interpretation of traditional stories helps us to learn precisely who we are and what we are about. Actually we find ourselves in the stories of God. These stories, Shea further suggests, create a world, adopt an attitude, and suggest a behavior. These musty, dusty accounts from the ancient Near East are not simply our heirlooms. They are our identity papers. When David is narrated, we are narrated. When David cannot confront reality, we cannot confront reality.

This "story" implies that we must go behind the text. Our concern is not to determine the intention of the original author for the purposes of historical analysis, although such a quest is invaluable. Instead, our quest is hermeneutical—we are anxious to learn how the story or stories concern us. Thus our quest is to uncover the basic human experiences of life and death, success and failure, hope and despair. According to J. Shea, in interpreting the stories, we seek to release the God who lives there. We might add: by releasing God, we are able to find ourselves. Biblical stories, and here the David stories, are more than narratives that arouse tension and then resolve it. Such stories are accounts of our tension and our efforts to resolve them. David locks arms with us. We avoid the generation gap because David's story is our story.

In terms of identity W. Doty suggests that we are what we relate. In our stories we are actually attempting to become other than we are. We are trying to experiment with possible futures, we are hoping to gain insights as to where we have been. The individual is always searching for new guides, new "how to" books. In our response to the Word of God in community we instinctively sense the need to model ourselves on other humans and their plights. In relating to that Word, we have actually concluded that human experiences are really not so vastly different. David in the tenth century B.C. is somehow a revelation of ourselves.

We cannot help expressing our gratitude to the original authors of these stories as well as to those editors who compiled the final canonical text. Though we are often at a loss to know the criteria for making a book a biblical book, we can still see that they were concerned with perennially human plots, problems, and persons. In this sense the book of the synagogue, which is the book of the Church, is our family album. We are there. David's story is our story.

WE BEGIN WITH OURSELVES AND WORK BACKWARDS

What determines the stories that we tell? Where is the starting point? Do we begin with the biblical stories and move forwards? Or do we start with ourselves and move backwards? Before answering such questions, we might further ask: where does our need for stories originate? Is it simply a question of choosing this story or that story or is our selection process a more human undertaking?

Our need for stories—and indeed particular types of stories— begins with ourselves. It is our situation that determines what we shall choose and what we shall eliminate. As T. P. Burke sees it, stories have a claim on us because of their correspondence with our experience. We do not seek to make stories intelligible or acceptable. Rather, we use them to offer as satisfactory an interpretation of our experience as possible. In this process the past becomes meaningful because of our present situation.

If this means that at times we must select certain stories and reject others, then so be it. The story continues to have value because it touches us in our prudence and folly, in our security and anxieties. This implies a mutual trust. We trust ourselves to the point where we will let the story speak to us both candidly and unembarrassedly. We trust the story, even though it may be painful, because it may somehow bring relief to our situation. We cannot get along without the story and ironically the story cannot get along without us.

OUR SITUATION AND HENCE OUR NEED FOR CERTAIN STORIES

In seeking to respond to the Word of God in community, we must search out the state of that community. What has been our situation in recent years? What needs have we experienced so that we may select the right stories? We have certainly witnessed the breakup of some of the old patterns of security. We have had our Vietnams and our Watergates. We have seen the death of some theological assumptions and some Church institutions. Thus "Father said" and "Holy Mother the Church says" no longer have the same impact. We have awakened to the fact that theological assumptions and Church institutions can be very human. We have also noted an ever-expanding sense of human ingenuity. We have placed men on the moon and have begun to revere the computer. At the same time we have observed no little confusion, e.g., the sudden collapse of the Pahlavi government in Iran, a successful assassination in Egypt, and unsuccessful attempts in Rome and Washington. We also have greater inflation and dwindling oil supplies. In the age of super-technology we must confess our bewilderment and confusion.

Such a description is hardly exhaustive. However, it does suggest some of the problems that we face, some of the dilemmas that we must somehow resolve. What questions do we raise as a result of these problems and hence which stories do we pick? One crucial question seems to be the following: can we still be trusted? If so, how shall we exercise our trust and freedom?

If the question is correct, then we must decide on the right kind of stories. Will it be the splitting of the Reed Sea and hence escape from slavery? Will it be return from exile and hence beginning all over again? Which part of the Old Testament shall we open up to?

W. Brueggemann and others have suggested that we turn to the wisdom traditions of Israel, hence the traditions imbedded in Job, Proverbs, Qoheleth—and in the Roman Catholic canon—in Ben Sira and Wisdom. Part of the reasoning for this suggestion is that trust and freedom are among their primary concerns. They are not interested in quoting authority, e.g., "Thus says the Lord." They are not content to invoke a *deus ex machina* as in certain Pentateuchal traditions. Rather, these traditions urge people to look at reality, assess it, and apply it to themselves. As R. E. Murphy puts it, wisdom is concerned with imposing a tentative order on chaotic human experience.

Our first reaction to the above suggestion is to begin reading Job and Qoheleth and to forget about David. However, the David of many of the biblical stories—and hence "our" kind of David—is precisely the exemplar of trust and freedom. He faced life head-on and met its challenges. He became a master at coping. He accepted responsibility but did not always live up to it. David's story is, therefore, our story.

G. von Rad has called the tenth century B.C. a period of "enlightenment." Besides David's conquests, his bureaucracy, his capital of Jerusalem, the literature of the period also witnessed to this enlightenment. The first comprehensive history of Israel—the Yahwist—stems from the time of David and Solomon. In fact, the author who defends the Davidic dynasty is at pains to point out that David must have due regard for the conquered nations. Abraham was to be David's model. As Gn 12:3 states, "'all communities of the earth shall find blessing in you.'" The dealings of Abraham with the Canaanites (see Gn 18), of Isaac with the Philistines (see Gn 26), and Jacob with the Arameans (see Gn 29-32) were patterns to be followed by the new king. Even the fact that one had the leisure to write such a comprehensive history suggests that the climate was different. The writing also suggests that there were those in Israel who doubted if there was any connection between David and the patriarchs and Moses.

The times (and hence the stories) called for a new approach to theology. It was no longer sufficient to have God come and lead the patriarchs or direct Moses. It was a time for a different type of faith. We might call it a freedom faith. With new opportunities there were new ventures, with new worlds there were new possibilities. One had to seize the situations, if one was to cope with it at all.

Such is the faith of David. His theologians present him as a free man and the reason for this is that God chose to trust him. According to W. Brueggemann God acts best when God trusts humans with their moment in history. God frees humans from the need to please by law, cult, or piety. God runs the risk that humans will ultimately bring about a more human world. This is an overwhelming statement about what people are ordained to be by God. The story of David and his times is the story of ourselves and our times.

THE SOURCES FOR THE DAVID STORY

Where shall we find the stories of David so that we can tell our story? What value, moreover, do these stories have? A *first* and indeed rich source is the story of David's rise in First Samuel 16-31. Here we have the story of David and Goliath, of David as the Robin Hood in the area of the Negeb, of David who hires himself out to be a Philistine general but who still remains faithful to Israel, of David who could have killed Saul but spared him twice. It may be summed up in the song of the women of Jerusalem: "'Saul has slain his thousands, and David his ten thousands'" (1 Sm 18:7).

Much of this reflects popular storytelling. David is the guerrilla fighter who lives by expediency and imposes taxes on peaceful farmers. He is David as we want him to be. The story of David's rise legitimates his succession to the throne and absolves David of any faults or complicity in the disaster that befell the house of Saul. The David who thus emerges is the hero who has just slain Goliath, not the lusting king who must kill his subject to cover up his sin.

A *second* source is the so-called "Succession Narrative" which runs from Second Samuel 6 (9)-20 to First Kings 1-2. It is concerned with the problem of the succession to the throne at the death of David. It is quite likely the work of an eyewitness, someone privy to all the intrigues of the Davidic household. Here the weaknesses of David are portrayed in glaring fashion. The man who can control an empire cannot run his own household. Murder and incest play a significant role. David loves his children but he loves them to excess so that Joab must remark that the king loves those who hate him and hates those who love him (see 2 Sm 19:7).

A *third* source is the so-called additions to Second Samuel, i.e., chaps. 21-24. These chapters give us some interesting insights into the makeup of the man, although they can never match the richness of the two previous sources.

A *fourth* and theologically indispensable source is the work of the Yahwist, especially his description of sin in the garden.

A *fifth* source is the David of the Chronicler, i.e., First Chronicles 11-29. We will not make use of this source. For one thing, it often restates material already found in First and Second Samuel. Besides, the book is a later effort to rally around the Davidic throne when no throne existed. Its historical value has increased in the eyes of scholars. But for us—at least for our task—it offers us a David who is less than real and hence not one to answer the situation we have described.

SOME DAVID STORIES

A *first* insight into the David for our times is the scene where the illegitimate child of David and Bathsheba has become ill (see 2 Sm 12:13-25). When David learns of the illness, he fasts and sleeps on the ground clothed in sackcloth. When the elders urge him to get up and eat properly, he refuses. When David learns, however, that the child has died, he immediately puts off his sackcloth and fasting. For his court the action was totally confusing. Proper etiquette demanded that one do penance only when death had actually arrived. But for David this makes no sense. He replies to his courtiers: "'While the child was living, I fasted and wept, thinking, "Perhaps the Lord will grant me the child's life." But now he is dead. Why should I fast? Can I bring him back again? I shall go to him, but he will not return to me'" (2 Sm 12:22-23).

As W. Brueggemann notes, David has a new understanding of what life and death are about. One must take life as it comes, with an attitude of freedom, not Stoic indifference. Death is part of life and one must accept it. Or, put another way, life means to go on living even in the face of death. The story continues that David comforted his wife and then went and slept with her. The strength of David is not to give in to weakness. To cope with death is to learn the art of living.

A *second* incident is the scene depicted in First Samuel 21 where David has to flee from Saul and comes to Ahimelech, the priest of Nob, to ask for the holy bread. Ahimelech tells David that the rules of the holy war hold: his men must have been away from their wives for three days. The account is not totally clear. To be sure, David gives an evasive answer: "'Whenever I go on a journey, all the young men are consecrated—even for a secular journey'" (1 Sm 21:6).

The ultimate question is a distinction between the profane and the holy. Holy bread demands continence. David appears to reject this notion of holiness. The need in which both he and his men find themselves is such that the categories of profane and holy no longer hold. Or perhaps he is lobbying for a new understanding of what is holy. In any event the canon of sacredness must give way to expediency. The greater good is the welfare of his men. The preservation of what is holy is of lesser importance.

A *third* incident is the scene depicted in 2 Sm 23:13-17. David is fighting the Philistines and is surrounded by some of his best warriors. He longs for the water that comes from his home town, saying, "'Oh, that someone would give me a drink of water from the cistern that is by the gate of Bethlehem!'" (2 Sm 23:15). Upon hearing this wish, three of his warriors break through the enemy lines and draw the water from the Bethlehem cistern. When they present the same to David, he pours it on the ground, adding: "'The Lord forbid that I do this! Can I drink the blood of these men who went at the risk of their lives?'" (2 Sm 23:17).

The incident affirms David's solidarity with his men. In W. Brueggemann's study, his own needs are not such that they prevent him from recalling his common humanity with these men. David thus refuses to enjoy what these men have acquired at enormous risk to their lives.

A *fourth* scene illustrates God's abiding trust in David. The text is found in Second Samuel 7 and is known as the dynastic oracle (see vv 11-16). We tend to read these words in a rather nonchalant way. We reason, after all, that covenant is such a common category. However, this is no ordinary covenant. Unlike the Sinai covenant, the Davidic covenant has no conditions attached. It is more aptly called a royal grant, i.e., an outright gift of the dynasty and its succession with no strings attached. The only other example we have of this is the covenant with Abraham in Genesis 15. Most likely the Genesis scene simply reflects the scene here in Second Samuel.

When we pause to reflect on this account, it is staggering. God chooses to trust this individual at this moment. God promises to back him up and support him. It is only too obvious that God loves David and so trusts him. However, the trust is not without its responsibilities. Yet in a few verses this passage illustrates that not to be trusted is not to be David, that not to be respected is not to be David, that not to be awarded freedom is not to be David. If David's story is to be our story, the same must be true of us: to be trusted, respected, and awarded freedom.

A *fifth* story is the story of the garden (Gn 2:4b-3:24). There appear to be some parallels to link the David-Bathsheba incident of Second Samuel 11-12 with the Yahwist's account. Thus David finds Bathsheba beautiful and takes her (2 Sm 11:2, 4; see Gn 3:6). David realizes that he has sinned (2 Sm 12:13; see Gn 3:7, 10). The death sentence is announced (2 Sm 12:5, 13-14; see Gn 2:17). However, the birth of a son shows God's graciousness (2 Sm 12:24; see Gn 3:21; 4:1).

If this analysis is valid (J. Blenkinsopp and W. Brueggemann offer further evidence to support this thesis), then this implies something about the Yahwist. He discerned something in David and his family that is applicable to the entire human family. The fault of David, viz., the refusal to accept limitations and so play God, is the continuing human fault. The fall of David is the continuing human fall. For our case, therefore, David's story is truly our story.

A *sixth* and final scene is David's reaction to Nathan's parable in Second Samuel 12, i.e., after Nathan tells the parable of the poor man and his ewe lamb. David's first reaction is emotional: "'As the Lord lives, the man who has done this merits death!'" (2 Sm 12:5). His second reaction is judicial: "'He shall restore the ewe lamb four-fold because he has done this and has had no pity'" (2 Sm 12:6). Once Nathan turns the tables on David by saying, "'You are the man!'" (2 Sm 12:7), David's final reaction is noteworthy. As the trusted and free individual, David knows through his faith that he is dealing with a person, not an impersonal will. Hence the beautiful expression in 2 Sm 12:13: "'I have sinned against the Lord.'" Even in his sinfulness there is something noble about David. He will not pass the buck. He will not suggest that weak human nature is the cause. He admits his own sinfulness before Yahweh. To be sure, he has been unfaithful to the trust. But the basis of that trust remains, viz., a personal relationship with Yahweh. We are not really surprised when we hear Nathan say, "'The Lord on his part has forgiven your sin; you shall not die'" (2 Sm 12:13).

We are not far removed from the world of Genesis 3. Certainly the man passes the buck to the woman who passes the same to the serpent (see Gn 3:12-13). But throughout there is a person with whom one must deal, not an impersonal will. True trust and responsibility are possible only where there is a relationship with people. We do not expect machines to be trusting and responsible, only the people who operate the machines.

THE LINK BETWEEN DAVID AND OURSELVES

In the light of these six incidents we must conclude that there is more than a least common denominator between ourselves and David, between our story and his. Some of the old patterns of security, both civil and ecclesiastical, are breaking up. We may tend to be as reactionary as the audience of the Yahwist. However, the David story teaches us not to withdraw into the womb or retreat to the sanctuary where God presides. Rather, the David story impels us to face life head-on, to go forth courageously even in the face of the demise of these patterns of security. Do we dare to be human in a changing world? Do we dare to make David's story our story?

We have seen the demise of certain theological assumptions. Without disparaging authority within the community, we have seen the death of certain theological institutions. Perhaps we have learned the hard way the following dictum: if your theology does not work out, you don't change your history, you change your theology (contrast 2 Sm 7:14-16 with 1 Kgs 2:4; 9:4-9). Perhaps the most insidious theological assumption was the focus on heaven, not earth—on individuals, not community. In the light of these changes do we dare to live with a certain number of unanswered questions? Do we dare to let the David story have an impact on our story?

We have watched the sinful humanity of both civil and ecclesiastical institutions. For many, this was a bewildering experience because we did not admit the possibility of sin in our heroes and heroines. The David story is a healthy corrective. We find our hero with all the trappings of the loving, caring guerrilla fighter in the account of David's rise. Yet we are forced to read the Succession Narrative where the hero now appears as a lusting male and an inept father. Do we dare to go further and take David's repentance and so make reconciliation an ingredient of sinful humanity? Can we accept the young shepherd who slew Goliath (but see 2 Sm 21:19) and at the same time not dismiss the mature king who lusted for Bathsheba? Do we dare to make David's entire story our story?

Especially in our technological world we have noted enormous advances which are the result of human ingenuity and talent. At

82

the same time we run the risk of making things people and perhaps some people gods. We feel compelled to tinker and toy with the givens of history. But do we also feel compelled to respect people as people? In the face of an ever expanding human knowledge do we feel driven to respect the person precisely as a person and not simply another ingredient in a highly mechanized world? If respecting the person as such is a limitation, do we dare to live with limitations? Do we dare to accept the David story in Genesis 2-3? Can we live freely and fully and yet with limitations? Can David still have an impact on us?

We have been privy to a world of confusion in many segments of the Church and the world. Things have changed, are changing, and the presumption is that they will continue to change. Are we content to let this world slip by without making our contribution? Are we happy to label it sinful and arrogant and yet not lift a finger to offer some direction and hope? The David story reminds us that this is our world, we have no other.

We may not presume to call on a God who will summon Moses or Joshua and resolve everything for us. Our God is a God who trusts us in the face of change and confusion. The monarchy of David could never revert to the tribal existence at the time of the Judges. The monarchy was there to stay. To cope meant to dialogue with monarchy and make it work. The Yahwist assures us that we can and must make a difference. Will we allow David's theologian to have an impact on our theology in our world at our moment in history?

A DAVIDIC CREED

The David story is basically a response (or lack of response at times) to the Word of God in community. The following creed is a summary of the key elements in that story. It is a creed that flows from the successes and failures of the David story and hopefully it will be one that will flow over into our own story.

We believe in a God:

(1) who holds that the goal of existence is life, not survival or security or success;

(2) who teaches us to search for authority in our world of experience too;

(3) who entrusts to us the task of having a peculiarly human world;

(4) who asks us to be responsible for our own destiny and the destiny of our community;

(5) who maintains that life is for enjoyment, celebration, and appreciation;

(6) who risks trusting us, although not blind to our weaknesses;

(7) who compels us to respect persons and never denigrate them to the level of things;

(8) who imparts to us the ability to be free *for* others, although we naturally search to be free *from* others;

(9) who urges us to question the structure of our community on the condition that people will be better served;

(10) who commands us to search out the good in all human institutions because they may be good and hence human;

(11) who is willing to give us our moment in history simply because God is our God and we are God's people;

(12) who asks us to accept certain givens in life and to learn to cope because life is like that;

(13) who places limitations on our world so that our giving will be limitless;

(14) who beckons that we treat God as God treats us, viz., as persons;

(15) who respects us as God respected David.

WE BELIEVE IN THE GOD OF DAVID.

BIBLIOGRAPHICAL SUGGESTIONS

Blenkinsopp, Joseph. "Theme and Motif in the Succession History (2 Sm IX 2ff) and the Yahwist Corpus," *VTS* 15 (1966) 44-57.

Brueggemann, Walter. "David and His Theologian," *CBQ* 30 (1968) 156-181.

_____ . "Scripture and an Ecumenical Life-Style," *Int* 24 (1970) 3-19.

_____ . "Israel's Moment of Freedom," *The Bible Today* #42 (April, 1969) 2917-2925.

_____ . "Kingship and Chaos: A Study in Tenth Century Theology," *CBQ* 33 (1971) 317-332.

_____ . *In Man We Trust. The Neglected Side of Biblical Faith.* Richmond: John Knox, 1972.

_____ . "On Trust and Freedom: A Study of Faith in the Succession Narrative," *Int* 26 (1972) 3-19.

Burke, T. Patrick. "The Theologian as Storyteller and Philosopher," *Horizons* 4 (Fall, 1977) 207-215.

Clements, Ronald E. *Abraham and David.* SBT. Naperville: Allenson, 1967.

Coats, George W. "The God of Death," *Int* 29 (1975) 227-239.

Craghan, John F. "Three Old Testament Theologians of Hope," *American Ecclesiastical Review* 167 (1973) 363-386.

Cross, Frank M., Jr. *Canaanite Myth and Hebrew Epic.* Cambridge: Harvard University Press, 1973, 219-273.

Doty, William G. "The Stories of Our Times," *Religion as Story.* Edited by J. B. Wiggins. New York: Harper & Row, 1975, 93-121.

Ellis, Peter F. *The Yahwist: The Bible's First Theologian.* Notre Dame: Fides, 1968; Collegeville: The Liturgical Press, 1976.

Lemche, Niels P. "David's Rise," *JSOT* 10 (November, 1978) 2-25.

Maly, Eugene H. *The World of David and Solomon*. Englewood Cliffs: Prentice-Hall, 1965.

Murphy, Roland E. "The Hebrew Sage and Openness to the World," *Christian Action and Openness to the World*. Edited by J. Papin. Villanova: Villanova University Press, 1970, 219-244.

Rad, Gerhard von. "The Beginnings of Historical Writing in Ancient Israel," *The Problem of the Hexateuch and Other Essays*. New York: McGraw-Hill, 1966, 166-204.

_____ . "The Joseph Story and Ancient Wisdom," *Ibid*. 292-300.

Shea, John. *Stories of God*. Chicago: Thomas More, 1978.

Weinfeld, Moshe. "The Covenant of Grant in the Old Testament and in the Ancient Near East," *Journal of the American Oriental Society* 90 (1970) 184-203.

Whybray, Roger N. *The Succession Narrative. A Study of II Samuel 9-20. I Kings 1-2*. SBT. Naperville: Allenson, 1968.

Wolff, Hans W. "The Kerygma of the Yahwist," *Int* 20 (1966) 131-158 = (with W. Brueggemann), *The Vitality of Old Testament Traditions*. Atlanta: John Knox, 1975, 41-66, 132-138.

CHAPTER 9

The Invitation to
Prophetic Ministry

Biblical passages to be read: Is 40-55; the Book of Amos.

WORD AND RESPONSE

Most of us enjoy the prophetic books. Amos, Hosea, Jeremiah, Ezekiel, etc., have a dramatic ring. We learn of their perceptions, their bravado, their real humanity. It becomes obvious that the Word of God had a special impact on them and compelled them to carry out their prophetic roles. When we have finished reading a given prophet, we are prepared to admire, but not to imitate.

We suffer from antiquarianism. We gladly admit that the prophets reacted generously to God's Word and that their reaction had repercussions on their communities. However, we dare not concede that we are also called upon to react generously and thus have an impact on our communities. The prophetic books are thereby condemned to the neutral existence of ancient Near Eastern theology. We thus invoke the principle that studying the prophetic Word is necessarily divorced from living the prophetic Word. Unfortunately such antiquarianism can be a crippling disease.

Response to the Word of God in community must raise the question: what does Amos or Hosea mean *now*? To read the prophetic books is to be involved in the ongoing challenge of the Word in ever new settings. A spirituality that sees prophetism as only an academic exercise denies the vitality of God's Word and hence refuses the hermeneutical demand of actualizing the Word. To read a given biblical prophet means to envision our community under the impact of that same Word. A sound spirituality will resist all forms of antiquarianism.

Negatively, a prophet is not a mere fortuneteller or social agitator. As a matter of fact, a prophet can be both of these but only because of a more basic reality. That reality is the fact that the prophet speaks for God. The prophet offers to the community, therefore, God's outlook on reality, God's way of thinking, God's value system, God's assessment of the concrete situation. To invoke a valuable Old Testament tradition, the prophet stands in God's council. The prophet is privy to the deliberations of God and the council. As a later tradition in Amos puts it, "Indeed, the Lord does nothing without revealing his plan to his servants, the prophets" (Am 3:7). Or the prologue of Second Isaiah: "A voice cries out: In the desert prepare the way of the Lord! . . . A voice says, 'Cry out;' I answer, 'What shall I cry out?'" (Is 40:3, 6).

C. Westermann emphasizes the messenger dimension of the prophet (note the formula: "Thus says the Lord"). He notes that in the Old Testament the word is a personal event to which speaking as well as hearing belongs—it is a kind of happening that moves from one person (the one speaking) to another (the one hearing). Hence the prophet's purpose is to move, to cover distances, to span the chasm between God and humans.

J. Muilenburg added another dimension. Prophets are speakers for Yahweh, apostles sent to particular times to speak particular words. They do more than repeat inherited and traditional clichés; they attempt to make God's Word immediate, relevant, and contemporary. He also noted that prophets are like Moses, i.e., his covenant mediators, intercessors for the people, speakers for God.

The prophet operates within the context of covenant. It is the relationship of Yahweh to Israel, of Israel to Yahweh, and of Israelites to one another. The prophet makes God's viewpoint have an impact on the people, reminding them that their relationship with Yahweh is jeopardized if they exclude sisters and brothers. Prophets find their proper identity in serving Yahweh and the people. They cease to be genuine prophets when they exclude either God or the people to concentrate on self.

THE MACHINERY OF PROPHECY

It may be suggested at the risk of being overly mechanical that the prophet is involved in five steps: the prophet *experiences, perceives, assesses, reacts,* and *communicates.* The prophet is always part of his/her own time and culture. (1) The prophet *experiences* what is happening in that time and culture. (2) The prophet then *perceives* that something is missing, something is wrong, something does not jell. (3) The prophet next *assesses* that perception against the background of covenant. He/she sees people as God's people, kings as subject to God, and sin as betrayal of covenant and oppression of God's people. (4) The prophet *reacts* to that value judgment, pondering it, suffering with it, dialoguing with it. (5) The prophet finally *communicates* the experience, the perception, the assessment, and the reaction to the people of God. He/she does it in such a way that the people immediately know what God is about. The language of prophecy is poetry. It speaks to their needs and their world. Though people may dislike the message, they do not misunderstand. Communication is the king.

Around the year 760 B.C. the prophet Amos (1) *experiences* the social revolution of his time: there are a few rich people and an ever widening oppressed proletariat. (2) He *perceives* that something is wrong. Selling the poor man for a pair of sandals and trampling the heads of the weak into the dust are not right (see Am 2:6-7). (3) He *assesses* his perception against the background of covenant: "For they know not how to do what is right, . . . storing up in their castles what they have extorted and robbed" (Am 3:10). To be Israelite means to be for others, to be in covenant means to protect those in covenant. (4) He *reacts* to that value judgment. He knows that he is sent: "'I was a shepherd and a dresser of sycamores. The Lord took me from following the flock, and said to me, 'Go, prophesy to my people Israel'" (Am 7:14-15). (5) He finally *communicates* in a language that the people cannot mistake. For example, a funeral elegy: "She is fallen, to rise no more, the maiden (against NAB) Israel; she lies abandoned upon her land, with no one to raise her up" (Am 5:2). Or a woe: "Woe to those who turn judgment to wormwood and cast justice to the ground" (Am 5:7).

CRITICIZING AND ENERGIZING

In a recent work on prophetism W. Brueggemann describes the prophetic task as offering a consciousness and perception alternative to the consciousness and perception of the principal culture around us. In his view the prophetic role involves two elements: (1) criticizing and (2) energizing.

We realize that we are all made to conform to certain patterns, even though our experience warns us that such conformity is wrong. In the criticizing role the prophet has to reveal the deceptions that conformity brings in its wake. The prophet thereby points out those seductive and manipulative powers that prevent us from being authentically human.

We also realize that we allow ourselves to become victims of despair. We suppress our very desire for change and accept the view that things cannot be turned around. In the energizing role the prophet has to proclaim the message of hope. This implies the rediscovery of deep-seated longing and the refusal to accept the majority view of pessimism.

JEREMIAH AND SECOND ISAIAH

Jeremiah lived in a period that saw the demise of one world power (the neo-Assyrian) and the sudden rise of another (the neo-Babylonian). He noted the practices of both kings and subjects. One such practice was seeking security at the price of freedom. His interpreters present him as an intrepid foe of every form of manipulation. (As R. P. Carroll has seen, much of the Book of Jeremiah is from the prophet's interpreters.)

The powers of oppression prefer to offer a form of security for the vision of freedom. It is not a question of being free for others but of tranquillizing oneself with overdoses of security. The outcome is the loss of personal contact with a personal God and the purchase of numbness in impersonal religion.

Nature religion continued to be a problem in Jeremiah's time. Some of his people falsely concluded that the loss of political independence was linked to their failure in nature religion. "'But since we stopped burning incense to the queen of heaven and pouring out libations to her, we are in need of everything and are being destroyed'" (Jer 44:18). For Jeremiah the price of security was demeaning and dehumanizing (see also Jer 2:12-13, 23-25). It made the relationship between God and Israel an impersonal one. It destroyed divine liberty since Yahweh was placed in a position of dancing *a priori* to the tune of the people.

Jeremiah also exercised this criticizing office when he destroyed the false security of God's presence. The people had been seduced into thinking that the temple, God's dwelling place, was impregnable. To criticize the establishment by preaching the destruction of the temple seemed heresy. However, the prophet felt compelled because the people had been manipulated. "Put not your trust in the deceitful words: 'This is the temple of the Lord' . . . I will do to this house just as I did to Shiloh" (Jer 7:4, 14).

Executive privilege was as much a threat in Jeremiah's time as it was during the days of Watergate. The people had been numbed into thinking that the king's power was absolute and hence the institution of monarchy was everlasting. W. Brueggemann remarks that kings love to say "forever" to everything. Monuments are supposed to last forever. Jeremiah, however, witnessed the manipulation of the ordinary people by kings. It was a flagrant violation of covenant. "Woe to him who builds his house on wrong, his terraces on injustice . . . The burial of an ass shall he be given, dragged forth and cast out beyond the gates of Jerusalem" (Jer 22:13, 19). Prophets do not hesitate to proclaim deathliness where deathliness is present. Prophets refuse to be numbed into complacency.

Towards the end of the Babylonian exile, i.e., ca. 540 B.C., Second Isaiah sought to overcome the depression afflicting his community in Babylon. Like the Priestly Writer, he used the oracle of salvation to good effect. He announced the start of a new relationship that was not grounded in his people's fidelity but in Yahweh's love. He proclaimed that Yahweh took due notice of Israel's plight. "Fear not, for I have redeemed you; I have called you by name: you are mine. When you pass through the water, I will be with you . . ." (Is 43:1-2).

Second Isaiah also energized by utilizing the Exodus theme. Israel posed two questions: (1) is our God able to help us? and (2) if able, will our God help us? The answer to these questions is reflected, in part, in the prophet's use of the Exodus tradition. He boldly addressed the task of announcing a new Exodus in keeping with ongoing creation (see Is 51:9-10). He spoke of the new miracles accompanying the new Exodus (see Is 41:17-20). Finally, he proclaimed a radically new event—the past was over and done. "Remember not the events of the past, the things of long ago consider not; see, I am doing something new . . ." (Is 43:18-19).

Second Isaiah also employed the *gō'ēl* or "redeemer" image to advantage. To a people caught in the morass of neglect and helplessness the prophet presented Yahweh as the next of kin. The family's honor was thus uppermost in Yahweh's actions. The dimension of intimacy is obvious: "Fear not, O worm Jacob, O maggot Israel; I will help you, says the Lord; your *gō'ēl* is the Holy One of Israel" (Is 41:14). And again: "Thus says the Lord, your *gō'ēl*, the Holy One of Israel: For your sakes I sent to Babylon: I will lower all the bars, and the Chaldeans shall cry out in lamentation" (Is 43:14).

THE MODERN MINISTER AND THE PROPHETIC ROLE

In assuming the prophetic role today's minister (the term "minister" includes both sexes and an almost inexhaustible series of service to God's people) must be in touch with himself/herself, the community, and God. (1) The minister must *experience* what is happening in his/her time and culture. (2) The minister must then *perceive* that the world has lost, at least partially, its sense of value. The minister cannot be anesthetized into slogans like "Well, that's the way it has to be!" The minister cannot accept the statement: "You shouldn't make waves!" (3) The minister then *assesses* the malaise of the world in terms of the relationship with God, people, and himself/herself. In other words the assessment is covenantal. In covenantal thinking/acting people always remain people. They are never degraded to the category of thing. In the covenantal assessment authentic humanity depends on keeping people people and things things.

(4) The minister then *reacts*. The minister reacts within himself/herself. If truly prophetic, the minister has not lost the art of being shocked or upset. Thus the powers of oppression have not numbed the minister to the inhumanity of the treatment of sisters and brothers. At this point society begins to label the minister eccentric because the minister finds his/her humanity, i.e., his/her Christianity, in honest concern for fellow human beings. (5) The minister finally *communicates* and indeed in a variety of ways. But communicate the minister must. He/she speaks a language and acts in a way that indicate to all that humanity's wound is real and must be healed, that humanity's plight is genuine and must be remedied, that humanity's need is blatant and must be dealt with.

As mentioned earlier, W. Brueggemann speaks of the twofold prophetic task of criticizing and energizing. Expressed another way, criticizing means that the minister must *tell it the way it really is* and energizing means the minister must *tell it the way it can be*.

TELLING IT THE WAY IT REALLY IS

Prime among the forces of oppression is the *ego syndrome*. It is that depersonalizing, dehumanizing power that finds the identity of people only in terms of themselves. The framework of covenant disappears because the person relates only to himself or herself, not to God and not to other sisters and brothers.

Among other things the ego syndrome manifests itself in the cult of pleasure. Our media inform us that we will go around only once and hence should grab all the gusto we can. We are told that we must have the latest fashion because we owe it to ourselves. We are seduced into thinking that we, as individuals, are number one.

The ego syndrome also reveals itself in the delineation of the beautiful people. Not infrequently the models are taken from the entertainment world. These models are oft estranged, seldom faithful people who have made it to the top in music and film. Unfortunately the powers of oppression present such beautiful people as the new Golden Calf we must worship.

The ego syndrome also betrays itself in the status quest, and here ministers are not exempt. We are duped into thinking that status creates true joy, that lack of status necessarily leads to unhappiness. To make it or not to make it, that is the question. We despair because our name is not at the head of the list or on the name plate. The powers of oppression teach us subtly, yet realistically, how to compete and vie—and indeed all too ruthlessly—by means of a manual entitled "How to get ahead and destroy your fellows in ten easy lessons." While ambition can be a creative force, we must also admit to its destructive power.

Besides the ego syndrome the minister must recognize the *economics of affluence.* It goes hand in hand with the ego syndrome. It is predicated on the assumption that we Americans must be the biggest and the best despite the hazards and hardships for fellow Americans and others. Accountability is minimal because the powers of oppression have become denizens of the anonymous computer. The result is Three Mile Island and Love Canal. The minister must criticize this lack of accountability. Otherwise we run the risk of perpetuating the murder of Naboth and the theft of his vineyard (see 1 Kgs 21).

The economics of affluence sees the minorities especially as means to its own ends. Wages, working conditions, treatment of employees are not consonant at times with human dignity. Like Amos we must note: "They drink wine from bowls and anoint themselves with the best of oils; yet they are not made ill by the collapse of Joseph" (Am 6:6). This numbness, this insensitivity to the value of the person and his/her inherent dignity tends to make us think that everything is all right. At this point the minister must observe that we have betrayed our liberty for a form of security.

TELLING IT THE WAY IT CAN BE

The minister must also energize. He/she is asked to provide the means whereby hope becomes possible again. Here the minister is called upon to rediscover the hopes and desires that have been all too effectively suppressed. Like Second Isaiah the minister must proclaim: "Fear not, for I have redeemed you, I have called you by name, you are mine" (Is 43:1).

But who are the people who need our energizing? Or, to put it another way, who are those people whose hopes and desires have been all too effectively suppressed? Who are hurting? The following groups include only some of those to whom the minister must proclaim the energizing word.

In the first place the *poor,* i.e., those whose means and way of life are subhuman, those whose quest is always bread for today, never for tomorrow. Here administrators must play a caring role. They are called upon to make hope possible on a larger scale and to make longing realizable for a larger number. The administrator as prophetic minister must envision the people beyond the computer and their plight beyond the surveys. When the needs of the poor are thus met, the energizing word is: "I will open up rivers on the bare heights, and fountains in the broad valleys; I will turn the desert into a marshland, and the dry ground into springs of water" (Is 41:18).

The *marginated* in the Church look to the prophetic minister to say with Ezekiel: "And I will put my spirit within you, and you shall live, and I will place you in your own land" (Ez 37:14). The silent majority of *fallen aways* is eager to hear an energizing word. Though they do not articulate their need, they want the prophetic minister to remind them that they are still persons, hence endowed with a unique dignity. The minister must tell them the way it can be. He/ she must communicate to them that the community needs them and, at the same time, that they need the community. The energizing word must be: "You are my witnesses, says the Lord, my servants whom I have chosen to know and believe in me and understand that it is I" (Is 43:10).

Among the fallen aways the *divorced and remarried* yearn to hear that they are not the neglected of the diaspora. The minister must inform them that the capital, Jerusalem, is still interested. When the minister notes the Christian dimension of their lives, he/ she must applaud it. It is always the task of the prophetic minister to uncover the presence of God when people least suspect or expect it. We are the community of Ezekiel: "I will seek the lost, and I will bring back the strayed, and I will bind up the crippled, and I will strengthen the weak" (Ez 34:16).

Those hurting include the *lonely,* the *shut-ins,* the *depressed.* It is always the task of the prophet to assure individuals that the community is still involved in their need, even if the community is represented only by the person of the prophetic minister. Counseling is a prophetic undertaking. It seeks to make the Word of God relevant and contemporary to those who cannot hear or will not hear it. We must frankly admit that in our society we have more hostages at home than we once had in Iran. Their complaint is that the Lord— the Church—has forgotten them. Prophetic ministry to them captures the vision of Second Isaiah: "Can a mother forget her infant, be without tenderness for the child of her womb? Even should she forget, I will never forget you. See, upon the palms of my hands I have written your name" (Is 49:15-16).

A significant group is also the *women*—both religious and lay— who serve in ministry or seek to serve in ministry. In the energizing task the point of departure must be the Word of God. That Word is always a many-splendored event/happening that transcends the barriers of background, position, and even sex. As energizer, the prophetic minister is the servant of the Word. We cannot manipulate the Word to cater to our own penchants. We must hear the Word to meet the needs of others.

With regard to women in ministry the clergy, as prophetic ministers, must look to the community and ask how the community can best be served. Women have already undertaken various forms of ministry. They seek to be acknowledged, to be recognized as servants of that same Word. Only an incarceration within clerical ego and a stultification of the power of the Word will force clerics to be threatened by women ministers of the Word. Here the energizing task is to support, encourage, and applaud those women who seek not to usurp the positions of clergy as servants of the Word but to make their own contributions in serving that same Word.

It was Second Isaiah who democratized the Davidic covenant. All the people could share the unique relationship of David with the Lord (see Is 55:3). It was the same prophet who taught his people not to limit God's power but to be as open as possible. Thus the energizing task vis-à-vis women in ministry is not unlike the thrust of Is 55:10-11: "For just as from the heavens the rain and snow come down and do not return there till they have watered the earth, making it fertile and fruitful, giving seed to him who sows and bread to him who eats, so shall my word be that goes forth from my mouth; it shall not return to me void, but shall do my will, achieving the end for which I sent it."

THE MANNER OF THE WORD AND THE MANNER
OF THE PROPHETIC MINISTER

In what situations does the prophetic minister perform his/her task of criticizing and energizing? Our first reaction is to look to some very solemn proclamation of the Word, e.g., from the pulpit. However, teaching, counseling, suffering, recreating, etc., are loci for the prophetic tasks. In these spheres as well as others, the prophetic minister is involved in the steps of experiencing, perceiving, assessing, reacting, and communicating.

To offer consolation is to announce that this is the way it is but this is the way it can be. To teach is to make the Word of God have an impact on our time, unmasking the powers of oppression and proffering the catalysts of hope. To suffer is to witness to God's Word as sustaining and supporting. Perhaps Ezekiel's most eloquent word was during the time of his dumbness when he silently acted out the tragedy of Jerusalem (see Ez 3:22-27; 24:26-27; 33:21-22). Our recreation is to testify to God's goodness to us in nature and other people. It can be the springboard for bringing the contagion of the Word of God to bear on those who have excommunicated themselves from the beauty of nature and other people. Our experience of such goodness and our communication of the same are calculated to offer the community God's outlook on reality.

The manner of the prophetic minister is, first and foremost, to let the Word saturate his/her very being. To serve the Word is more than an intellectual exercise. It is an undertaking that engages all the fiber and person of the prophetic minister. In the words of one prophet: "But it (the Word) becomes like fire burning in my heart, imprisoned in my bones; I grow weary holding it in, I cannot endure it" (Jer 20:9). It must be as intimate and personal to today's prophetic minister as the Word was to Ezekiel. "So I opened my mouth, and he gave me the scroll to eat. And he said to me, 'Son of man, eat this scroll which I give you and fill your stomach with it.' Then I ate it; and it was in my mouth as sweet as honey" (Ez 3:2-3). The Word of God must be as much a part of today's prophetic minister as the food he/she eats which, in turn, becomes part of his/her person.

It goes without saying that all prophetic ministers become discouraged. They grope at times in darkness because the Word—their word—has not had its desired effect on the world. Yet such ministers must derive hope from the fact that the word they preach and the word they are outstrips their physical existence. Come what may, the word is not condemned to a limbo of years in ministry. Future generations of sisters and brothers will learn what Ezekiel learned in his call from Yahweh: "But you shall say to them: Thus says the Lord God! And whether they heed or resist—for they are a rebellious house—they shall know that a prophet has been among them" (Ez 2:4-5).

BIBLIOGRAPHICAL SUGGESTIONS

Blenkinsopp, Joseph. *Prophecy and Canon*. Notre Dame: Notre Dame University Press, 1977.

Bright, John. *Jeremiah*. AB. Garden City: Doubleday, 1965.

Brueggemann, Walter. *The Prophetic Imagination*. Philadelphia: Fortress, 1978.

Buber, Martin. *The Prophetic Faith*. New York: Macmillan, 1949.

Carroll, Robert P. *From Chaos to Covenant. Prophecy in the Book of Jeremiah*. New York: Crossroad, 1981.

Clements, Ronald E. *Prophecy and Tradition*. Growing Points in Theology. Atlanta: John Knox, 1975.

Coote, Robert B. *Amos among the Prophets: Composition and Theology*. Philadelphia: Fortress, 1981.

Craghan, John F. "The Prophet Amos in Recent Literature," *BTB* 2 (1972) 242–261.

Eichrodt, Walther. *Ezekiel*. OTL. Philadelphia: Westminster, 1970.

Heschel, Abraham. *The Prophets*. New York: Harper & Row, 1962, 27–38, 103–139, 145–158.

Holladay, William L. *Jeremiah: Spokesman out of Time*. Philadelphia: United Church Press, 1974.

McKenzie, John L. *Second Isaiah*. AB. Garden City: Doubleday, 1968.

Mays, James L. *Amos*. OTL. Philadelphia: Westminster, 1969.

Muilenburg, James. "The Book of Isaiah, Ch. 40-66, Introduction and Exegesis," *IB*

5. New York: Abingdon, 1956, 381–773.

Muilenburg, James. "The 'Office' of the Prophet in Ancient Israel," *The Bible in Modern Scholarship*. Edited by J. P. Hyatt. New York: Abingdon, 1965, 74-97.

Rad, Gerhard von. *The Message of the Prophets*. New York: Harper & Row, 1967, 9–109, 161–228.

Raitt, Thomas M. *A Theology of Exile: Judgment/Deliverance in Jeremiah and Ezekiel*. Philadelphia: Fortress, 1977.

Reid, David P. *What Are They Saying About the Prophets?* New York: Paulist Press, 1980.

Vawter, Bruce. *The Conscience of Israel*. New York: Sheed & Ward, 1961, 1–97, 232–277.

Waldow, H. Eberhard von. "Message of Deutero-Isaiah," *Int* 22 (1968) 259–287.

Westermann, Claus. *Basic Forms of Prophetic Speech*. Philadelphia: Westminster, 1967.

—————— . *Isaiah 40-66*. OTL. Philadelphia: Westminster, 1969.

Wolff, Hans W. *Amos the Prophet*. Philadelphia: Fortress, 1973.

Zimmerli, Walther. "Message of the Prophet Ezekiel," *Int* 23 (1969) 131–157.

—————— . *Ezekiel*. Hermeneia. Philadelphia: Fortress, 1979. I = chaps. 1-24.

CHAPTER 10

The Invitation to A Prophetic Ministry Of Non-Manipulation

Biblical passages to be read: the Book of Hosea.

OUR SEEMINGLY NON-PROPHETIC SITUATION

Almost by definition we regard our experiences as personal and intimate. They are, we claim, incidents or events that touch only ourselves or, at best, only a select few. Both the disasters and the successes of our lives are filed away under "personal and confidential." We feel that we cannot open the file since we would be revealing part of ourselves. While there is certainly for most people a proper realm of privacy, we seem to go beyond that realm by becoming secretive. Whether we are willing to admit it or not, we have chosen to limit our practice of religion to a pseudo-covenant that admits only a relationship between God and ourselves. It is enormously difficult for us to break free from the gravitational hold of ego to embrace a God who identifies in terms of other people. In no way, therefore, can the personal become communal.

What is our vision of this covenant God? Is this God the divine dispenser or celestial administrator who deals with impersonal clients in an impersonal way? Is this God so fettered by our "transactions" that every display of emotion or feeling is automatically impossible? Have we so painted this God into a corner that the only escape is purely mechanical liturgy whereby attendance devoid of dispositions assures the ongoingness of the relationship? Are we guilty of the death of personalism in relating to this covenant God?

Response to the Word of God in community must take these

questions seriously. Such a notion of spirituality necessarily provides for the overlapping of personal and communal and cannot escape the implications of these questions. It is not surprising that reflection on these questions can derive profit from the prophet Hosea, a book where private and public are intermingled to the advantage of the people of God. Basically the reading of this prophetic book is the call to a prophetic ministry of non-manipulation.

HISTORICAL BACKGROUND

H. W. Wolff divides the Book of Hosea in the following manner: (1) 1:2-5:7—the prosperous days of the northern kingdom of Israel toward the end of Jeroboam II's (782-753 B.C.) reign; (2) 5:8-8:14—the crucial events of the Syro-Ephraimitic War (ca. 734-732 B.C.) when the northern kingdom (Ephraim) and Aram (Syro) formed an alliance against Judah; (3) 9:1-12:15—a quiet period before and after the accession of the neo-Assyrian king, Shalmaneser (727-722 B.C.); and (4) 12:1-14:10—the period immediately preceding or at the beginning of the siege of Samaria, hence ca. 725-724 B.C. Hosea preached, therefore, from approximately 755 to 725 B.C. It was a period that moved from enormous prosperity to the edge of disaster.

As we have already noted several times, the Canaanite fertility rite exercised a great influence on God's people. In the northern kingdom, where the majority of the people were farmers, the confusion of Yahweh and Baal, the Canaanite god of fertility, continued to hold sway. In this cyclic conception of history the proper performance of the rites with their sacral intercourse was guaranteed to result in the blessings of fertility on marriages, cattle, and crops. As a result, Yahweh could be manipulated after the manner of Baal. This implied that Yahweh was no longer free. As a result, the covenant relationship was reduced to the level of confusion of persons, viz., Yahweh and Baal.

HOSEA, HUSBAND AND PROPHET

Hosea 1-3 is still one of the classical problems in Old Testament research. The problem is: what is the relationship of these three chapters and what can they tell us, if anything, about the historical Hosea and his wife Gomer? What creates the problem is the nature of these three chapters: (1) chapter 1—biography; (2) chapter 2—oracles; and (3) chapter 3—autobiography. Most likely the three chapters reflect three different sources. Not a few exegetes have thrown up their hands and concluded that it is impossible to say anything conclusive about the prophet and his marriage, maintaining that everything is purely symbolic. Admittedly, because of the nature of the sources, a history of the marriage is excluded. However, by excluding history, we need not exclude some knowledge of the setting and background of this significant prophet.

According to H. H. Rowley the prophet was instructed by Yahweh to marry a woman of weak moral character ("a harlot's wife"—Hos 1:2*) and to give symbolic names to the children. Chapter 2 shows that Gomer was unfaithful to Hosea by committing adultery in the form of prostitution, most likely as a devotee of the Canaanite shrines. This same chapter shows that Gomer longed for her husband after her lovers failed her. In chapter 3 Gomer has fallen into slavery. However, Hosea's love for her is so overwhelming that he reclaims her from slavery and sets about to renew the marital relationship. While we certainly cannot write an historical account because of the sources, H. H. Rowley's conclusion does justice to the text and serves as a reasonable working hypothesis, one supported in large measure by the rest of the prophet's message.

In a recent comprehensive commentary on Hosea, F. I. Andersen and D. N. Freedman point out that the prophet's life and the history of his marriage and family shaped the meaning of his proclamation. It was the turmoil and anxiety of his relationship with Gomer and the children that exerted a lifetime influence on the preaching of the Word. Specifically, it was his personal experience of love and concern, of infidelity and frustration, of hope and longing that provided his insight into the relationship between Yahweh and Israel. In this view the personal experience became a communal patrimony. Hosea gained a unique perception of Yahweh's reactions because he had confronted the same problems in his wife and family. This analogy led him to communicate Yahweh's sense of neglect and desperation.

HOSEA 1-3

Those responsible for the final form of the book did not work haphazardly. They opted for a careful compilation process, not a scissors and paste method. In a detailed study E. M. Good has suggested that in Hosea 1-3 the two narratives (1:2-9; 3:1-5) and the

---

* There is a discrepancy between the chapter and verse division of the Hebrew text and the Vulgate in the Book of Hosea. Hebrew 2:1-2 = Vulgate 1:10-11; Hebrew 2:3-25 = Vulgate 2:1-23; Hebrew 12:1 = Vulgate 11:11; Hebrew 12:2-15 = Vulgate 12:1-14. We will employ the Hebrew numbering (followed by NAB) rather than the Vulgate numbering (followed by the Revised Standard Version and the New English Bible). The Jerusalem Bible prints the Hebrew numbering in ordinary roman type on the top and the Vulgate numbering in italics on the bottom.

three oracles (2:1-3; 2:4-17; 2:18-25) are so knit together that the central oracle on wife and children (2:4-17) is highlighted. Thus the two narratives sandwich the three oracles. The first narrative (1:2-9) provides information about the unfaithful wife theme and the symbolic names of the children. The first oracle (2:1-3) takes up these symbolic names and announces a happy outcome. The second oracle (2:4-17) returns to the unfaithful wife theme and discusses her punishment and restoration. The third oracle (2:18-25) focuses on the punishment of the unfaithful wife and takes up the children's names once more. Finally the second narrative (3:1-5) goes back to the theme of the second oracle, viz., the unfaithful wife's punishment and restoration. In this arrangement the central oracle on the wife and nation (2:4-17) receives the main accent.

In a perceptive study of Hos 2:4-17, 18-25, W. Brueggemann has shown how the author has interwoven the official language of covenant with the personal elements of the prophet's experience. He speaks of these two units as covenant broken and restored.

Hos 2:4-15 deals with the broken covenant. Yahweh indicts his wife Israel: she did not recognize her husband as the giver of the grain, the wine, and the oil (2:10); she chose to go after her lovers and neglect her husband (2:15). Yahweh threatens his wife Israel: she will be stripped naked and become like an arid land (2:5—a reference to the desert experience); she will lose her grain and wine and watch the end of her formerly joyous liturgies (2:11, 13). Yet Yahweh summons his wife to renew the covenant: she is to remove her harlotry from before her and her adultery from between her breasts (2:4); "Then she shall say, 'I will go back to my first husband, for it was better with me then than now'" (2:9).

In Hos 2:16-17 the prophet describes the possibility of a renewed covenantal relationship. The prophet borrows from the Exodus tradition, speaking of the wilderness experience as the honeymoon of Yahweh and his bride. Yahweh longs for the rendezvous in the desert where he and his estranged wife can be reconciled. "So I will allure her; I will lead her into the desert and speak to her heart. From there I will give her the vineyards she had . . ." (2:16-17). As W. Brueggemann notes, the four verbs used here underline Yahweh's status as the giver of gifts, not Israel's rightful reward from a manipulated fertility deity.

In the third oracle (2:18-25) the prophet's promises correspond to the threats of 2:4-15. Instead of infertility there is a new covenant including the beasts of the field, the birds of the air, and the things crawling on the ground (see 2:20). Instead of being stripped naked, Israel will enjoy a new marital relationship founded on mutual love (see 2:21-22). Instead of the end of liturgies there will be a chorus of response in which Yahweh, the heavens, the earth, and the grain/wine/oil will participate. Both spouses (2:18) and children (2:25) will be reconciled.

MARRIAGE AS COVENANT MODEL

Hosea is the first Old Testament writer to use marriage as a covenant model—a tradition followed by Jeremiah (see Jer 2:2-3) and Ezekiel (see Ez 16; 23) as well as by the author of Ephesians in the New Testament (see Eph 5:22-33). When one thinks of the Canaanite influence, this was a daring move. Thus Yahweh is like Baal in that Yahweh has a wife. However, Yahweh is unlike Baal in that his wife is the people of Israel.

This insight offers a greater appreciation of the intimacy and demands of the covenant relationship. The quality that is to be sought here is unrelenting marital fidelity. We are reminded of the image of bone and flesh in Gn 2:23 and its implication of abiding covenantal backing and support, i.e., through thick and thin. In the opposite direction the rupture of this relationship is the sin of infidelity. In Hosea it is specifically adultery in the form of prostitution. Covenant as marriage necessarily means an exclusive relationship. Hosea's experience with Gomer taught him the anguish and pain that Yahweh found in his marital relationship with Israel. By loving Gomer, Hosea came to understand something of Yahweh's deep love for his wife.

DEMYTHOLOGIZING

Hosea had to resolve this problem: how present Yahweh to a largely agricultural audience hooked on the fertility cult? His response was to show how covenantal fidelity brought fertility while covenantal infidelity caused infertility. (This equation is obviously weak, as the author of Job, among others, shows.) In developing this theological approach, Hosea did not adopt the stance of Deuteronomy: "'Destroy without fail every place on the high mountains, on the hills, and under every leafy tree where the nations you are to dispossess worship their gods'" (Dt 12:2). Instead, Hosea strove to neutralize the fertility myth. He chose to demythologize it, i.e., to remove from it what could not be reconciled with Israelite faith but to preserve and refocus the positive elements it contained.

When speaking of the marriage between Yahweh and Israel, the prophet does not hesitate to describe the God of Israel as a seducer: "So I will allure her . . ." (Hos 2:16). At the same time, however, the setting for seduction is the desert with its memories of Israel's honeymoon days. The move of the daring lover is to reawaken covenantal loyalty: "She shall respond there as in the days of her youth, when she came up from the land of Egypt" (Hos 2:17). Although nature religion sought to assure the fertility of marriage by sacral intercourse and its implication of loyalty to Baal, Hosea speaks of marriage in covenantal terms: "I will espouse you in right and justice, in love and in mercy; I will espouse you in fidelity . . ." (Hos 2:21-22).

Elsewhere the prophet successfully interweaves the language of agriculture with the language of covenant: "'Sow for yourselves justice, reap the fruit of piety; break up for yourselves a new field, for it is time to seek the Lord, till he come and rain down justice upon you'" (Hos 10:12). When Israel chooses to trade Yahweh for Baal, when Israel resorts to covenantal infidelity, the prayer of the prophet is the petition for infertility: "Give them, O Lord! give them what? Give them an unfruitful womb, and dry breasts!" (Hos 9:14).

THE PERSONALISM OF KNOWLEDGE

A key word in Hosea's theological vocabulary is "know/knowledge." Our first inclination is perhaps to stress the intellectual dimension of the term. Thus we gain or acquire "knowledge." Perhaps we are less inclined to underline the volitional aspect of the term, although we do speak of "really knowing a person." For the prophet Hosea it is this volitional dimension which emerges from his message. Against the background of certain ancient Near Eastern texts "to know" means "to acknowledge." It is used in treaty contexts where the vassal is called upon to "know" his overlord by remaining faithful to the oath of obedience. In Hos 13:4 the prophet introduces Yahweh as the covenant God from the days of the Exodus. He adds: "You know no God besides me, and there is no savior but me." Elsewhere Hosea exposes the emptiness of Israel's oath. He speaks of their violation of covenant, noting: "While to me they cry out, 'O God of Israel, we know you!'" (Hos 8:2).

In the light of the fertility cult this vocabulary is another example of the prophet's daring demythologizing. "To know" is used in Hebrew and other languages in the sense of sexual knowledge (see Gn 4:1; 19:8). However, when he speaks of the renewed covenant relationship, he stresses the "acknowledgement" aspect of the word, i.e., recognizing Yahweh as covenant lord/husband. The covenantal language of Hos 2:21-22 supports such a conclusion: "I will espouse you in right and in justice, in love and in mercy; I will espouse you in fidelity and you shall know the Lord." Elsewhere the prophet describes his people as hardened in sin, especially infidelity which prevents them from returning to Yahweh: "For the spirit of harlotry is in them, and they do not recognize the Lord" (Hos 5:4).

In Hos 4:1-3 the prophet employs a covenant lawsuit, a literary form adapted from Israel's court trials and legal procedures wherein Israel is indicted for violation of covenant. (There is also a borrowing from international treaty usage whereby Yahweh is suzerain and Israel vassal.) In 4:1a the prophet summons the people. This is followed by a statement of violation of covenant: "There is no fidelity, no mercy, no knowledge of God in the land. False swearing, lying, murder, stealing and adultery! in their lawlessness, bloodshed follows bloodshed" (4:1b-2). Finally in 4:3 there is the sentence, specifically the implementation of curses of infertility against God's people. "Knowledge" has a personal, volitional ring. It is the failure to recognize Yahweh as lord/husband. (Note how the generic terms of covenantal infidelity in 4:1b are followed by the specific crimes of 4:2.)

THE IMPERSONALISM OF MECHANICAL RENEWAL

It is one thing to offend a person, it is quite another thing to fake making up with the offended person. Hosea came to know the shallowness of Israel's renewal. It was a painful experience because he concluded that it pained Yahweh. It was a frustrating experience because he reasoned that it frustrated Yahweh as well. For the prophet only a renewal that sprang from the human heart and spirit was truly worthy of the covenant relationship.

There is reason for suggesting that Hos 5:15-6:6 is a liturgy of covenant renewal, or better, of attempted covenant renewal. It begins in 5:15 with Yahweh's waiting for the moment of repentance: "I will go back to my place until they pay for their guilt and seek my presence. In their affliction, they shall look for me." Hos 6:1-3 is the liturgical formula, a "confiteor" recited by the people in view of reconciliation. It employs the standard expression of repentance: "'Come, let us *return* to the Lord'" (6:1). The formula continues, using the language of killing and restoration on the third day. There is some extrabiblical treaty background for this formula, implying that the vassal is regarded as dead because of disobedience but then restored by the overlord in view of renewing the oath of fealty. "The third day" is the day for covenant (re)making (see Ex 19:11, 15, 16). Against this background Israel is dead because of violation of covenant but eager to be raised up by renewal of covenant: "He will revive us after two days; on the third day he will raise us up, to live in his presence" (6:2). For Hosea the sham liturgy merely reflects Israel's sham covenantal sense: "Let us know, let us strive to know the Lord . . ." (6:3).

Yahweh's reaction is completely unexpected. The covenant lord/husband retaliates by exposing the people's sense of loyalty: "Your piety (i.e., covenantal fidelity) is like a morning cloud, like the dew that early passes away" (6:4). Yahweh's indignation continues in v 5, reaching its final expression in v 6: "For it is love (i.e., covenantal fidelity) that I desire, not sacrifice, and knowledge of

God rather than holocausts." For God's people it is all too easy to provide sacrificial offerings. However, it is much more difficult for them to carry out what the offerings symbolize, viz., their giving of self to Yahweh.

For the prophet this is simply mechanical liturgy. It is a question of going through all the motions yet of being totally unwilling to reform. Because there is no sense of interior renewal, the liturgy degenerates into a form of insolence. It is also a form of oppression whereby covenant is reduced to impersonalism. It is this impersonalism that provokes Yahweh's violent outburst in 6:5: "For this reason I smote them through the prophets, I slew them by the words of my mouth." It is only too obvious to the prophet that Yahweh cannot tolerate this viciousness. Ultimately Yahweh cannot accept the status of a fertility deity. Yahweh cannot be constrained to grant blessings because of liturgical exactness and rubrical precision. What is required is a total awareness of the person of Yahweh and a total realization of the heinousness of fakery. Here the human spirit has reached the nadir of malice.

DIVINE PATHOS

Hos 6:4-6 may give the impression that Yahweh will be unyielding, that Yahweh has embarked on a plan whose smooth execution will inevitably lead to the destruction of the covenant people. Evenness, consistency, resolution—these are the qualities which we naturally project on the God of Israel. However, the Hebrew Bible attests that Yahweh is not a least common denominator of the ancient Near East but a God ever concerned in paradoxical ways about his son/wife Israel.

Hos 11:1-11 opens with a touching picture of Yahweh as father, specifically a father because of the Exodus: "When Israel was a child I loved him, out of Egypt I called my son" (11:1). Hosea then describes Israel's lack of response to so caring a father by contrasting it with the father's unstinting love: "Yet it was I who taught Ephraim to walk, who took them in my arms; . . . I fostered them like one who raises an infant to his cheeks . . ." (11:3, 4). In vv 5-7 the author logically announces the punishment awaiting so recalcitrant a son. Clearly the moment for paternal strength has arrived. But it is at this moment that Hosea pictures Yahweh in the most human of feelings, exposing Israel's God to the vicissitudes of human emotions: "How could I give you up, O Ephraim, or deliver you up, O Israel? How could I treat you as Admah or make you like Zeboiim (cities destroyed along with Sodom and Gomorrah—see Dt 29:22)? My heart is overwhelmed, my pity is stirred." As J. L. McKenzie has remarked, blind rage will not be the determining factor, since God

106

is God and not human. Here divine compassion transcends the categories of human justice.

In 13:4-11, however, Hosea depicts Yahweh as regaining control of himself. In a clearer state of mind Yahweh reviews Israel's past performance and concludes that only swift retribution is reasonable. Thus Yahweh, once the shepherd defending his sheep from the attacks of vicious animals (see Hos 9:10 where Yahweh finds Israel in the desert and offers protection), assumes the role of attacker: "I will attack them like a bear robbed of its young, and tear their hearts from their breasts; I will devour them on the spot like a lion, as though a wild beast were to rend them" (13:8).

Hosea pursues this line of thinking in 13:12-16. Yahweh dismisses all vacillation. If Yahweh exhibited softness or hesitation in the past, Yahweh now makes amends for such weakness by resolutely pursuing the course of action expressed in 13:4-11. Only Israel's destruction will satisfy the demands of Israel's God. There is no longer room for compassion. "Shall I deliver them from the power of the nether world? shall I redeem them from death? Where are your plagues, O death! where is your sting, O nether world! My eyes are closed to compassion" (13:14).

Hos 14:2-9 jars the seemingly faultless logic of 13:4-16. Here Yahweh has reverted to the "weakness" of 11:7-8. The piece begins on a note of conversion: "Return, O Israel, to the Lord, your God . . . Take with you words, and return to the Lord . . ." (14:2, 3). In 14:5 Yahweh is again the loving father rather than the cold judge: "I will heal their defection, I will love them freely; for my wrath is turned away from them." For us the passages smack of reversible logic and continuity of opposed emotions.

A. Heschel has rightly stressed this divine pathos. For the God of Israel humans are not abstractions or generalizations. In order to deal with humans as humans, he writes, God must become aware of them emotionally. Since this God is not the divine onlooker but active participant in the drama of covenant, this God must relate to his people, not as ideas, but as concrete individuals exposed to misery and frustration. An emotionally detached deity may be the god of some equally detached philosophers but it is certainly not the God of Israel. Divine pathos means divine concern. For this God people are always people, never things.

JESUS AND THE PERSONAL/COMMUNAL

The writers of the New Testament support the view that personal events/happenings in the life and work of Jesus were essentially communal events/happenings. They took the words and actions of Jesus and interpreted them to meet the needs of their various communities. They made both the life-style and the death-style of this first century A.D. Jew the model for all who would seek genuine humanity. They handed on Jesus' awareness of human pain, Jesus' concern over human malice, and Jesus' conviction about human forgiveness as the pattern for ongoing human reaction. The story of the New Testament is the story of human involvement and human interaction. The death of Jesus symbolized the death of all impersonalism in dealing with God.

Response to the Word of God in community demands that we adopt the non-manipulative way of Jesus of Nazareth. Such a way rejects mechanical liturgy in favor of church services that overflow into human concern and support. Such a way sponsors the display of emotion and feeling for the needs of others in place of a weekly contribution devoid of further commitment. Such a way insists on the acquisition of human identity by reaching out instead of focusing within. In the final analysis our personal gifts, blessings, perceptions, etc., must contribute to the common good. Hosea by way of Jesus must have an impact today.

BIBLIOGRAPHICAL SUGGESTIONS

Andersen, Francis I. & Freedman, David N. *Hosea*. AB. Garden City: Doubleday, 1980.

Brueggemann, Walter. *Tradition for Crisis: A Study in Hosea*. Richmond: John Knox, 1968.

Buss, Martin J. *The Prophetic Word of Hosea, A Morphological Study*. BZAW. Berlin: Töpelmann, 1969.

Craghan, John F. "The Book of Hosea, A Survey of Recent Literature on the First of the Minor Prophets," *BTB* 1 (1971) 81-100, 145-170.

Eichrodt, Walther. "The Holy One in Your Midst, the Theology of Hosea," *Int* 15 (1961) 259-273.

Fensham, F. Charles. "The Covenant-Idea in the Book of Hosea," *Die Ou Testamentiese Werkgemeenskap in Suid-Afrika* 7/8 (1964-1965) 35-49.

Good, Edwin M. "The Composition of Hosea," *Svensk Exegetisk Årsbok* 31 (1966) 21-63.

Heschel, Abraham. *The Prophets*. New York: Harper & Row, 1962, 39-60, 247-267.

Huffmon, Herbert B. "The Covenant Lawsuit in the Prophets," *JBL* 78 (1959) 285-295.

McKenzie, John L. "Divine Passion in Osee," *CBQ* 17 (1955) 287-299.

_____ . "Knowledge of God in Hosea," *JBL* 74 (1955) 22-27.

Mays, James L. *Hosea*. OTL. Philadelphia: Westminster, 1969.

Robinson, H. Wheeler. *The Cross of Hosea*. Philadelphia: Westminster, 1949.

Rowley, Harold H. "The Marriage of Hosea," *BJRL* (1956-1957) 200-233 = *Men of God*. London: Nelson, 1963, 66-97.

Vawter, Bruce. *Amos, Hosea, Micah*. Old Testament Message. Wilmington: Michael Glazier, 1982, 77-127.

Ward, James M. *Hosea: A Theological Commentary.* New York: Harper & Row, 1966.

_____ . "The Message of the Prophet Hosea," *Int* 23 (1969) 387–407.

Wijngaards, Joanne N. "Death and Resurrection in Covenant Context," *VT* 17 (1967) 226–239.

Wolff, Hans W. "Guilt and Salvation, A Study of the Prophecy of Hosea," *Int* 15 (1961) 274–285.

_____ . *Hosea.* Hermeneia. Philadelphia: Fortress, 1974.

CHAPTER 11

The Invitation to Communal Concern

Biblical passages to be read: Is 1-12, 28-32, 36-37.

WITH LIBERTY AND JUSTICE FOR SOME

Our pledge of allegiance insists that in the American way liberty and justice are for all. More realistically, it is a condition to be attained, not a fact already achieved—neither here nor elsewhere. Injustices and inequities abound. Yet our reaction may be to drown out the cry of the poor and abused with "God's in his heaven, all's right with the world." But therein seems to lie the problem. We think of people as candidates for heaven, not as individuals who already possess an inherent dignity and a corresponding claim to a fully human life on earth. We are so engaged in continuing the evils of rank individualism that we all but crush the sense of communal concern. We thereby denigrate our pledge of allegiance to: with liberty and justice for those who can get it!

We are, first and foremost, a people with rights. Only reluctantly and then after some prodding are we a people with obligations. We have been trained to ask what society owes us, what other people must do for us. Our spontaneous question is: what's in it for me? We have not been disciplined—at least not adequately—to ask what we owe society, what we must do for other people. Our spontaneous question is seldom: what's in it for them? We have forgotten that the truly human priority is to insist on the rights of others.

The institution tends to be anonymous. More often than not, it is interested in plans and programs, not people and their plight. Accountability may be minimal, since institutions have a pronounced

111

penchant to provide for themselves and, when challenged, to exhibit only ephemeral repentance. We tend to regard the titles of our leaders as indications of status attained, not of obligations yet to be fulfilled.

Response to the Word of God in community must involve itself in communal concern. To be in covenant means to protect those in covenant. To be a strong community means to provide for the weakest in that community. A reflection on the word and work of Isaiah of Jerusalem (Is 1-39, although not everything is by the eighth century B.C. prophet) is a challenge to our sense of community. Such reflection is calculated to have us pose the question: how do we interpret our pledge of allegiance?

SOME FEATURES OF THE PROPHET

Isaiah of Jerusalem (sometimes called First Isaiah) preached in the southern kingdom of Judah, principally, it would seem, in the city of Jerusalem. His time was one of foreign invasion and concomitant hardship. From his call in 739 B.C. (hence a contemporary of Hosea) to his last dated preaching in 701 B.C., Isaiah never ceased to advocate a vision of God which necessarily entailed concern for all God's covenanted people. His easy access to the king may suggest that he himself belonged to the higher echelons of Jerusalemite society. In any event his word was felt by courtier and commoner alike.

A first obvious feature of his message is God's holiness. A recurring epithet in the whole book of Isaiah is "the Holy One of Israel." The basis for this expression was his experience of God's overpowering holiness at the time of his call. "'Holy, holy, holy is the Lord of hosts!'" (Is 6:3) in the seraphim's chant made the prophet immediately aware of his own lack of holiness and the subsequent need for cleansing. However, the experience of God's holiness also became the standard by which he assessed the people. They were not demonstrating that holiness which covenant called for, i.e., concern for all the people. Thus Isaiah opposed whatever detracted from Yahweh's holiness.

A second feature is the kingship of Yahweh. While the prophet clearly perceived the transcendence of Israel's God in the inaugural vision in the temple (see Is 6:1-13), he also realized that this God was part and parcel of the actions of the people. In this vision Isaiah refers to Yahweh as "the king" (Is 6:5). "King" implied that human kings were not absolute, that they were accountable to the Holy One of Israel. To engage in whatever form of politics, especially warfare, meant that the human king's action could not be at variance with that of the divine king. To disregard Yahweh's kingship would mean to court disaster.

As T. C. Vriezen has made clear, a third feature of his message

112

is the need for faith. In a world of neo-Assyrian might, when Judean kings were tempted to ask aid from that power or tempted to rebel against it by seeking Egyptian aid, the basic thrust of the prophet was faith. When King Ahaz was deliberating the possibility of bringing in the neo-Assyrian war machine against the kingdoms of Damascus and Israel, Isaiah's words to Ahaz were: "Unless your faith is firm, you shall not be firm!" (Is 7:9).

To believe meant to lean on Another, to be rooted in Another, to have a vision of reality not dictated by military might but by the need for holiness. When Judah hoped that her alliance with Egypt would bolster her efforts to overthrow the neo-Assyrian yoke, the prophet proclaimed: "For thus said the Lord God, the Holy One of Israel: By waiting and by calm you shall be saved, in quiet and trust your strength lies. But this you did not wish" (Is 30:15).

THE BREAKDOWN OF COMMUNITY

The prophet's analysis of his community is that his people are consumed with following their own whims and pleasures. Accountability to the community is minimal, concern for self is maximal. It is a situation that will ultimately prompt action on God's part.

In the song of the vineyard (Is 5:1-7) Isaiah gets his audience to condemn itself. It is likely that he poses as a ballad singer while the crowds take part in the festivities of the grape harvest. He describes how his friend made every effort to ensure a good harvest. However, the yield was only wild grapes. At this moment the prophet announces his friend's final decision concerning the unproductive vineyard, viz., he will simply allow it to go to ruin.

Isaiah then makes the point of his ballad. The vineyard is really God's people. The house of Israel and the men of Judah have long been special objects of God's love. However, election implies productivity. Using a play on words in Hebrew, Isaiah proclaims that God sought judgment (*mišpāṭ*) only to find bloodshed (*mišpāḥ*). God looked for justice (*ṣᵉdāqà*) only to find outcry (*ṣᵉ'āqà*), i.e., the cry of the poor whom fellow Israelites have manipulated. The ballad is ultimately the song of Israel's condemnation.

In 1:10-17 the prophet—not unlike Hosea and Amos—attacks purely mechanical liturgy. People find it easier to contribute to the cult and attend ceremonies rather than provide for the needs of the total community. According to Isaiah a liturgy devoid of communal concern ceases to be liturgy. To worship Yahweh means to care for Yahweh's people: "Wash yourselves clean! Put away your misdeeds from before my eyes; cease doing evil; learn to do good. Make justice your aim: redress the wronged, hear the orphan's plea, defend the widow" (1:16-17).

Is 3:1-15 deals with the crisis of leadership. Vv 2-3 name the

113

leaders: the military personnel, judges, prophets, etc. Since they have not provided for their people (v 1), Yahweh will replace them with youngsters (v 4). The outcome will be chaos with lack of respect and mutual oppression in its wake (vv 5-7). In vv 13-15 the prophet announces how God will further deal with this failure of leadership. Borrowing from the legal practices of his day, he paints a picture of how poorly his people fare in a covenant lawsuit. In v 13 Yahweh arises to perform the office of judge. In the beginning of v 14 we have those charged: the elders of the people and the princes. The rest of v 14 is the charge: "It is you who have devoured the vineyard; the loot wrested from the poor is in your houses." V 15 is the haunting question addressed to the leadership: "What do you mean by crushing my people, and grinding down the poor when they look to you?" For the prophet this is but another lack of holiness in interhuman relationships.

For the prophet not only the men but also the women are responsible. Their focus is solely on themselves. In 3:16-17, 24 he describes the wealthy women as flaunting their position: ". . . (they) walk with necks outstretched, ogling and mincing as they go, their anklets tinkling with every step . . ." (3:16). At this point Isaiah announces that Yahweh will make the punishment fit the crime: their perfume, girdle, coiffure, and rich gown will become respectively a stench, a rope, baldness, and a sackcloth shirt (see 3:24). The parade of wealth is ultimately a demonstration of concern for self.

The woe oracle probably derives from Israel's funeral celebration (see 1 Kgs 13:30; Jer 22:18-19). It now expresses the pain that will come upon various groups whose behavior works against the community—hence the presence of lament and grief originally associated with a funeral. Characteristic of the woe oracle is reversal of imagery. This is a divine indictment of sinful behavior borrowed from the very language or imagery of the indictment.

Is 5:8-25; 10:1-5 is a series of seven woes directed against different segments of the population. Several of them are especially noteworthy for violation of interhuman justice. Is 5:8-10 deals with the greedy who buy up the real estate of the poor until they are the sole proprietors of a huge empty space: "Woe to you who join house to house, who connect field with field, till no room remains, and you are left to dwell alone in the midst of the land!" (5:8). Their punishment will be that ten acres will yield only six gallons of wine (5:10). Is 5:22-23 is concerned with the drunkards (see also Is 5:11-13) and manipulators of the legal system: "To those who acquit the guilty for bribes, and deprive the just man of his rights" (5:23). Similarly Is 10:1-4 looks to those who enact unjust legislation and refuse justice to the poor: "Woe to those who enact unjust statutes and who write

114

oppressive decrees, depriving the needy of judgment and robbing my people's poor of their rights, making widows their plunder and orphans their prey!" (10:1-2). In the prophet's view there will be no escape for such leaders on the day of punishment (10:3). *Corruptio optimi pessima est!*

THE KING AND THE PEOPLE

Isaiah was not content to face only certain levels of leadership. He was particularly concerned about the Judean king. From all appearances he regarded the Davidic dynasty as a God-given institution for meeting the needs of the covenant people. The liturgy for the coronation of the Davidic prince expressed the people's hope for better times. However, it also indicated the means for achieving that hope, viz., social justice for all the people. Psalm 72 captures both the hope of the people and the task of the institution. "He [the Davidic prince] shall govern your people with justice and your afflicted ones with judgment. The mountains shall yield peace for the people, and the hills justice. He shall defend the afflicted among the people, save the children of the poor and crush the oppressor.... From fraud and violence he shall redeem them, and precious shall their blood be in his sight" (Ps 72:2-4, 14).

In two oracles, Is 9:1-6 and 11:1-9 (best known for their use in the Christmas liturgy), Isaiah endorsed a view of monarchy consonant with justice and righteousness for the community. In his judgment the institution could still be the vehicle for social justice.

In Is 9:2-4 the prophet reflects the military situation of his time. Through God's intervention, however, the people will overthrow the burden of the foreign oppressor. Is 9:5 reads: "For a child is born to us, a son is given us; upon his shoulder dominion rests. They name him Wonder-Counselor, God-Hero, Father-Forever, Prince of Peace." The "son" is the king. He becomes God's adoptive son when he assumes his kingly office (see Ps 2:7). "Wonder-Counselor, God-Hero," etc., are throne names for the new king. In 9:6, however, the scene switches to the application of these names. A king who is truly worthy of the name will provide for the common good. He will meet their needs. "His dominion is vast and forever peaceful, from David's throne, and over his kingdom which he confirms and sustains by *judgment and justice,* both now and forever" (9:6).

According to the poem, peace results when the king looks to the good of the entire community. In a recent work on Isaiah, W. L. Holladay describes the impact of a coronation. It is a time when people feel that they have turned a corner. They nourish the hope that the government will now respond to human needs. "Long live the king" really implies "Let the people live."

Although some authorities refer Is 11:1-9 to the postexilic period, there are still good reasons for suggesting that it is the work of Isaiah of Jerusalem. It is also likely that he borrows from the ritual of coronation.

The gifts of the spirit in Is 11:2 ("A spirit of wisdom and of understanding," etc.) are those gifts that the king needs in order to discharge his office properly. Is 11:3 shows the proper use of such gifts: "Not by appearance shall he judge, nor by hearsay shall he decide." It continues in 11:4: "But he shall judge the poor with justice, and decide aright for the land's afflicted. He shall slay the ruthless with the rod of his mouth, and with the breath of his lips he shall slay the wicked." Finally in 11:5 there is a description of one item of the king's clothing which concerns social justice: *"Justice* shall be the band around his waist, and *faithfulness* a belt upon his hips."

WAR OR PEACE

Isaiah was not a political scientist who viewed military engagements as the amassing of soldiers and machinery to defeat a given enemy. He was not simply pro-Judah or pro-Assyria. He was always pro-Yahweh. The only military strategy which he consistently advocated was faith and trust in the King who resided in the temple, not the king who lived in the palace.

Is 10:5-15 offers the prophet's view of the place of neo-Assyria in God's plan. To be sure, neo-Assyria was Judah's overlord. But for the prophet it was more. In 10:5 he proclaims that neo-Assyria is doing God's bidding, that this powerful nation is actually "my rod in anger, my staff in wrath." However, neo-Assyria refuses to abide by Yahweh's limited disciplinary action against the covenant people. "Rather, it is in his heart to destroy, to make an end of nations not a few" (10:7). Neo-Assyria has exceeded Yahweh's mandate. Consequently Yahweh will take action against neo-Assyria. Is 10:15 spells out neo-Assyria's role as means, not end in Yahweh's plan: "Will the axe boast against him who hews with it . . . As if a rod could sway him who lifts it, or a staff him who is not wood!" The poem clearly establishes Yahweh's hegemony over the greatest power of the ancient Near East at that time.

At the death of the neo-Assyrian King Sargon in 705 B.C. many of the vassal nations sought to overthrow their political allegiance. Thinking that the time was right, the kingdom of Judah entered into an alliance with the twenty-fifth dynasty in Egypt. In Is 30:1-7 the prophet decries the futility of such an alliance. His judgment is not based merely on political expediency but on theological perception. To seek the aid of Egypt is to deny the aid of Yahweh: "Woe to the rebellious children, says the Lord, who carry out plans that are not mine, who weave webs that are not inspired by me, adding sin upon sin. They go down to Egypt but my counsel they do not seek" (30:1-2). Actually the people to whom they are transporting their riches are good for nothing (30:6). For the prophet, political powers should respect the Power at work.

Is 30:1-3 also describes the failure of the Egyptian alliance because of faith perception: "Woe to those who go down to Egypt for help, who depend upon horses; who put their trust in chariots because of their number and in horsemen because of their combined power, but look not to the Holy One of Israel nor seek the Lord" (31:1). He sharpens the contrast in 31:3: "The Egyptians are men, not God, their horses are flesh, not spirit."

Isaiah 31 also contains two passages, 31:4-5 and 31:8-9, which in W. L. Holladay's view were added by Isaiah himself. Unlike 31:1-3, these two passages contain good news for Judah. In 31:4-5 God is a lion undaunted by neo-Assyria who shields Jerusalem. In 31:8-9 neo-Assyria is the power that will fall. If these passages are by the prophet, they do not support prophetic ambivalence. Rather, they endorse a policy in which Yahweh's plan takes precedence over the plans of all the powers, not excluding neo-Assyria.

In 701 B.C. the army of the neo-Assyrian king, Sennacherib, marched against Jerusalem and its king, Hezekiah, because of the latter's violation of his oath of fealty to the overlord. It is extremely difficult, if not virtually impossible, to reconstruct what actually took place (see 2 Kgs 18:13-19:37; Is 36-37; 2 Chr 32). The prophet clearly opposed the rebellion. However, according to 2 Kgs 19:20-34 = Is 37:21-35 Isaiah predicted that the city would be spared (see Is 29:1-6 as interpreted by 29:7-8). On the other hand, although the city was not taken, the surrounding area of Judah was utterly devastated. One gets the impression that here too Isaiah was not pro-Judah and anti-Assyria, but rather pro-Yahweh. The prophet's insistence was on the plan of Yahweh, not on the expediency of rebellious Judah or on the military might of arrogant neo-Assyria.

WITH LIBERTY AND JUSTICE FOR ALL

In the light of the message of Isaiah of Jerusalem our response to the Word of God in community must reflect certain concerns. That response must reject apathy and promote mutual concern. Some of the elements in that response would seem to include the following:

The prophetic task involves freeing not only the oppressed but also the oppressors. In this sense we are asked to go beyond Moses as our prophetic model. He freed the oppressed. But in opposing the oppressors, the Egyptians, did he ultimately free them? A vision of social justice is inadequate that does not ultimately seek to eradicate oppression by freeing the sources of oppression. This implies that the oppressors must provoke us, not only to indignation and anger,

117

but also to dialogue and consciousness-raising. Prophetic ministry seeks to make God's Word have an impact on everyone.

In liberating the oppressors, we must insist on a theology of titles after the manner of Isaiah. The modern prophet is called upon to point out the implications of titles. A title without service is really no title. By experience we know that our titles automatically imply a relationship to others. Yet we tend to understand titles only in and for themselves. They suggest some degree of promotion. However, promotion really means that we have promoted the welfare of our sisters and brothers. Ultimately a title minus service is a disservice.

We must deal with the institution. Here the vision of Isaiah offers considerable insight. Admittedly, as J. Miranda notes, institutions have a pronounced inability to admit errors and correct them. Yet prophetic ministry must consist, in part at least, in criticizing the institution if it does not fulfill its basic reason for existence: the service of the community. It is once again a question of the sabbath for humans, not humans for the sabbath. While we must be realistic, we must also be sustained by the hope that Isaiah had for the institution—yet a hope that did not prevent him from criticizing that same institution.

Isaiah also challenges the modern prophet to uncover the evils which fester in the community at large. Perhaps it is not too far from the mark to suggest that the quest should concentrate on purely egocentric ventures. Each of the evils discussed by the prophet ultimately involves an egotistical stance—the community is excluded. Without using the term, Isaiah advocates a covenant-oriented theology wherein neglect of sisters and brothers necessarily entails neglect of Yahweh. Isaiah challenges the modern prophet to work out the logical conclusions of covenant and have the courage to point out the distortions of covenant. To be in covenant means to sustain others. An ego trip is by definition a caricature of covenant.

Given the arms race, given the ever greater chances for global warfare, what is the modern prophet called upon to say? It would certainly be wrong to equate the neo-Assyrian threat with our own potential for disaster. Granted the differences, is there yet a link between Isaiah and ourselves? The answer seems to be a vision of faith which transcends the blueprints of annihilation. The question can no longer be: can we make a bigger and better bomb? It must be: dare we have a vision of God and hence of humanity whereby the lust for power is made subservient to the desire for peace? Without disparaging political science, we must be open to a vision wherein only Yahweh is king and all other "kings" his servants. Isaiah was not simply pro-Judah or pro-Assyria. He was always pro-Yahweh. A vision of God must come before the choosing of sides.

BIBLIOGRAPHICAL SUGGESTIONS

Blank, Sheldon H. *Prophetic Faith in Isaiah*. New York: Harper, 1958.

Buber, Martin. *The Prophetic Faith*. New York: Macmillan, 1949, 126-154.

Childs, Brevard S. *Isaiah and the Assyrian Crisis*. SBT. Naperville: Allenson, 1967.

Clifford, Richard J. "The Use of *HÔY* in the Prophets," *CBQ* 28 (1966) 458-464.

Cogan, Morton. *Imperialism and Religion: Assyria, Judah and Israel in the Eighth and Seventh Centuries B. C. E.* SBLMS. Missoula: Scholars Press, 1974, 65-96.

Exum, J. Cheryl. "Of Broken Pots, Fluttering Birds and Visions in the Night: Extended Simile and Poetic Technique in Isaiah," *CBQ* 43 (1981) 331-352.

Gottwald, Norman K. *All the Kingdoms of the Earth*. New York: Harper & Row, 1964, 147-208.

Holladay, William L. *Isaiah: Scroll of a Prophetic Heritage*. Grand Rapids: Eerdmans, 1978, 1-113.

Janzen, Waldemar. *Mourning Cry and Woe Oracle*. BZAW. Berlin: de Gruyter, 1972.

Jensen, Joseph. *The Use of tôrā by Isaiah*. Catholic Biblical Quarterly Monograph Series. Washington, D.C.: Catholic Biblical Association of America, 1973.

_____ . "Weal and Woe in Isaiah: Consistency and Continuity," *CBQ* 43 (1981) 167-187.

_____ . *Isaiah 1-39*. Old Testament Message. Wilmington: Michael Glazier, forthcoming.

Kaiser, Otto. *Isaiah 1-12. Isaiah 13-39*. OTL. Philadelphia: Westminster, 1972, 1974.

Kissane, Edward J. *The Book of Isaiah*. Revised edition. Dublin: Browne & Nolan, 1960. 2 vols.

Melugin, Roy F. "The Conventional and the Creative in Isaiah's Judgment Oracles," *CBQ* 36 (1974) 301-311.

Miranda, José P. *Marx and the Bible*. Maryknoll: Orbis, 1980.

Rowley, Harold H. "Hezekiah's Reform and Rebellion," *BJRL* 44 (1961-1962) 395-461 = *Men of God*. London: Nelson, 1963, 98-132.

Scott, Robert B. Y. "The Literary Structure of Isaiah's Oracles," *Studies in Old Testament Prophecy*. Edited by H. H. Rowley. Edinburgh: Clark, 1950, 175-186.

_____ . "The Book of Isaiah, Ch. 1-39, Introduction and Exegesis," *IB* 5. New York: Abingdon, 1956, 149-381.

Scullion, John J. "Approach to the Understanding of Is. 7:10-17," *JBL* 87 (1968) 288-300.

Vriezen, Theodor C. "Essentials of the Theology of Isaiah," *Israel's Prophetic Heritage. Essays in Honor of James Muilenburg*. Edited by B. W. Anderson & W. Harrelson. New York: Harper & Row, 1962, 128-146.

Ward, James. *Amos and Isaiah*. New York: Abingdon, 1969, 143-279.

_____ . "Isaiah," *IDBSup*, 456-461.

Whedbee, J. William. *Isaiah and Wisdom*. New York: Abingdon, 1971.

CHAPTER 12

The Invitation to Prayer

Biblical passages to be read: Pss 1; 2; 23; 37; 65; 72; 91; 100; 110; 121; 128; 145.

THE ANCIENT HEBREW PSALTER AND MODERN CHRISTIAN PRAYER

For many of us the responsorial psalm in our liturgy is an obstacle that prevents us from rushing on to the next reading. We repeat the response but must acknowledge that it has little meaning for us. When we discover that the psalms are forms of prayer, we throw up our arms and duly observe that there seems to be an irreversible chasm separating us from our biblical roots. We are forced to admit that we could go on our trek with God without such excess baggage.

Even when we accept the psalms as a traditional form of prayer stemming from both the synagogue and the Church, we still do not feel comfortable with the cultural setting. For those of us who have grown up in the city, Psalm 23 appears to have little impact: "The Lord is my shepherd; I shall not want. In verdant pastures he gives me repose; beside restful waters he leads me; he refreshes my soul" (Ps 23:1-2). What does it mean when we speak of our God as "shelter/shade/refuge/fortress" (see Ps 91:1-2)? Again we tend to think of death as the cessation of the vital processes and the condition for the beatific vision. Such a view seems far removed from the thought of the psalmist: "The breakers of death surged round about me, the destroying floods overwhelmed me" (Ps 18:5-6 = 2 Sm 22:5-6). Perhaps our greatest difficulty lies with the attitude of vindictiveness evident in some of the psalms. For example, "O daughter of Babylon, you destroyer, happy the man who shall repay you the evil you have done us! Happy the man who shall seize and smash your little ones against the rock!" (Ps 137:8-9).

However, both canon and hermeneutics suggest that we attempt to uncover the positive values in the psalms, values that will serve as our response to the Word of God in community. Canon implies a certain commonality between Israel's experience and our own. Hermeneutics demands that we seek to engage the question behind the text, that we seek to recover the experience of Israel and see that experience as somehow applicable to our own situation. As L. Alonso Schökel has observed, we must underline the archetypal symbols not conditioned by culture, such as water, light, space, etc.

THEOLOGICAL PREMISES OF ISRAEL'S PRAYER

The Old Testament does not provide us with a systematic treatment of Israel's theological premises in any given book. Rather, the Old Testament prefers to tell the story, pray the prayer, or recite the rubric, leaving us the somewhat uncongenial task of inquiring into the attitude or frame of mind that produces the story, prayer, or rubric. In the other direction such a task is often the unearthing of common bonds in the most uncommon places.

For Israel Yahweh is unique. From her experience with Yahweh Israel recognizes that her God cannot be reduced to the status of the deities of the ancient Near East. Yahweh is not the embodiment of such powers as fertility or death. Yahweh is always the vibrant One. Israel's formula of taking oaths presumes this quality in her God: "as Yahweh lives . . ." (see 2 Sm 12:5; 1 Kgs 2:24). At prayer Israel realizes that her God is not an impersonal object to be cajoled by human praise or human misery but a totally concerned person to be invoked in situations of joy or pain.

Covenant presupposes that Yahweh has to do with Israel and that Israel has to do with Yahweh. According to the covenant relationship, Yahweh freely chooses to be partner to the needs and problems of Israel. By the same token, Israel acknowledges that she must look to the God of the covenant to be sustained and encouraged in the vicissitudes of life. Since communication between the two partners is essential, prayer is a necessary ingredient in the lines of communication. Without prayer Israel fails to carry out the implications of covenant.

The individual and the community interact in prayer. The Psalter is the community's prayer book, yet it provides for the prayer needs of individuals. This presumes that the community is in some way caught up in the needs of individuals. On the other hand, individuals cannot divorce themselves from the needs of the community. To be involved in prayer means to be involved in the history of this people, not only its past, but also its present. To be a praying Israelite means to be a member of a praying community. Once again Israel rejects every form of one-on-one relationship with Yahweh, even in the most personal and intimate expressions of prayer.

THE FAITH OF THE PSALMIST

R. E. Murphy and others have enriched our appreciation of the faith of the psalmist. Such authors have ferreted out the faith qualities of Israel's writers/singers of prayer and have presented such qualities for our own manner of prayer. In our response to the Word of God in community, we are encouraged to judge Israel's prayers from Israel's point of view. We are also forewarned that the undertaking will be a very rewarding one as well.

Liturgy and psalms go together. When we are tempted to regard the psalms as a purely private form of prayer, we are urged to consider the history of the Psalter. In that history the community took over the compositions of some individuals and enhanced their value by making them prayers of the community. It was the great contribution of the Scandinavian scholar, S. Mowinckel, to show that the Psalter has its setting in liturgy. He demonstrated that, generally speaking, the psalms were initially composed for use in the liturgy. The liturgical setting does not denigrate personal prayer. Rather, it implies that a healthy personal prayer life must be linked to the concerns of the community. To speak of liturgy is to speak of a world of concerns which must transcend the individual. Liturgy, therefore, overlaps with covenant.

In their compositions Israel's writers/singers used a variety of literary genres. The presupposition is that human life is never a unilinear development but rather a series of ups and downs with a variety of experiences. Hence these writers/singers composed royal psalms for the key moments in the life of the Davidic king (and hence in the life of the people). They composed psalms of trust for the expression of unrelenting confidence in the God of Israel. For the times of conflict, turmoil, frustration—whether communal or individual—they produced the laments. For the needs of astonishment and bewilderment at God's capacity to begin anew, they wrote the psalms of declarative praise. To profit from Israel's prayer book, we must be willing to identify these literary genres. This is not merely an academic exercise but a truly human attempt to discover the attitudes and feelings of the ancient author and adapt them to our own contemporary needs. At the same time we must not lose sight of Israel's creativity in using literary genres.

Yahweh's presence is an indispensable element in the faith of the psalmist. The psalmist does not have to badger the individual or the community to discover the presence of Yahweh. Such a presence is simply a given. In a psalm adapted from Canaanite literature Yahweh is the God of the storm who is manifest both in nature and the setting of worship: "The voice of the Lord twists the oaks and strips the forests, and in his temple all say, "Glory!"" (Ps 29:9). In fact, Yahweh is so omnipresent that it is utterly impossible to avoid his/her presence: "Where can I go from your spirit? from your presence where can I flee? If I go up to the heavens, you are there; if I sink to the nether world, you are present there" (Ps 139:7-9; see also Am 9:1-4). Another manner of expressing Yahweh's presence is Yahweh's "face": ". . . your presence, O Lord, I seek, hide not your face from me . . ." (Ps 27:8-9; see also Ex 23:17; 34:23). As the laments show, even Yahweh's apparent absence is another manifestation of his/her presence.

Yahweh's holiness and human sinfulness are also ingredients in the faith dimension of the psalms. Israel could pray these psalms over the centuries because she had the capacity to identify, among other things, with the human experience of sinfulness. The Psalter presupposes that God's people are not perfect: "Turn away your face from my sins, and blot out all my guilt. A clean heart create for me, O God, and a steadfast spirit renew within me" (Ps 51:11-12). Hence the Psalter is not a collection of pious prayers for those who have not experienced human failure and human weakness. At the same time this awareness of human sinfulness impinges on the awareness of divine holiness. Israel realizes in her expression of prayer that Yahweh cannot and will not condone sin: "Do me justice, O Lord! for I have walked in integrity, . . . Search me. O Lord, and try me; test my soul and my heart " (Ps 26:1-2).

THE FUNCTION OF THE PSALTER YESTERDAY AND TODAY

The Psalter may still strike us as being a bulky, unmanageable collection of ancient prayers. The very mention of 150 psalms saps the energy of many a would-be devotee of the psalms. Without articulating our need perhaps, we are searching for a key which will unlock the treasures to be found there. We feel we need some guide, some plan to make our way through the maze of laments, royal psalms, psalms of confidence, etc. More basically, we are searching for a hermeneutical guide or plan that will help us to discover the basic humanness of these prayers and hence the link between ancient Israel and ourselves. We argue implicitly that the human condition has not changed that radically over the centuries.

In an original article W. Brueggemann addresses this question. He speaks in terms of function, arguing that there are basic human movements that call for specifically different types of prayer. He maintains that there is no set dialectic or stereotyped mode in our lives. Rather, we experience moments when we are unwilling to let go of the old securities which have worked reasonably well up to now. We enter upon a new world where pain and frustration are uppermost, but a pain and frustration that the certainties of the past will not resolve or clarify. We then experience moments when we are willing to accept a new world with an outlook of hope. We know of a newness that the past did not and could not provide. We reach out and accept the newness in the wake of discouragement and frustration. We thus emerge with a different outlook on life and ourselves. Hence our expression of prayer must betray this difference.

W. Brueggemann proposes orientation-disorientation-reorientation as a useful way of seeing the function of the psalms and, therefore, of praying those psalms in the appropriate situation. This chapter will discuss some of the psalms of orientation, leaving the psalms of disorientation and reorientation to the following chapters. Although W. Brueggemann's essay will not go unchallenged, it seems an eminently practical way of relating to our prayer needs by bridging the hermeneutical chasm. Thus the Psalter is made to reveal its typically human character and to invite us to respond genuinely to the Word of God in community.

PSALMS OF ORIENTATION

In W. Brueggemann's analysis psalms of orientation are characterized by lack of movement. They do not envision radical inability to cope with present pain and frustration or the tension-releasing embrace of God's gift of newness. The psalms of orientation speak to the times of normalcy and equilibrium. We do not experience violent upheavals in our world. Rather, we continue to enjoy an evenness where life has its reliable and certain laws of normalcy. Indeed we do not want to see these laws of normalcy disappear since in this view there is a place for everything and everything is in its place. The following types of psalms, among others, seem to fit this world-view: wisdom psalms, psalms of descriptive praise (hymns), psalms of trust, and royal psalms.

WISDOM PSALMS

As the first psalm in the Psalter, Psalm 1 sets the tone for the entire anthology (see also Jer 17:7-8): "Happy the man who follows not the counsel of the wicked nor walks in the way of sinners . . . but delights in the law of the Lord . . . He is like a tree planted near running waters . . . Not so the wicked, not so . . ." (vv 1-4). There is a touch of envy in the word translated as "happy." Its force is: "How enviable is the situation of the man who . . ." This is certainly the type of psalm that functions well in black and white life situations. The grayness of in-between situations is not even contemplated. Psalm 1, therefore, speaks to circumstances of clear-cut retribution.

125

Thus the good person will prosper (obviously here on earth) while the evil person is doomed to suffer—at least eventually here on earth. While Psalm 1 serves a valuable purpose as the introduction to the Psalter, by itself it caters to the state of orientation.

Psalm 37 establishes a link between religious observance and the good life: "Trust in the Lord and do good, that you may dwell in the land and enjoy security" (v 3). Yahweh's care for the righteous is continual: "The Lord watches over the lives of the wholehearted; their inheritance lasts forever" (v 18). There is no doubt but that the righteous will emerge as victors while the wicked are utterly vanquished: "He (the Lord) will promote you to ownership of the land; when the wicked are destroyed, you shall look on." In the psalmist's view there appears to be the equation between righteous works and fitting rewards (once again, in this life). It is interesting to note that wisdom writers, such as the author of the Book of Job and Qoheleth, will take issue with such a facile equation.

Psalm 128 identifies fear of the Lord with walking in his/her ways. The psalm then develops the blessings flowing from this stance and indeed from the male point of view: "For you shall eat the fruit of your handiwork . . . your wife shall be like a fruitful vine . . . your children like olive plants . . ." (vv 2-3). While the psalm attests Yahweh's reliability, it also tends to bind the God of Israel to contractual dispensing of the goods of life. It is a psalm that addresses those who presently experience the happiness of both married life and family life.

We can certainly recognize the value in serving/fearing Yahweh, but we must also be aware of easy equations and facile clichés in the distribution of this world's goods. Wisdom psalms have a special place in the lives of those who are financially well off, not concerned about tomorrow's food or preoccupied about next month's rent or fuel. The psalm reflects the stability of life where we can be grateful but also avaricious in clutching our prosperity. It is difficult to experience depression in its various forms and still pray this psalm.

PSALMS OF DESCRIPTIVE PRAISE (HYMNS)

C. Westermann distinguishes between psalms of descriptive praise and psalms of declarative praise. While both classes praise God, the psalms of descriptive praise (which are properly hymns) picture an ongoing situation and hence ongoing security, while the psalms of declarative praise assert what has recently occurred, viz., God's new provision/interruption in terms of miracle and wonder. We will treat the psalms of declarative praise under reorientation.

In Psalm 65 the author acknowledges Yahweh as the God of fertility. The Lord is the farmer par excellence who cooperates with the people in the whole agricultural process: "Thus have you prepared the land: drenching its furrows, breaking up its clods, softening it with showers, blessing its yield" (v 11). The psalm praises the God of Israel for ongoing concern and attention. In view of the harvest-laden wagons and the abundance of flocks the Israelite feels compelled to shout and sing for joy. Fertility bespeaks the presence of Yahweh. However, it is a presence that must be acknowledged. God has once again met the needs of the people.

Psalm 100 is praise of Yahweh on the occasion of a procession to the temple. The opening verses reveal the atmosphere of joyful exuberance in the composition: "Sing joyfully to the Lord, all you lands; serve the Lord with gladness; come before him with joyful song" (vv 1-3). Using the imagery of the shepherd and the flock, the psalm elaborates the covenant as the basis for such outpourings of praise: "his we are; his people, the flock he tends" (v 3). According to the psalm the present demonstration of God's abiding concern is in keeping with the traditional stance of divine fidelity. God is the dependable One whose record of performance is always consistent: "the Lord, whose kindness endures forever, and his faithfulness, to all generations" (v 5). A community that experiences such a pattern of divine behavior easily joins in the liturgical celebration.

Like Psalm 100, Psalm 145 describes Yahweh as the quintessence of love and graciousness: "The Lord is gracious and merciful, slow to anger and of great kindness" (v 8; see Ex 34:6). The psalm exhorts all creation and God's own people to take part in the expression of glory to Yahweh. God deserves such glory because of his/her work in creation itself and the history of Israel: "Let all your works give you thanks, O Lord, and let your faithful ones bless you" (v 10). The psalm especially notes God's fidelity to Israel in the process of reversal: "The Lord lifts up all who are falling and raises up all who are bowed down" (v 14). The God of this psalm is a person who carefully oversees both material creation and human history. This is a God of credentials, a God of proven sensitivity both to the world at large and Israel in particular.

In a recent article J. Goldingay suggests viewing the psalms of descriptive praise in a dynamic, non-mechanical manner. He points out that the believer's life with God is an alternating one. Thus today's declarative praise (accent on newness and abruptness) can become tomorrow's descriptive praise. As a result, descriptive praise can be the fruit of a new orientation (reorientation) which then becomes an integral element in praise of God's ongoing goodness.

PSALMS OF TRUST

Psalm 23 ("The Lord is my shepherd") is perhaps the best known psalm. It traditionally serves as a reading for wakes and burials—hence its character as a psalm of trust is a given. In the ancient Near

East kings were often called shepherds (see Ez 34)—a title that assumed that they would provide for their flocks/people. Yahweh's manner of providing is verdant pastures and restful waters (v 2). Under the protection of a committed shepherd fear is unreasonable, confidence is the only fitting response: "Even though I walk in the dark valley I fear no evil; for you are at my side . . ." (v 4). God's rod wards off enemies, his staff assures guidance (v 4). Besides being a shepherd, Yahweh is also a host who spreads the table and anoints the head with oil (v 6). In this banquet setting the psalmist is confident that Yahweh's covenantal qualities ("goodness and kindness"—v 6) will perdure. Here the psalmist experiences no upsetting power or force at work. Given the shocks of life, he finds there is no basis for frustration or despair. The God of this psalmist is a God who backs up covenantal words with covenantal actions.

Psalm 91 opens by addressing God as "shelter/shadow/refuge/fortress" (vv 1-2). Vv 10-13 develop the implications of this address: "For to his angels he has given command about you . . . upon their hands they shall bear you up . . . you shall tread upon the asp and the viper . . ." No evil, no affliction, the company of angels including safety on the rocky roads, and protection from wild animals and snakes are a significant demonstration of Yahweh's pledged word. Vv 14-15 are a divine oracle: ". . . I will deliver him . . . I will be with him in distress . . . and glorify him." The author of this psalm does not disguise the dangers of human life—they are simply a fact. However, the assurance of Yahweh's help is also a fact. Even in the face of formidable odds, this psalmist can cope. Yahweh is the reality that creates equilibrium. Nothing is too great an obstacle.

In Psalm 131 the psalmist looks to the mountains, realizing that help will certainly be forthcoming: "I lift up my eyes toward the mountains; whence shall help come to me? My help is from the Lord . . ." (vv 1-2). He describes the relentless character of Yahweh: a guardian who does not fall asleep, a shade that protects against exposure to the dangerous Palestinian sun (vv 3-6). Moreover, Yahweh's protection is both universal and perpetual: "The Lord will guard your coming and your going, both now and forever" (v 8). For this psalmist reliability is the very essence of Yahweh. To be sure, there will be some demanding moments in his life. However, awareness of such moments does not create a loss of balance or the sense of direction. Yahweh is always there to help.

ROYAL PSALMS

The royal psalms relate to the key events in the life of the Davidic prince and hence in the life of the people of God. They reflect God's solemn promise to David to provide for the monarchy, although they also assume that the line of David will likewise provide for the people (see 2 Sm 7). They are, therefore, prayers for the institution, an expression of the peace and security which the people so often sought. It is significant that Israel continued to pray the royal psalms when there was no longer any monarchy. They are an abiding expression of God's concern for the king and, therefore, for the people. (In the New Testament the royal psalms are employed to interpret the Christ Event, especially in the Acts of the Apostles.)

Psalm 2 finds its setting in the coronation of the Davidic prince. In the transition from one king to another, vassal states inevitably seek an opportunity to rebel and throw off the Davidic yoke (vv 1-3). This weak human attempt allows Yahweh to enjoy a belly laugh: "He who is throned in heaven laughs, the Lord derides them" (v 4). At this point the official reads the protocol confirming Yahweh's vested interest in the Davidic prince: "'I myself have set up my king on Zion, my holy mountain'" (v 6). The following verse proclaims adoptive sonship, viz., the Davidic prince is God's son: "'You are my son; this day I have begotten you'" (v 7). As a result, the Davidic prince is given rule over the nations, indeed a tightfisted rule (vv 8-9). For the people the recitation of this psalm evokes the theme of "Happy days are here again!" God's pledged word guarantees peace, security, and hope.

As noted earlier, Psalm 72 is a royal psalm probably employed on the coronation of the new Davidic king in Jerusalem as well. On this occasion abiding peace and the regaining of the vast territory of the Davidic empire were among the principal objects of prayer: "May he rule from sea to sea, and from the River to the ends of the earth. His foes shall bow before him, and his enemies shall lick the dust" (vv 8-9). Beyond this, the psalm envisioned the tribute brought by the vassal kings from the far west (Tarshish and the isles) and the far south (Arabia = Sheba, and Seba) (vv 10-11). For the worshipers it was a return to the halcyon days of yore when David and Solomon ruled a vast empire and received tribute from their vassals. At the heart of the prayer is the awareness that the Lord still stands by the people and hence the focus of the psalm may be verified in the newly crowned king.

According to M. Dahood, Psalm 110 is an ancient royal psalm which celebrates the king's victory in battle. A member of the court addresses the king, reciting Yahweh's oracle: "The Lord said to my Lord: 'Sit at my right hand . . .'" (v 1). The royal throne, according to M. Dahood, consists of registers depicting the conquered enemies, hence the enemies constitute the king's footstool. The "dawn" and "dew" of v 3 are the gift of youth conferred by Yahweh. In the battle Yahweh was the king's support. According to v 4 the Davidic king is recognized as priest of the "Eternal One" (the title of a Canaanite god

129

now employed for Yahweh) according to that covenant which makes him the legitimate ruler of God's people. In this view (as well as in the traditional coronation view) Yahweh's power is the basis of the institution. It is such power that can provide solidity and security. The psalm, therefore, speaks of God's fidelity and concern, even though historically the Davidic kings as a whole did not live up to the duties of their office.

PSALMS OF ORIENTATION AND OUR WORLD

While the laments and the psalms of declarative praise are much more interesting than the psalms of orientation, still the latter have a claim to a rightful place in our lives. By speaking this way, we are assuming that there are times and periods apart from disorientation and reorientation when we do recognize a certain balance and a certain harmony in our lives. If there is a blessing for every occasion, then there must be a psalm for our varied experiences.

The wisdom psalms, while they tend to paint a black and white picture of reality, are an invitation to live this life. While we certainly do not disparage the afterlife, we tend to see this life as a sort of passage, as a mere condition for making it or not in the hereafter. The wisdom psalms urge us to live life, not merely to tolerate it. They invite us to enjoy life, not merely to put up with it. Although the righteousness = prosperity equation is faulted by experience itself, nonetheless we should capture the attitude underlying the wisdom psalms, viz., to regard life as a gift, specifically as a gift to be enjoyed in community because this is the Creator's will and our human intuition. The wisdom psalms in the final analysis are a prodding to recapture the joy of living.

The psalms of descriptive praise speak of divine intervention and human interaction. They are an appeal to praise our God for the ongoingness of creation. They assume that we humans can recognize our God both in the created world and in history. They presume that we are able to put aside our focus on self in order to concentrate on the faithful One. The psalms of descriptive praise seek to celebrate the goodness of life because of the Giver of life. Such psalms announce the death of egocentricity and the rebirth of theo/anthropo-centricity. They appeal to our ability to recognize the ongoingness of creation in other people. The God of Israel seldom chooses to operate alone. To praise the co-creators is to praise the Creator.

While life does have its problems, frustrations, and agonies, life also attests to the presence of a covenant God who inspires trust and confidence in the midst of life's concerns. Such trust and confidence does not dismiss the reality of these concerns. While admitting that reality, we must see psalms of trust and confidence moving us in the direction of covenantal fidelity. It is not without significance that the ability to trust often emerges after the experience of pain and anxiety. Our God is a God with credentials. These psalms are the radical ability to recall our history with our God and to live trusting lives on the basis of that recollection.

The royal psalms must lead us to focus on the institution, on Church as we know it with both its virtues and vices. The royal psalms may serve as an incentive to reflect on the two-pronged reality of the Church, viz., the presence of our God and the presence of us humans. While we must be concerned with criticizing our Church, we must also be anxious to energize it. This energizing must force us to uncover a God who will sustain and protect us. This is the dimension of stability and equilibrium which not even our greatest acts of malice can obliterate. The royal psalms, far from teaching us to abdicate the scene, instruct us to recognize the presence of God on that same scene. The sinful institution is always linked to the sinless One.

BIBLIOGRAPHICAL SUGGESTIONS

Alonso Schökel, Luis. "Psalm 30 as Christian Prayer," *HomPastR* 72 (July, 1972) 22-27.

_____ . "The Poetic Structure of Psalm 42-43," *JSOT* 1 (1976) 4-11.

_____ . *Treinta Salmos: Poesia y oració*n. Estudios de Antiguo Testamento. Madrid: Ediciones Cristianidad, 1981.

Anderson, Bernhard W. *Out of the Depths.* Philadelphia: Westminster, 1970.

Barth, Christoph. *Introduction to the Psalms.* New York: Scribner, 1966.

Beuken, W. A. M. "Psalm 39: Some Aspects of the Old Testament Understanding of Prayer," *HeyJ* 19 (1978) 1-11.

Blank, Sheldon H. "Men Against God: The Promethean Element in Biblical Prayer," *JBL* 72 (1973) 1-13.

Brueggemann, Walter. "Psalms and the Life of Faith: A Suggested Typology of Function," *JSOT* 17 (June, 1980) 3-32.

_____ . *Praying the Psalms.* Winona: Saint Mary's Press, 1982.

Dahood, Mitchell. *The Psalms.* AB. Garden City: Doubleday, 1965-1970. 3 vols.

Dupont, Jacques. "Messianic Interpretation of the Psalms in the Acts of the Apostles," *The Salvation of the Gentiles. Essays on the Acts of the Apostles.* New York: Paulist Press, 1979, 103-128.

Goldingay, John. "The Dynamic Cycle of Praise and Prayer in the Psalms," *JSOT* 20 (July, 1981) 85-90.

Greenberg, Moshe. "On the Refinement of the Conception of Prayer in Hebrew Scriptures," *Association for Jewish Studies Review* 1 (1976) 57-92.

Gunkel, Hermann. *The Psalms. A Form-Critical Introduction.* Facet Books—Biblical Series. Philadelphia: Fortress, 1972.

Guthrie, Harvey H. *Israel's Sacred Songs: A Study of Dominant Themes.* New York: Seabury, 1966.

Hayes, John H. *Understanding the Psalms.* Valley Forge: Judson, 1976.

Heschel, Abraham. *Man's Quest for God. Studies in Prayer and Symbolism.* New York: Scribner, 1954.

——————— . *Who Is Man?* Stanford: Stanford University Press, 1966.

Lewis, Clive S. *Reflections on the Psalms.* New York: Harcourt & Brace, 1958.

Mowinckel, Sigmund. *The Psalms in Israel's Worship.* New York: Abingdon, 1962. 2 vols.

Murphy, Roland E. "Israel's Psalms: Contribution to Today's Prayer Style," *Review for Religious* 34 (1975) 113–120.

——————— . "The Faith of the Psalmist," *Int* 34 (1980) 229–239.

Ringgren, Helmer. *The Faith of the Psalmists.* Philadelphia: Fortress, 1963.

Sabourin, Leopold. *The Psalms. Their Origin and Meaning.* New York: Alba House, 1969. 2 vols. One-volume paperback (minus the texts of the Psalms): 1974.

Scott, Robert B. Y. *The Psalms as Christian Praise.* World Christian Books. New York: Association Press, 1958.

Terrien, Samuel. *The Psalms and Their Meaning for Today.* Indianapolis: Bobbs-Merrill, 1952.

——————— . *The Elusive Presence. Towards a New Biblical Theology.* Religious Perspectives. New York: Harper & Row, 1978, 278–349.

Wahl, Thomas. "Praying Israel's Psalms Responsibly as Christians: An Exercise in Hermeneutic," *Worship* 54 (1980) 386–396.

Weiser, Artur. *The Psalms.* OTL. Philadelphia: Westminster, 1962.

Westermann, Claus. *The Praise of God in the Psalms.* Richmond: John Knox, 1965, 15–51, 116–151.

——————— . "Psalms, Book of," *IDBSup,* 705–710.

——————— . *The Psalms. Structure, Content, and Message.* Minneapolis: Augsburg, 1980, 81–126.

Worden, Thomas. *The Psalms Are Christian Prayer.* London: Chapman, 1962.

CHAPTER 13

The Invitation to Lament

Biblical passages to be read: Pss 6; 22; 27; 44; 69; 80; Jer 12:1-2,
4b-5; 15:10-11, 15-21; 17:14-18; 2 Cor 11-12.

THE CRISIS OF PAIN

We suffer the death of a loved one. We contract a serious illness. We become the object of malicious gossip and slander. We find it increasingly more difficult to pay the rent or the mortgage. We are rejected by our friends. To be sure, we do acknowledge that life has its moments of great joy and happiness, its times of good health and sufficient money, its periods of acceptance and appreciation. But when tragedy strikes, we realize that we are weak, vulnerable humans subject to the fluctuations of interest rates, the caprices of friendship, and the vulnerability of the human body. These are the times of rejection and dejection. Our world is falling apart and we attempt to rebuild it in the old-fashioned way.

The efforts at rebuilding are perhaps the greatest source of disillusion. We look to the tried and true remedies of the past. In a faith context we rehearse the doctrines of our Church community. We recall that the God who afflicts us is also the God who loves us. In the assets department we yearn to hear that the market will reverse itself and that the interest rates will go down. In the health situation we review the miracles of modern medicine and strain to learn that the new treatment will work in our case. These efforts demonstrate that we still long for the securities of the past, that we are not willing to let go and accept a newness not predicated on Church doctrines, market rates, or miracle medicines. We want the past to be revived, but we do not want to face a future with a new set of variables.

In our pain we experience loneliness. We feel that we are individuals tagged by Church and society at large to go it alone. We long for community, even if that community is only one other person who can commiserate and empathize. It is precisely in the desperation of such moments that we begin to grasp a dimension of redemption. We now know that pain and frustration must be communicated in order to become redemptive. Pain not shared is pain that cannot be healed.

ISRAEL'S LAMENTS

Israel's laments are parade examples of coping with pain, hence of communicating frustrations. Such laments, whether individual or communal, usually follow this structure: (1) an introduction containing invocation and cry for help; (2) a main section including both complaint and supplication; and (3) a conclusion that is not really fixed but often anticipates divine help.

Psalm 6, an individual lament, opens with a cry for help: "O Lord, reprove me not in your anger, nor chastise me in your wrath" (v 2). According to v 7 enemies are the cause of the psalmist's problem: "My eyes are dimmed with sorrow; they have aged because of all my foes" (v 8). Because there is no belief in an afterlife, the author suggests that prolonging his life will mean prolonging his praise of God on earth: "For among the dead no one remembers you; in the nether world who gives you thanks?" (v 6) In the conclusion of the psalm the author announces that the Lord has intervened and, therefore, all his enemies will receive their just punishment (vv 9-11).

Psalm 27, an individual lament, combines complaint and confidence. False witnesses who breathe out violence hound the psalmist: "Give me not up to the wishes of my foes; for false witnesses have risen against me, and such as breathe out violence" (v 12). He seeks to enjoy God's presence (which is limited to this life) and does not hesitate to cry out: "Hide not your face from me; do not in anger repel your servant. You are my helper; cast me not off; forsake me not, O God my savior" (v 9). The psalm concludes with a statement of confidence: "I believe that I shall see the bounty of the Lord in the land of the living" (v 12).

Psalm 69, another individual lament, is the outpouring of an innocent Israelite who yet trusts that God will redress the wrong he has suffered: "Those outnumber the hairs of my head who hate me without cause" (v 5). Because of his affliction he is actually experiencing the waters of Sheol or the underworld: "Save me, O God, for the waters threaten my life; I am sunk in the abysmal swamp where there is no foothold ... I am wearied with calling, my throat is parched; my eyes have failed with looking for my God" (vv 2-4). The basis of

divine intervention is the covenant: "Answer me, O Lord, for boun-
teous is your kindness; in your great mercy turn towards me" (v 17).
In the conclusion the psalmist anticipates such intervention: "For
the Lord hears the poor, and his own who are in bonds he spurns
not" (v 34).

In Psalm 44, a communal lament, God's people have experienced
a devastating military defeat. In vv 2-9 the psalmist describes God's
consistent pattern of victory in the past: "But you saved us from
our foes, and those who hated us you put to shame" (v 8). In vv 10-17
the psalmist then announces the present calamity: "You marked
us out as sheep to be slaughtered . . . you sold your people for no
great price . . . you made us the reproach of our neighbors . . ." (vv 12-
14). After protesting the innocence of the people, the psalmist boldly
challenges God to resume the old pattern: "Awake! Why are you
asleep, O Lord? Arise! Cast us not off forever" (v 24).

In Psalm 80, another communal lament, the community has
experienced some political misfortune, although the specific situation cannot be recovered. In vv 9-12 the psalmist sums up the Exodus-
Conquest tradition: "A vine from Egypt you transplanted; you drove
away the nations and planted it . . ." (v 9). But in vv 13-14 the community charges that Yahweh has neglected the people, exposing
them to the attacks and ravages of enemies and wild animals. The
psalm concludes with a petition for new life, assuring Yahweh that
divine support will mean human fidelity: "Then we will no more
withdraw from you; give us new life, and we will call upon your
name" (v 19).

ISRAEL'S REALISM

As W. Brueggemann has pointed out, the laments deal with the
genuine experiences of life. They describe life precisely the way it
is. They do not flee the scene of pain to a world of make-believe
where the ache is not real and the anguish is not genuine. On the
contrary, the laments teach us that to dwell on the euphoric dimension of life to the exclusion of its frustrating side is to cease to be
human. The problem is there and we can ignore it only to our own
detriment.

The laments clearly show that theology means relating to a
person. C. Westermann has remarked that in western theology God
becomes an object. Hence we talk *about* God, but not *to* God. The
laments, however, unequivocally state that we dare not neglect the
personal element of theology. In the laments we deal *with* a person.
We do not simply announce our list of woes, expecting computer-
like attention to them. As A. Heschel put it so beautifully, in speech
we seek to inform but in prayer we seek to partake.

The basis of this dialogue is covenant. In our problems and difficulties we imply that, while this God has a claim on us, we also have a claim on this God, whether as individuals or a community. Covenant supplies the boldness which is so characteristic of the laments. Thus we have the right to complain to God and ask for a hearing. Israel's experience is that we can always talk back to God and accuse God but we can never ignore God.

Concretely the laments presuppose that my problem is God's problem, that our problem is God's problem. Covenant is not reducible to the times of unimpaired relationships and uninterrupted ecstasies. Covenant is more often than not reducible to the times of impaired relationships and interrupted ecstasies. Through covenant the God of Israel must become privy to the heartbreaks and anxieties facing both the nation as a whole and the Israelite as an individual. Covenant means that there is someone who will hear, covenant means that there is someone to turn to. Covenant means that we are not alone.

In another study W. Brueggemann noted the dissimilarities between Kübler Ross' grief process and the laments. In place of denial the laments insist on address. Thus the laments are directed to someone who is interested, whereas the grief process focuses on the non-reality of the pain and anguish. Whereas depression sets in as an element of the grief process, expression takes over in the laments. Israel expects that her plea will get a hearing and her expression bears this out. Unlike the grief process, the laments are grounded in a framework of relationship. It is not a question of being alone in the hospital bed or of being abandoned at home by the family. In the laments an "I and Thou" always pervades. As a result, the laments look forward to intervention. The laments imply that we are treated as persons even in our most vulnerable situations. The grief process lacks that frame of reference.

THE ECLIPSE OF THE OLD SECURITIES

In the laments Israel tells it the way it really is. The first step in dealing with disorientation is to articulate the problem. At this juncture we realize that the psalms of orientation are not suited to this articulation. The wisdom psalms provide too facile a solution and the psalms of descriptive praise do not envision disruption and lack of harmony. To hear ourselves complain is to state that we have moved to a level of being radically different from that of orientation.

The laments admit various degrees of acceptance or denial. In Ps 44:2-9 there is the litany of Yahweh's saving interventions. There is the hope that the past can somehow be revived: "O God, our ears have heard, our fathers have declared to us, the deeds you did in their days, in days of old" (v 2). In Ps 6:9-11 there is the solemn proclamation of divine intervention, hence of acceptance. But herein lies the beauty of the Psalter. There are psalms for those who hesitate to bid farewell to the old securities and there are psalms for those who reach out to accept the presence of the new realities.

C. Westermann has noted that the laments are not simply the acknowledgement of a distressing situation. Rather, the laments give way to petition and ultimately to praise. Hence the laments are not really laments—they are complaints, powerful forms of protest grounded in a person who can intervene. It is this dimension of expectation that prevents the laments from becoming catalogues of grievances.

The transition from complaint to vow/praise is not easily explainable. How does one move from desperation to exclamation? For example, "My eyes are dimmed with sorrow, they have aged because of all my foes. Depart from me, all evildoers, for the Lord has heard the sound of my weeping . . ." (Ps 6:8-9). According to a prevalent view the priest intervenes at the sanctuary and reads a divine oracle, assuring the petitioner of God's acceptance of the lament. Whatever the explanation, the conclusions of the laments (with the exception of Psalm 88) look forward to a new state of being. At the end of the disorientation stage the petitioner exists on a new level, indicating that the whole experience was ultimately not the clutching of the old clichés but the searching for new realities. Letting go of the past is the condition for growth in the future.

Response to the Word of God in community can identify with the plight of the psalmists. The evildoers (Ps 6:9), the false witnesses (Ps 27:12), the waters of Sheol (Ps 69:2-3), and the enemy oppressors of the people (Pss 40:11; 80:7) are symbolic of our own demises. The loss of loved ones, the experience of debilitating diseases, the disappearance of financial stability are modern counterparts to the psalmists' world. The acceptance of death, the coping with disease, the embrace of a less financially secure life are the new levels of being towards which the ancient laments may be directed. To accept, to cope, to embrace mean to proclaim, to announce, to assert that we are covenant persons ever intent on new ways of living, not simply existing.

JEREMIAH'S CONFESSIONS

It is a common view that the so-called Confessions of Jeremiah are individual laments. For some exegetes (for example, J. Bright) these Confessions offer us an intimate look at the frustrations and agony of the prophet. Many of these exegetes would suggest a time after 609 B.C., i.e., after the death of King Josiah when the relatively easy prophetic ministry from 626 B.C. onwards gave way to the more difficult proclamation of the fall of Judah and Jerusalem—a message not readily accepted, especially by the institution. According to this view the prophet bared his soul in these Confessions and most likely shared such intimacies with a select group of disciples.

Other exegetes (for example, R. P. Carroll) maintain that the Confessions do not provide any biographical information about the prophet. One view here is that the laments are liturgical pieces uttered in the context of the cult and hence not related to the prophet's experiences. Another view is that they are the product of later reflection by exilic Deuteronomists, i.e., a school steeped in the application of Deuteronomy to the situation of exile. A variation of this view is that the Confessions are liturgical compositions calculated to portray the community's response to the destruction of Jerusalem and subsequent exile. In this view the prophet serves as the community's intercessor.

This second view regards the Confessions as interpretations of the prophet's career. It is at least possible that these interpretations are somehow grounded in the dimensions of the prophet's personality. Interpretation does not mean distortion. Whether or not they relate instances (to some degree) of the prophet's life, they are still instructive as insights into the meaning and application of lament.

In Jer 12:1-2, 4b-5 Jeremiah contends with God. In vv 1-2 the prophet points out how the wicked flourish, adding in v 4b their boast, viz., "God does not see our ways." It is the age-old problem of evil. God's reply merely reiterates the mystery involved: "If running against men has wearied you, how will you race against horses? And if in a land of peace you fall headlong, what will you do in the thickets of the Jordan?" (v 5).

In Jer 15:10-11, 15-21 the text relates a crisis in Jeremiah's vocation. The prophet begins by announcing his despair, then asking God: "Tell me, Lord, have I not served you for their good? Have I not interceded with you in the time of misfortune and anguish? You know I have" (v 11). The prophet then urges that Yahweh take vengeance on his persecutors (v 15). After describing his faithful execution of the prophetic office in vv 16-17, Jeremiah attacks God in these terms: "Why is my pain continuous, my wound incurable, refusing to be healed? You have indeed become for me a treacherous brook, whose waters do not abide!" (v 18). Vv 19-20 are God's reply, chiding the prophet but also promising assistance: "For I am with you, to deliver and rescue you, says the Lord" (v 20).

In Jer 17:14-18 the prophet expands on his incurable wound. He begins with a plea for a hearing: "Heal me, Lord, that I may be healed; save me, that I may be saved, for it is you whom I praise" (v 14). He then notes the obduracy of his audience, viz., their demands to see the words of woe actually fulfilled (v 15). After urging that disaster was not his doing (v 16), the prophet pleads: "Do not be my ruin . . . Let my persecutors, not me, be confounded . . . Bring upon them the day of misfortune" (vv 17-18).

As interpretations of Jeremiah, these laments portray the vulnerability involved in fidelity to one's prophetic mission. They also suggest that weakness and frailty are not alien elements in the discharge of that mission. Although he opts for a more biographical stance, J. Bright notes that it is even in rebellion that God calls his servants. Vocation and weakness, fidelity to vocation and coping with weakness are expressions of the prophetic calling but, more basically, of the human condition.

These Confessions also stress the covenantal dimension in another direction. Whereas in the laments of the Psalter, the individual's/people's problem and concern become God's problem and concern, in the Confessions God's problem and concern also become Jeremiah's problem and concern. In his pleas for a resolution to the agonies of prophetic ministry, Jeremiah nonetheless reciprocates by acceding to God's plea. His fidelity to preaching the Word in the most adverse circumstances implies that lament is a two-way street. The God of the covenant is a God interested in the needs of the nation and individuals. By seeking relief from our situation, we are thereby assuming the obligation of providing relief for God's situation—other people.

JESUS AND THE CROSS

The Gospel writers (not unlike the redactors of the Book of Jeremiah) were not bent upon a blow by blow account of the last moments of the historical Jesus. Rather, they sought to interpret the death of Jesus for their respective audiences. Both Mt 27:46 and Mk 15:34 place Ps 22:1, an individual lament, on the lips of the dying Jesus: "'My God, my God, why have you forsaken me?'" Lk 23:46 puts Ps 31:6, a psalm of declarative praise, on the lips of the dying Jesus: "'(Father), into your hands I commend my spirit.'" (Ps 31:10-14 is a description of the psalmist's distress.) (Unlike the Synoptics, John goes his own way in Jn 19:30.) In his study of the words of Jesus on the cross, J. Reumann concludes that use of Psalm 22 and a critical study of the Gospels view the cross as lament in suffering and thanksgiving for what God did through Jesus.

Against the background of the two-pronged aspect of lament it would not be unrealistic to suggest that the use of Ps 22:1 does not focus merely on Jesus' plea. While it does imply that Jesus' problem and Jesus' difficulty were now the Father's problem and the Father's difficulty, it also assumes that the Father's problem and the Father's difficulty were also Jesus' problem and Jesus' difficulty. Since the Father's world of concern was the salvation of all, Jesus embraced that world by embracing death. Resurrection demonstrated that the embrace of death was ultimately the embrace of life. As in the laments of the Psalter, Jesus was clearly on a new level of being.

PAUL'S THEOLOGY OF WEAKNESS

In Second Corinthians 11–12 Paul addresses his manner of ministry. Although this is a letter and not a lament, this section suggests the stance of lament in coping with weakness, a stance not unlike that in the Confessions of Jeremiah.

In replying to his opponents, Paul notes that he too can boast about his Jewish background (11:22), his labors (11:23-29), and his visions (12:1-4). However, Paul chooses to go another route by boasting about his weaknesses. "If I must boast, I will make a point of my weaknesses" (11:30). In 12:5 he states: ". . . but I will do no boasting about myself unless it is about my weaknesses." For Paul weakness is not simply a statement about the status quo. Rather, weakness has an inherent power to extricate a person from the incrustations of ego and thus to look beyond oneself to Christ. As M. Neumann points out, far from disparaging his ministry, weakness becomes a badge of apostolic authority and legitimation: "Therefore I am content with weakness, with mistreatment, with distress, with persecutions and difficulties for the sake of Christ; for when I am powerless, it is then that I am strong" (12:10).

Human weakness and divine presence go hand in hand. Far from preventing union with God, weakness makes the Apostle aware that his strength derives from outside himself. In his request about the thorn in the flesh (12:7), Paul receives this reply: "'My grace is enough for you, for in weakness power reaches perfection'" (12:9). To sing of his weakness is to announce the presence of God after the manner of the presence in the desert tabernacle (see Ex 40:35): "And so I willingly boast of my weaknesses instead, that the power of Christ may *rest* upon me" (12:9). Paul was clearly in touch with his Old Testament roots.

THE PANGS OF LETTING GO

The laments are a school of prayer. They do not merely list the vicissitudes of life. They encourage the modern practitioner to bring these upsetting experiences to the attention of God and hence to the attention of the community. They urge us to meet life head-on, i.e., not to fake it and pretend that it is not so, but to acknowledge our weaknesses and cope with them. They insist that we not look back to the old securities but that we embrace the present crisis as a faith opportunity. Instead of meaning demise, the crisis can mean growth, even if and especially if the resolution of the crisis is not what we first anticipated.

The laments are a study in human weakness. They do not represent a Stoic venture whereby we surmount all the obstacles by dint of our own energies. The laments bid us to look beyond ourselves to a generous God who creates us in the image of his Son, i.e., as weak humans. Our task is not to eliminate each weakness by the meticulous application of an iron will. Instead, our task is to bring these weaknesses to light and then acknowledge that our God will say something to our world in and through those weaknesses. We are invited after the manner of Jesus, Jeremiah, and Paul, as well as the psalmists, to accept our ministry and to live it to the full with its concomitant share of pain and frustration. To cope with tragedy and anguish is to announce that we do not travel the road alone. God chooses to find a conspicuous dwelling place in the hearts of those who continue to accept their humanness and make it the catalyst for ministry.

The laments of Jeremiah and Jesus demand that we open ourselves up to the larger contours of our God's world of concerns. Jeremiah and Jesus are intrepid examples of looking beyond their own needs to the larger needs of the community. We are forcefully reminded that covenant is a two-edged sword. By asking help in our world of frustration, we are implicitly offering help for God's world of frustration, viz., other people. Such laments are another example of the fact that a one-on-one relationship with our God is a distortion. To cry for help means to be willing to hear the community's cry for help. To lament in this sense is truly to respond to the Word of God in community.

BIBLIOGRAPHICAL SUGGESTIONS

Anderson, George W. "Enemies and Evildoers in the Book of Psalms," *BJRL* 48 (1965-1966) 18-29.

Blank, Sheldon H. "The Confessions of Jeremiah and the Meaning of Prayer," *HUCA* 21 (1948) 331-354.

_____ . *Jeremiah: Man and Prophet.* Cincinnati: Hebrew Union College Press, 1961, 105-128.

Bright, John. "Jeremiah's Complaints: Liturgy or Expressions of Personal Distress?" *Proclamation and Presence. Old Testament Essays in Honour of Gwynne Henton Davies.* Edited by J. I. Durham & J. R. Porter. Richmond: John Knox, 1970, 189-214.

_____ . "A Prophet's Lament and Its Answer: Jeremiah 15:10-21," *Int* 28 (1974) 59-74.

Brueggemann, Walter. "From Hurt to Joy, From Death to Life," *Int* 28 (1974) 3-19.

_____ . "The Formfulness of Grief," *Int* 31 (1977) 263-275.

_____ . "Psalms and the Life of Faith: A Suggested Typology of Function," *JSOT* 17 (June, 1980) 3-32.

Carroll, Robert P. *From Chaos to Covenant. Prophecy in the Book of Jeremiah.* New York: Crossroad, 1981, 107–135.

Gerstenberger, Erhard. "Jeremiah's Complaints: Observations on Jer. 15:10-21," *JBL* 82 (1963) 393–408.

_____ . "Psalms," *Old Testament Form Criticism.* Trinity University Monograph Series in Religion. Edited by J. H. Hayes. San Antonio: Trinity University Press, 1974, 198–207.

_____ . (with W. Schrage) *Suffering.* Biblical Encounter Series. New York: Abingdon, 1980, 11–135.

Heschel, Abraham. *Who Is Man?* Stanford: Stanford University Press, 1966.

Kübler Ross, Elisabeth. *On Death and Dying.* New York: Macmillan, 1969.

Neumann, Matthias. "Ministry, Weakness, and Spirit in II Corinthians," *Clergy Review* 59 (1974) 647–660.

Plastaras, James. *The God of Exodus.* Milwaukee: Bruce, 1966, 49–59.

Raitt, Thomas M. *A Theology of Exile: Judgment/Deliverance in Jeremiah and Ezekiel.* Philadelphia: Fortress, 1977, 106–127.

Reumann, John. "Psalm 22 at the Cross," *Int* 28 (1974) 39–58.

Sölle, Dorothee. *Death by Bread Alone. Texts and Reflections on Religious Experience.* Philadelphia: Fortress, 1978.

Stanley, David M. *Boasting in the Lord: The Phenomenon of Prayer in Saint Paul.* New York: Paulist Press, 1973.

_____ . "Power and Weakness," *The Way* 16 (1976) 176–188.

Westermann, Claus. *The Praise of God in the Psalms.* Richmond: John Knox, 1965, 52–81.

_____ . "The Role of the Lament in the Theology of the Old Testament," *Int* 28 (1974) 20–38.

_____ . *The Psalms. Structure, Contents, and Message.* Minneapolis: Augsburg, 1980, 29–45, 53–70.

CHAPTER 14

The Invitation to Newness

Biblical passages to be read: **Pss** 30; 40; 98; **Is** 43:10-17; 51:9-10; 52:7-10; **Lk** 15; **Col** 1:15-20.

THE DEMISE OF CELEBRATION

We do not like to be surprised. We claim that we are masters of our own fate, that we call the shots, that we are in charge. To be surprised implies that others have a certain control over our fate, that others will call some of the shots, that others are to some degree in charge. We perceive autonomy as the supreme value. Consequently anything that even appears to diminish our autonomy must be resisted at all costs.

Checks and balances, cause and effect, energy expended and results obtained—these are our pragmatic business principles which tend to dominate other dimensions of our lives. It is difficult to sit back and acknowledge a beautiful reality which we did not buy or manufacture. The sunset, the symphony, the sonnet—these realities are not the result of our manipulation. Yet how often do we accept them as the raw material of existence and never stop to reflect on their inherent qualities? They beg to be properly esteemed, not merely tabulated and stored away in our computers. Where we have little influence, we tend to have little interest.

People are gifts. They are the ever new handiwork of the Creator, displaying an almost infinite variety of talents and abilities. In our assertive business style we are apt to regard them as means to our own ends. Thus they become the means of production for us—either for pleasure or for business. We hesitate to uncover the Creator's image, to discover the warmth of their love or the depth of their

143

compassion. Perhaps we feel that their utterly human qualities will expose the shallowness of our utterly inhuman tendencies.

Our world yearns to be transformed. "World" too often means natural resources and untapped sources of energy. We do not pay sufficient attention to the world of broken humans who seek to be energized and reinstated as persons. They have little in terms of collateral or security. For us they are not the beautiful people. Yet these are the ones eager to make the passage from chaos to cosmos. They ask us to be their transforming agents.

We have lost the ability to party. We prove unfaithful to our biblical roots by refusing to celebrate the accomplishments of others. We have thereby lost the sense of mystery, viz., to praise goodness or talent which is the gift of Another and not the end product of our manipulative forces. We resist saying, "It is good, very good!" We cannot congratulate others because we will not acknowledge the God of surprises.

Response to the Word of God in community means to counteract the gravitational forces of ego by recovering the ability to praise, especially to praise where newness is unexpectedly present. We are invited to review our biblical heritage and rediscover the ongoing yet unexpected aspect of the Creator's work. We are invited to reassess our appreciation of newness.

PSALMS OF DECLARATIVE PRAISE AND THANKSGIVINGS

We noted earlier that C. Westermann distinguishes between psalms of descriptive praise (hymns) and psalms of declarative praise. While both praise God, they do so in different ways. In the psalms of descriptive praise God's ongoing care and hence God's ongoing security is highlighted. In the psalms of declarative praise, however, God's new provision/interruption is accentuated. Thus in terms of function the psalms of descriptive praise (hymns) are proper to orientation whereas the psalms of declarative praise are proper to reorientation.

Although many exegetes posit a difference between hymns (including C. Westermann's psalms of declarative praise) and thanksgivings, the latter considers psalms of declarative praise and thanksgivings the same reality. He points out, among other things, that the vocabulary of thanksgiving overlaps with that of praise. For example, Ps 145:10: "Let all your works give you thanks, O Lord, and let your faithful ones bless you." Without pressing this identification of forms, W. Brueggemann suggests that in terms of function the psalms of declarative praise and the thanksgivings are basically the same. They do not merely describe but actually assert the newness that has come to pass.

The psalms of declarative praise and the thanksgivings have to do with surprises, specifically in areas and situations where people do not anticipate surprise. The surprise is not the result of human cause and effect, it belongs to the category of gift. In the move from disorientation to reorientation amazement and bewilderment occupy center stage. The person or persons involved did not achieve this newness by their own efforts, although they perhaps longed for it. They simply attest that God has transformed them by extricating them from what seemed to be an impossible situation. Although their old world has collapsed, a new one has been created.

Celebration is the only adequate response to this newness. We cannot simply retreat to a neutral corner and reflect philosophically on a passage from one state of mind to another. On the contrary, we must proceed immediately to the very heart of the community and proclaim the newness. In turn, the community is asked to respond. This newness cannot remain the private patrimony of the individual or individuals. It must become the focus of the community's praise/thanksgiving. When God works as the author of surprises, the entire community is to become the bearer of the good news. Such goodness is a contagious event/happening.

NEWNESS IN THE PSALTER

The structure of the psalm of declarative praise/thanksgiving is rather simple. The first element is an introduction or call to praise/thank. Frequently the choir leader exhorts the group or congregation to respond. The second element is an account of the newness that Yahweh has brought about. The third element is a conclusion, i.e., a renewed call to praise/thank.

Psalm 30 is a psalm of declarative praise/thanksgiving of an individual who has been delivered from death. In v 2 the psalmist announces his intention to extol Yahweh. Next he describes the passage from disorientation to reorientation: "I cried out to you and you healed me . . . You preserved me from among those going down into the pit. Sing praise to the Lord, you his faithful ones" (vv 3-5). After describing the brokenness of his life ("But when you hid your face I was terrified" [v 8]), he shows the giftedness of his new situation: "You changed my mourning into dancing; you took off my sackcloth and clothed me with gladness . . ." (v 12). The sacred dancing is the manner of celebration—a celebration to which he has also invited the community (see v 5).

Psalm 40 combines two psalms: a psalm of declarative praise/thanksgiving (vv 2-11) and a lament (vv 12-18). The opening verses describe how Yahweh responded to the psalmist's petition by freeing him from the clutches of death: ". . . he stooped toward me and heard my cry. He drew me out of the pit of destruction, out of the mud of the swamp . . ." (vv 2-3). The unexpected is: "He set my feet upon a crag; and he put a *new* song into my mouth, a hymn to our God" (v 4). However, this miracle is not for the psalmist alone. Besides sharing his rescue in the cultic center, he also remarks: "Many shall look on in awe and trust in the Lord" (v 4). Indeed this surprise is not merely a passing incident in Yahweh's relationship with Israel. By nature Yahweh is a God of surprises: "How numerous have you made, O Lord, my God, your wondrous deeds! And in your plans for us there is none to equal you . . ." (v 6).

According to S. Mowinckel Psalm 98 is an enthronement psalm, part of an enthronement festival in Jerusalem honoring Yahweh as king. For the Scandinavian scholar the festival was not limited to observing that Yahweh had become king at a given point in time. Rather, the festival celebrated the ongoingness of Yahweh's kingship—it was always fresh and new. (Ps 93:1 may also be translated: "Yahweh has become king.") Thus the psalm, while it recognizes what happened in the past, is still able to call forth a fresh awareness on the part of the people. Liturgy was not intended to get stale.

Psalm 98 captures this freshness in the opening verse: "Sing to the Lord a *new* song" (v 1). The following verses suggest motives for the celebration: "for he has done wondrous deeds . . . in the sight of the nations he has revealed his justice. He has remembered his kindness and his faithfulness toward the house of Israel . . ." (vv 1-3). Jubilation is Israel's form of acknowledgement, a jubilation that does not neglect the proper musical instruments: "Sing joyfully to the Lord, all you lands; break into song; sing praise. Sing praise to the Lord with the harp . . . with trumpets and the sound of the horn sing joyfully before the King, the Lord" (vv 4-6). The psalmist does not limit Israel's praise to the lands (v 4) but includes the entire world vv 7-8). Praise should overflow into all of nature. Such a king (v 9) deserves this tribute.

NEWNESS IN SECOND ISAIAH

New yet ongoing. This summarizes the message of contagious joy that Second Isaiah proclaimed to his exilic audience in Babylon. To the questions "can our God help us and, if so, will our God help us?" (see Is 40:12-31), this prophet announces that Yahweh's intervention is so radically new, so unexpected, so much a gift that they must forget the past: "Remember not the events of the past, the things of long ago consider not; see I am doing something *new*!" (Is 43:18-19). At the same time this newness is in keeping with God's ongoing plan of creation/redemption. The God who breaks through the despair and hopelessness of exile is the God who overcame the unruly waters of chaos. The God who gifts Israel is the God who continues to create: "But now, thus says the Lord, who *created* you, O Jacob, and *formed* you, O Israel: Fear no, for I have redeemed you . . ."

(Is 43:1). To an audience that once dismissed the possibility of good news, Second Isaiah communicates the mandate issued to Zion/ Jerusalem: "Go up onto a high mountain, Zion, herald of glad tidings; cry out at the top of your voice, Jerusalem, herald of good news! Fear not to cry out and say to the cities of Judah: Here is your God!" (Is 40:9). This presence is a newness not anticipated because of disorientation yet not totally unprecedented because of ongoing creation.

Newness means the appropriate praise for Yahweh's dramatic action. Is 42:9 ("See, the earlier things have come to pass, *new* ones I now foretell . . .") provides the setting for acknowledging Yahweh's regal status in Is 42:10-17. This passage intones the new song for the new yet old demonstration of Yahweh's kingship: "Sing to the Lord a *new* song, his praise from the end of the earth . . ." (Is 42:10). Kedar in the Arabian peninsula and Sela in Edom (v 11) are to catch the exuberant notes of the jubilation. The king now dons his warrior's uniform and flexes the might of his person against the enemies (v 13). For this audience Yahweh was silent too long. Indeed that stillness appeared to be their God's only possible response to their plight. But Yahweh now breaks the silence. His battle cry shatters the despair of the past and releases hope for their future: "I have looked away, and kept silence, I have said nothing, holding myself in, but now, I cry out as a woman in labor, gasping and panting" (v 14). Israel learns that Yahweh is truly a God of surprises, that not even their previous wickedness can repress their God's capacity to give anew.

Is 51:9-10 presents Israel thinking in terms of the old securities. Israel's mighty champion has been asleep too long, oblivious of the needs of the people. Hence Israel urges the repetition of the old days: "Awake, awake, put on strength, O arm of the Lord! Awake as in the days of old, in ages long ago!" (v 9). The past seems to provide the pattern for Israel's liberation. In Is 51:9 Israel cites the creation myth where Yahweh conquers the sea monster: "Was it not you who crushed Rahab, you who pierced the dragon?" In Is 41:10 Israel recalls Yahweh's dramatic victory at the Reed Sea: "Was it not you who dried up the sea, the waters of the great deep, who made the depths of the sea into a way for the redeemed to pass over?"

Yahweh will indeed respond to these petitions but not in a way that will diminish the power to give. Thus Yahweh will once again defeat the monster and dry up the sea. But it will be a radically new way. Now the Exodus will pass through the desert (see Is 40:3-5; 43: 19-20; 44:3-4). The fierce champion who will lead Israel on this new way is also a shepherd who carries the lambs in his bosom and guides the ewes with care (Is 40:11). Yahweh's manner is always old yet new, one transcending the limitations that Israel places on the demonstration of might and concern. Yahweh will not be reduced to purely human parameters.

Is 52:7-10 is part of an enthronement hymn honoring Jerusalem. To those who doubt whether or not Yahweh will truly comfort Israel (see Is 40:1), this hymn offers an unambiguous reply. The guttered Jerusalem will be the sacrament of Yahweh's willingness to surprise. Thus the prophet pictures messengers running with the greatest possible speed to the devastated city: "How beautiful upon the mountains are the feet of him who brings glad tidings . . . announcing salvation and saying to Zion, 'Your God is King!'" (v 7). Unexpectedly watchmen in the destroyed city behold Yahweh restoring Jerusalem before their very eyes. At this point the ruins are invited to celebrate: "Break out together in song, O ruins of Jerusalem!" (v 9). Significantly the prophet does not limit the audience to only Israel. The nations of the earth also experience the marvel. Good news is never a miser's booty—it is always a public treasure (see also Is 44:23; 49:13).

THE NEWNESS IN CHRIST

In Colossae in Asia Minor certain Christians were denying Christ's unique role in the cosmos. In effect, they were rejecting the newness that God's action in Christ had achieved. Epaphras (see Col 1:7) reported these unorthodox tendencies to Paul. The result was Paul's letter to the Colossians probably written from Rome ca. 61-63 A.D.

Instead of celebrating the newness of Jesus' role as savior, these Christians maintained that there were intermediaries between God and the universe that brought about creation and exercised control over human destinies. As a result, they were unable to sing the hymn of reconciliation whereby Jesus overcame the chaos which separated the human world from God. Paul's reply is to urge the community to sing the hymn of Col 1:15-20, the hymn that reflects the movement from disorientation to reorientation.

Like Lady Wisdom (see Prv 8:22-31), Christ directs the work of creation as God's image (see Wis 7:26) and the first-born of all creatures (Col 1:15). Everything was not only created in him but indeed continues to be created through him and for him: "In him everything in heaven and on earth was created, things visible and invisible, whether thrones or dominations, principalities or powers; all were created (a Greek perfect—hence creation in the past continues in the present) through him, and for him" (v 16). When chaos threatened to disrupt the harmony of this universe, the Father became once again the God of surprises, i.e., God raised the dead body of Jesus. Christ is thereby "head of the body, the church; he who is the beginning, the first-born of the dead . . ." (v 18). Because of the gift of the resurrection absolute fullness resides in Christ—no intermediaries are necessary (v 19). It is the blood of the cross that reconciles all the disruptive forces both on earth and in the heavens (v 20). To acknowledge Jesus' role is to proclaim that chaos can lead to cosmos, that God's wisdom can outstrip our folly, that the Father's power can overcome our weakness.

LUKE'S DOCTRINE OF SURPRISES

Lk 15:1-3 shows Jesus surrounded by the IRS and sinners. The Pharisees and the scribes conclude that Jesus welcomes sinners and dines with them. At this point Luke has Jesus present the parables of the Lost Sheep (vv 4-7), the Lost Coin (vv 8-10), and the Prodigal Son (vv 11-32). Luke chooses to have Jesus vindicate the right not to put limits on God's goodness. Obviously in Luke's community some were requiring stringent conditions for sinners.

In the parables of the Lost Sheep and the Lost Coin both the shepherd and the woman appear to be preoccupied with what is relatively insignificant, viz., one sheep out of a hundred and one coin out of ten. But this is precisely what the Pharisees and the scribes are guilty of, viz., perverting values. They are more concerned about things than people, viz., sinners. If the finding of one sheep and one coin causes joy, then the finding of lost humans should provoke all the more joy. To join in the celebration means to join in the recovery of proper values.

The parable of the Prodigal Son is a classical example of God's capacity to (for)give, a capacity not based on human merits or credentials. The younger son does not dare to be surprised: "'Treat me like one of your hired hands'" (v 20). However, the father refuses to be manipulated by purely human criteria of forgiveness. The kiss, the change of wardrobe, and the celebration all indicate the generosity of a father who transcends the mechanical treatment of humans. The reason given by the father is the unexpected switch from disorientation to reorientation: "'Let us eat and celebrate because this son of mine was dead and has come back to life. He was lost and is found'" (vv 23-24).

The elder son cannot accept the imbalance in the father's actions. There is no possibility of surprise—only the ironclad law of reward and punishment. By refusing to join in the celebration (v 28), he refuses to budge from his entrenched theological position. His language is also indicative of his unwillingness. He refers to his younger brother as "'this son of yours'" (v 30), whereas the father speaks of "'this brother of yours'" (v 32). For Luke the father and the younger son show what God is like while the elder son reveals what his critics are like. In Luke's community the celebration of God's freedom takes precedence over the vindication of human punishment.

149

We are challenged to reject "new" as a dirty three-letter word. We are urged to admit a God of surprises who refuses to adjust to our narrowly defined categories of propriety and decorum. Ours is a God who chooses to give because that is the nature of our God.

We are asked to imitate our God in the transformation of chaos into cosmos. We are invited to look at our world of broken humans, to initiate actions not based on merit and demerit, and to be the catalyst in the disorientation-reorientation process. We are urged to effect surprises for others because we believe in a God of surprises.

We are encouraged to see our gifts as gifts for others. To console, to counsel, to instruct—these are talents that must have others as their beneficiaries. To be gifted means to be gift to others. Our humanity can counteract the inhumanity in our world. Our God chooses to act in and through us.

We are asked to observe the goodness in others and praise them. We humans find it relatively easy to praise God but much more difficult to praise fellow humans. Our God continues to surprise us by the accomplishments of others. Response to the Word of God in community demands that we set aside our ego to focus on the attributes of our God in others. Gifts, talents, abilities—all these should move us to sing, "It is good, it is very good!"

We are called upon to rediscover our sense of celebration. Our Eucharist is not intended to be an exercise in boredom but an ever new faith opportunity. We are asked to share the burdens of the community by sharing the bread and the wine. They are the symbols of our fragile world, a world that seeks to move from disorientation to reorientation. Eucharist is to provide the creative energy to profess belief in a God who would yet work surprises for others through us. To celebrate Eucharist is to restore our God's capacity to give through us. We do not need any more elder sons who remain outside and refuse to celebrate the sacrament of divine surprise.

BIBLIOGRAPHICAL SUGGESTIONS

Ackroyd, Peter R. *Exile and Restoration.* OTL. Philadelphia: Westminster, 1968, 118-137.

Anderson, Bernhard W. "Exodus Typology in Second Isaiah," *Israel's Prophetic Heritage. Essays in Honor of James Muilenburg.* Edited by B. W. Anderson & W. Harrelson. New York: Harper & Row, 1962, 177-195.

_____ . "Exodus and Covenant in Second Isaiah and Prophetic Tradition," *Magnalia Dei. The Mighty Acts of God. Essays on the Bible and Archaeology in Memory of G. Ernest Wright.* Edited by F. M. Cross, Jr. et al. Garden City: Doubleday, 1976, 339-360.

Brueggemann, Walter. "Psalms and the Life of Faith: A Suggested Typology of Function," *JSOT* 17 (June, 1980) 3-32.

_____ . *Praying the Psalms.* Winona: Saint Mary's Press, 1982, 27-37.

Buber, Martin. *The Prophetic Faith.* New York: Macmillan, 1949, 203-235.

Crossan, John D. *In Parables. The Challenge of the Historical Jesus.* New York: Harper & Row, 1973, 53-78.

Fitzmyer, Joseph A. "Reconciliation in Pauline Theology," *No Famine in the Land. Studies in Honor of J. L. McKenzie.* Edited by J. W. Flanagan & A. W. Robinson. Missoula: Scholars Press, 1975, 155-177.

Gerstenberger, Erhard. "Psalms," *Old Testament Form Criticism.* Trinity University Monograph Series in Religion. Edited by J. H. Hayes. San Antonio: Trinity University Press, 1974, 207-226.

Guthrie, Harvey. *Theology as Thanksgiving.* New York: Seabury, 1981.

Lohse, Eduard. *Colossians and Philemon.* Hermeneia. Philadelphia: Fortress, 1971, 1-183.

McKenzie, John L. *Second Isaiah.* AB. Garden City: Doubleday, 1968.

Mowinckel, Sigmund. *The Psalms in Israel's Worship.* New York: Abingdon, 1962. I, 106-192.

Muilenburg, James. "The Book of Isaiah, Ch. 40-66, Introduction and Exegesis," *IB* 5. New York: Abingdon, 1956, 381-773.

Raitt, Thomas W. *A Theology of Exile: Judgment/Deliverance in Jeremiah and Ezekiel.* Philadelphia: Fortress, 1977, 218-222.

Rogers, Patrick V. *Colossians.* New Testament Message. Wilmington: Michael Glazier, 1979.

Smart, James D. *History and Theology in Second Isaiah: A Commentary on Isaiah, 35, 40-66.* Philadelphia: Westminster, 1965.

Stuhlmueller, Carroll. *Creative Redemption in Deutero-Isaiah.* AnBib. Rome: Biblical Institute Press, 1970.

Westermann, Claus. *The Praise of God in the Psalms.* Richmond: John Knox, 1965, 81-116.

_____ . *Isaiah: 40-66.* OTL. Philadelphia: Westminster, 1969, 3-30.

_____ . *The Psalms. Structure, Contents, and Message.* Minneapolis: Augsburg, 1980, 47-51, 71-80.

CHAPTER 15

The Invitation to Wisdom

Biblical passages to be read: Prv 10-15; Wis 1-10.

UNDERACHIEVING IN LIFE

"**G**od's in his heaven, all's right with the world." Whether we admit it or not, this principle colors much of our lives. We have been educated to underachieve in life by focusing on heaven. As a result, life becomes solely the condition for the afterlife. Our living is reduced to certain actions we must perform, to certain laws we must observe, to certain fees we must pay. We tolerate living, we put up with living, we make deals with living. Somehow we are afraid to live simply for the sake of living. We speak of "getting something out of life"—we constrain life to grant us a few favors. We conclude that living is some*thing* that we will undertake only in heaven. We have been sold "a pie in the sky by and by."

Rank individualism has followed in the wake of our heaven-oriented "living." As W. Brueggemann has perceived, we feel we are going to make heaven single file. We seek to procure our niche by paying our dues but we do so individually. Other people become merely the condition for our getting ahead into heaven. We do not see ourselves as engaged in mutual efforts to foster a truly human community. We are individuals drowning in a sea of self-pursuit and self-fulfillment. Success means the attainment of our individual goals, not the promotion of our communal needs. Salvation means checking off our separate merits. Heaven is never the communion of saints but the compensation of isolated humans. Heaven is more place or thing rather than person or persons.

Authority tends to replace involvement. In our biblical tradition we prefer the mighty acts of God whereby the deity singlehandedly engineers the escape and delivers the people. We also thrill to "Thus says the Lord." Salvation is served up ready-made. We choose edicts and pronouncements over observation and experience. We are less and less likely to assess ecclesiastical and civil statements against the reality of living. Election and office insulate our abdication from the scene. We surrender our willingness to provide perception and constructive criticism for our leaders.

We are more indentured servants than trusted partners. We do not see our world as the place for interacting with others to achieve genuine living. We regard our God as the supreme celestial foreman who does not need our contribution. We cower in our distrust of self, thinking that this will somehow glorify the foreman. We have lost the capacity to make mistakes and gain insight in the process. We refuse to take initiative, judging that we will not make any difference anyway. We have given up on ourselves, regarding this submission as the sacrament of acceptance.

The wisdom writers of the Old Testament (the authors of Job, Proverbs, Ecclesiastes, Wisdom, Ben Sira) as well as other wisdom influenced writers could not and would not tolerate underachieving in life. The wisdom dimension of the canon, therefore, serves as a healthy corrective when copping out takes precedence over stepping forward. We are reminded that this segment of our Bible preserves values which demand that we review our life-style to determine if it is really a *life*-style. Wisdom challenges us to live to the full.

THE SEMANTIC RANGE OF "WISDOM"

A brief survey of the use of the Hebrew words for "wise" (*ḥākām*) and "wisdom" (*ḥokmâ*) reveals the exceedingly wide range of these terms. It also suggests that wisdom is not the privileged possession of a few but the acquired talent of many.

According to 1 Chr 22:15-16 David informs Solomon that he has already provided the following for the latter's temple: ". . . and every kind of craftsman skilled (literally "wise") in gold, silver, bronze, and iron." Similarly the women who do the spinning for the desert tabernacle likewise possess "wisdom" (see Ex 35:25). In the prophetic books the counseling skills of high officials figure prominently. More often than not, their skill does not produce true wisdom: "Utter fools are the princes of Zoan! the wisest of Pharaoh's advisers give stupid counsel" (Is 19:11; see also Jer 51:35). In the wisdom books themselves "wisdom" can connote cleverness (see the lack of cleverness in the ostrich in Jb 39:17). It is also employed for rules of conduct: "My son, if you receive my words and treasure my commands, turning your ear to wisdom, inclining your heart to understanding . . . (Prv 2:1-2). In Qoh 8:17 the accent is on academic wisdom: "However much man toils in searching, he does not find it out; and even if the wise man says that he knows, he is unable to find it out."

G. Fohrer has noted that a study of this wide range reveals an emphasis on a practical mastery of the questions of life rather than a theoretical one. The wise person is one who observes the problems of life and seeks to resolve them by experienced and competent action. Wisdom implies both cleverness and skill in handling detailed aspects of life.

THE ORIGINS OF WISDOM

Some regard wisdom as merely a literary phenomenon. Although there is an abundance of both Egyptian and Mesopotamian wisdom literature, what actually gave rise to the literature? Others see wisdom as part of the formal education for diplomats and other civil servants. Yet the Book of Proverbs cannot be explained on the basis of an address to avid students in the foreign service. Still others consider wisdom as adaptation to the world and life—a humanism of sorts. But is this a characteristic of wisdom rather than its proper origin?

Having analyzed the three positions given above, J.-P. Audet suggests that the wisdom tradition predates the existence of schools and cities and reflects tribal and family structures. In his perceptive paper Audet argues that wisdom is basically a *paideia,* an education and initiation provided in the family circle for coping with the problems of living. This helps to explain wisdom's penchant for observations, counsels, recommendations, and precepts. As an example of this *paideia,* Audet cites Tb 4:1-19. Thus, "Perform good works all the days of your life, and do not tread the paths of wrongdoing. For if you are steadfast in your service, your good works will being success, not only to you, but also to all those who live uprightly" (vv 5-6). The head of a tribe or family is thereby concerned with preserving and handing on this education and initiation. (See chapter 5 for the Decalogue and tribal wisdom.)

The implications of this *paideia* approach to wisdom are far-reaching. It emphasizes the family setting and the local community as important centers for learning the art of living. It suggests that the wisdom acquired in these settings be challenged by actual experience, especially in larger societies. This approach also urges the significance of the home and local community in the development of moral living. Do's and don't's imposed from above will have little impact if the home and local community have not introduced members to the task of living as contributing members of society. The ability to deal with laws and their obligations begins long before the awareness of statutes or civil ordinances.

Obviously wisdom is a growth process. As R. B. Y. Scott has

pointed out, the wisdom tradition has other sources. The accumulated wisdom of a coherent traditional culture is one such source. Here human experience is not only evaluated but also expressed in brief common sayings, e.g., proverbs. Schools take up the educational process begun at home, adding observation to admonition. There also emerge counselors who provide advice for leaders of state. In Israel and elsewhere wisdom becomes institutionalized by the scribal profession. Besides, there are always gifted individuals whose intellectual curiosity and moral awareness lead them to study the environment and human behavior in depth. Finally proverbs, debates, tales, etc., are codified and employed for formal religious purposes.

The sources of wisdom point in the direction of communal concern. They look to genuine living, not only on the part of individuals but also of the community. These sources suggest that a variety of people contribute to our understanding of life, that wisdom is not the privileged patrimony of the counselor but also the challenge and obligation of all those who see themselves as vitally engaged in living. Genuine wisdom by nature eschews any and every form of egomania. To be wise is always to be wise for, with, and by others.

WISDOM LITERATURE AND WISDOM MOVEMENT

Just why Job, certain psalms, Proverbs, Ecclesiastes, Wisdom, and Ben Sira form a unique corpus is a matter of dispute. R. E. Murphy suggests that this literature is one that attempts to impose a (tentative) order on chaotic human experience. The authors responsible for this literature have attempted to look at life with discerning eyes and to offer suggestions for coping with the Scylla and Charybdis all too evident in human experience. According to J. L. Crenshaw this literature is the search for self-understanding in relating to things, people, and God. In contradistinction to G. von Rad and J. L. McKenzie, Crenshaw maintains that wisdom is more than practical knowledge of life and the world and more than an approach to reality.

This discussion of wisdom literature as opposed to wisdom language, wisdom tradition, wisdom thinking, etc., is not merely an academic exercise. It shows that, while wisdom literature is relatively limited in the Old Testament, wisdom influence is more widespread. Authors detect the presence or influence of wisdom in the Yahwist's account of the garden (Gn 2:4b-3:24), the Joseph Story (Gn 37, 39-50), Deuteronomy, the Succession Narrative (2 Sm 6[9]-20; 1 Kgs 1-2), First Isaiah (see Is 31:1-3), Amos (see 3:3-6, 8; 6:12), etc. Thus the ability to cope with limitations, to achieve success without directly invoking the deity, to recognize certain patterns of cause and effect in human relationships, etc., is a talent associated with the wise. While the debate on the proper delimitations of wisdom literature and wisdom movement will go on, what will continue to emerge is greater awareness of the role of wisdom in all echelons of Israel's life and in the various literary expressions of that life. Wisdom is not a stepchild in the Old Testament corpus.

CHARACTERISTICS OF THE WISDOM STANCE

Wisdom is *open to experience and nature.* The wisdom writers believe that there are ways of coping with and steering through chaos in human experience. One must be patient and observant, ever alert to note what works and what does not work. As G. von Rad has remarked, wisdom prefers facts to theories. If a given policy or modus agendi proves to be harmful or counter-productive, wisdom demands that it be set aside. The task of wisdom is to point out to the institution the folly of inhuman practices. What does not promote human dignity should not be sacrificed to the continuity of tradition.

Wisdom *trusts in experience and reality.* Wisdom does not regard experience and reality as enemies of the state. After seeing what makes for living and non-living, wisdom adopts an attitude of trust and confidence in the experience and reality it has perceived. Though life continues to have its dangers and its difficulties, the wise person can advance courageously because he/she has gained from his/her own previous experiences as well as those of others. Security is a state of being that results from the optimistic stance towards this challenging yet instructive world.

As W. Zimmerli has observed, wisdom *thinks resolutely within the framework of creation.* Creation is the invitation to assume the human task of transforming the world. Wisdom assumes that the Creator does not regard humans as puppets to be pulled capriciously according to the vacillations of the divine will. Rather, wisdom assumes that the Creator charges humans to be partners in the on-going task of human transformation. It is not a question of severing all ties with the Creator. It is a matter of acknowledging the marvel of the Creator's handiwork and of developing that marvel in human existence. Wisdom refuses to surrender the human initiative which goes with creation. At the same time wisdom insists on the line of demarcation between divine prerogative and human liberty.

Wisdom *finds its verification in reality.* Wisdom does not invoke "Thus says the Lord" or "The Lord says, 'Let my people go.'" Wisdom does not operate on the basis of such authority. In the perceptive phase of W. Zimmerli, authority rules categorically whereas counsel is debatable. It is this attitude that explains the somewhat bewildering juxtaposition of Prov 26:4-5: "Answer not the fool according to his folly, lest you too become like him. Answer the fool according to his folly, lest he become wise in his own eyes." This paradoxical approach leaves the wise person free to apply the benefit of experience according to the concrete situation. What is viable at one time need not be viable at another. In this sense wisdom is more gray rather than black and white.

In W. Harrelson's expression wisdom is *non-synthetic*. In traditional philosophy and theology we are trained to systematize our world of experience by clarifying our thoughts and offering a rational foundation for our pursuits and actions. Wisdom, however, prefers the non-manual approach. It prefers to have a considerable number of observations that are unmanageable for those who think in terms of coherent systems. Frequently it is sufficient to offer the right phase, the proper quip, the apt story rather than a cerebral digression. Wisdom thereby welcomes the presence of the so-called "ordinary people" in its ranks; their ability to speak the right word at the right time counts for wisdom.

THEOLOGICAL ADVANTAGES OF THE WISDOM STANCE

In an essay written some twelve years ago W. Brueggemann analyzed the contributions of wisdom in terms of an ecumenical life-style. The essay is an example of hermeneutic. It bridges the gap between the thought patterns of Israel's world and the demands of modern living. It comes to grips with the underlying human realities that intersect ancient Israel and the modern world.

First of all, the goal and meaning of life is healthy community life. Life is not to be equated with success or security. We are not necessarily "living" with the acquisition of the president's office or the purchase of the best home. Life means concern for others. It advocates posing the questions in terms of others, not oneself. In W. Brueggemann's adroit phrase the wise have concluded that *we* precedes *me* theologically, chronologically, and logically.

Secondly, authority for life flows from our experience. There are limitations that we can violate only at the greatest risk. To toy with nuclear warfare is the garden revisited. Even if the stockpile of bombs is "pleasing to the eyes, and desirable for gaining knowledge" (Gn 3:6), experience teaches that we may confuse power with holocaust, autonomy with total destruction.

Thirdly, humans are responsible for their world. The God of the Old Testament risks the gift of human freedom. Yet this is the only condition for a truly human response to our community. Wisdom insists that to honor this God means to promote the welfare of sisters and brothers. Wisdom means the death of ego and the resurrection of community. Wisdom demands the celebration of human liberty in a liturgy of communal concern.

Fourthly, wisdom advocates the enjoyment and appreciation of life. Israel's wisdom writers urged their people not to endure life but to celebrate it. Although most of them did not believe in an afterlife, wisdom need not be construed as opposing this belief (see Wis 1-6). What it does urge is the acceptance of life as gift. Life is more than existence and survival, more than toleration and acquiescence. Life is the profound awareness of our relationship with our God and our community and the demonstration of that twofold relationship in celebration.

Fifthly, wisdom establishes the priority of people over things. Wisdom observes that creation subordinates things to people, not people to things. Humans are charged to exercise control of the created world but not to the point of manipulating fellow humans. Human kingship/queenship means the preservation of such values.

JESUS AS WISDOM TEACHER

In his teaching Jesus displayed the techniques and attitudes of Israel's sages. He liked using parables because they were a very flexible means of sharing his outlook on experience and reality. For example, in Mt 13:44 Jesus talks about the treasure hidden in the field as symbolic of the arrival of the kingdom and the radical commitment required by it. Thus the routine world of a farmer is interrupted by the discovery of a treasure that creates an entirely new world. But this implies the reversal of his past—the selling of everything he has. This, in turn, leads to the farmer's new activity, viz., accepting the world that Jesus offers the disciples, a world grounded in his very person. At the same time Jesus realized that his community was hardly a collection of only the perfect. The parable of the wheat and weeds (see Mt 13:34-40) indicates that both good and evil were involved.

Elsewhere in the Gospel tradition Jesus appears as one who knew how to use pithy statements to advantage. When accused by his enemies of associating with tax collectors and offenders against the law, he replied: "'People who are healthy do not need a doctor; sick people do'" (Mk 2:17). When anxious to demonstrate the uniqueness of his message, he explained: "'No, new wine is poured into new skins'" (Mk 2:22).

For Jesus the goal and meaning of life was healthy community life. He was moved by everything that oppressed and depressed the human spirit. The kingdom of God meant that he was God's instrument in alleviating the human condition. Thus he spoke in the typically wisdom phrases of the beatitudes: "'Blest (i.e., to be envied) are you who hunger; you shall be filled. Blest are you who are weeping; you shall laugh'" (Lk 6:20-21). Wisdom meant concern for others, especially the disenfranchised.

Jesus urged his audiences to look at life and find authority in experience. The Gospel tradition connects his disclosure of his identity at Caesarea Philippi, viz., Suffering Son of Man (see Mt

159

16:21; Mk 8:31; Lk 9:22), with the conditions for discipleship: "'If a man wishes to come after me, he must deny his very self, take up his cross, and follow in my steps'" (Mk 8:34; see Mt 16:24; Lk 9:23). According to this tradition Jesus is represented as teaching Christian discipleship in terms of suffering and total commitment. For Jesus' interpreters it was a question of gaining insight from the experience of Jesus himself and accepting the limitations inherent in discipleship.

The message of Jesus was not the abdication of human responsibility. It could not be a pious relationship with the Father devoid of contact with the community. Thus Matthew writing for his divided Church presents the stance of Jesus in terms of concern for the outcast members of the community. The afterlife is linked to communal living on earth: "'For I was hungry and you gave me food, I was thirsty and you gave me drink. I was a stranger and you welcomed me . . .'" (Mt 25:35-40.)

The Gospel tradition shows Jesus as one who enjoyed life. Eating and drinking were part of life and Jesus relished parties and celebrations. Whereas John the Baptist was an ascetic, Jesus was not. A tradition associated with the role of wisdom reveals this dimension of his life-style: "'The Son of Man appeared eating and drinking, and they say, "This one is a glutton and drunkard, a lover of tax collectors and those outside the law!" Yet time will prove where *wisdom* lies'" (Mt 11:19; see Lk 7:34-35).

Jesus taught the priority of persons over things. He viewed institutions as means to assist people, not to oppress them. If it was a question of the preservation of human dignity or human institutions, then the institutions had to go. Hence he insisted: "'The sabbath was made for man, not man for the sabbath'" (Mk 2:27; see Mt 12: 8; Lk 6:5).

The greatest example of Jesus' wisdom stance is the Eucharist. Both Jesus and his interpreters reflect the understanding of reality in terms of a meal, a setting that argues in favor of enjoyment and appreciation. At the same time it is concerned with fostering healthy community life. The words of institution accentuate human interaction and human provision. In turn, they imply the assertion of responsibility. To participate is to be involved, to share is to be committed. It is also an exercise in finding authority in experience, viz., the experience of Jesus in terms of total self-giving. Sacrifice and Eucharist go together. Thus people will always remain people and never be perverted to the level of things. The setting recalls the invitation of Lady Wisdom: "Come, eat of my food, and drink of the wine I have mixed! Forsake foolishness that you may live; advance in the way of understanding" (Prv 9:5-6).

BIBLIOGRAPHICAL SUGGESTIONS

Audet, Jean-Paul. "Origines comparées de la double tradition de la Loi et de la Sagesse dans le Proche-Orient ancien," *Orientalists' Congress.* Moscow: 1962. I, 352-357.

Brueggemann, Walter. "Scripture and an Ecumenical Life-Style," *Int* 24 (1970) 3-19.

_____ . *In Man We Trust. The Neglected Side of Biblical Faith.* Richmond: John Knox, 1972, 104-110.

Collins, John J. "The Biblical Precedent for Natural Theology," *JAAR* 45 (1977) 70.

Crenshaw, James L. "Method in Determining Wisdom Influence upon 'Historical' Literature," *JBL* 88 (1969) 129-142 = *Studies in Ancient Israelite Wisdom.* Edited by J. L. Crenshaw. New York: Ktav, 1976, 481-494.

_____ . "In Search of Divine Presence," *Review and Expositor* 74 (1977) 353-369.

Fohrer, Georg. *"sophia," Theological Dictionary of the New Testament.* Edited by G. Kittel & C. Friedrich. Grand Rapids: Eerdmans, 1971. VII, 476-496 = *Studies in Ancient Israelite Wisdom,* 63-83.

Gordis, Robert. "The Social Background of Wisdom Literature," *Poets, Prophets and Sages.* Bloomington: Indiana University Press, 1971, 160-197.

Harrelson, Walter. "Wisdom and Pastoral Theology," *ANQ* 7 (1966) 6-14.

Harvey, Julien. "Wisdom Literature and Biblical Theology," *BTB* 1 (1971) 308-319.

Mack, Burton L. "Wisdom Myth and Mytho-logy," *Int* 24 (1974) 46-60.

McKenzie, John L. "Reflections on Wisdom," *JBL* 86 (1967) 1-9.

Murphy, Roland E. *Seven Books of Wisdom.* Milwaukee: Bruce, 1960, 143-157.

_____ . "The Concept of the Wisdom Literature," *The Bible in Current Catholic Thought.* Edited by J. L. McKenzie. New York: Herder & Herder, 1962, 46-54.

_____ . "Assumptions and Problems in Old Testament Wisdom Research," *CBQ* 29 (1967) 407-418 = 101-112.

_____ . "The Interpretation of Old Testament Wisdom Literature," *Int* 23 (1969) 289-301.

_____ . "The Hebrew Sage and Openness to the World," *Christian Action and Openness to the World.* Edited by J. Papin. Villanova: Villanova University Press, 1970, 219-244.

_____ . "Wisdom and Yahwism," *No Famine in the Land. Studies in Honor of J. L. McKenzie.* Edited by J. W. Flanagan & A. W. Robinson. Missoula: Scholars Press, 1975, 117-126.

_____ . "Wisdom—Theses and Hypotheses," *Israelite Wisdom: Theological and Literary Essays in Honor of Samuel Terrien.* Edited by J. G. Gammie et al. New York: Union Theological Seminary, 1978, 35-42.

Pfeiffer, Robert H. "Wisdom and Vision in the Old Testament," *ZAW* 52 (1934) 93-101 = *Studies in Ancient Israelite Wisdom,* 305-313.

Porteous, Norman W. "Royal Wisdom," *VTS* 3 (1960) 247-261.

Priest, John F. "Where Is Wisdom To Be Placed?" *Journal of Bible and Religion* 31 (1963) 275-282.

Rad, Gerhard von. *Old Testament Theology.* New York: Harper & Row, 1962. I, 418-453.

_____ . *Wisdom in Israel.* New York: Abingdon, 1972, 113-137, 144-176, 190-206.

Rohr Sauer, Alfred von. "Wisdom and Law in Old Testament Wisdom Literature,"

Concordia Theological Monthly 43 (1972) 600–609.

Scott, Robert B. Y. "Study of the Wisdom Literature," *Int* 24 (1970) 20–45.

_____ . *The Way of Wisdom in the Old Testament*. New York: Macmillan, 1971.

Whybray, Roger N. *The Intellectual Tradition in the Old Testament*. BZAW. New York: de Gruyter, 1974.

Zimmerli, Walther. "Concerning the Structure of Old Testament Wisdom," *Studies in Ancient Israelite Wisdom*, 177–207.

_____ . "The Place and Limit of the Wisdom in the Framework of Old Testament Theology," *Scottish Journal of Theology* 17 (1964) 146–158 = *Studies in Ancient Israelite Wisdom*, 314–326.

CHAPTER 16

The Invitation to Job

Biblical passages to be read: Jb 1-14; 29-31; 38-42.

THE QUESTION OF RELATIONSHIPS

Who is our God? Is he/she the divine architect with a once grandiose plan for humans but now one who chooses not to become involved? Is our God so tucked away from the reality of human life that our plight no longer has an impact? Is our God the meticulous bookkeeper who relates to us only in terms of debits and credits? Is our God merely the subject of conventional statements of religion totally divorced from our real world? More crucially, is our God capable of so entering into our human condition that he/she can be transformed as well? What are the extremes to which our God will go in the effort to identify with us humans? Will the real Yahweh please stand up?

Who are our real friends? Are they merely the ones who frolic with us when misfortune is only a faint possibility? Are they present only when they can grow fat on our wealth and absent when they will become lean in our poverty? Are they the mouthpieces for traditional pious platitudes which will do nothing to ease the pain and which they probably have never tested anyhow? Are they really capable of genuine empathy, capable of seeing distraught humanity and then articulating an energizing word? Are they the attendants at the wake and the funeral but the absentees in the months and years of post-funeral grief? Will our real friends please stand up?

Who is the real me? Is the real me an outside party in relating to God and society? Is the real me a "go by the book" believer who can recite the religious instruction answers but not live out their implications? Is the real me one who will confront this God, attack this God, and yet be willing to listen to this God? Is the real me able to be transformed, able to face the adversities of life and regard them, not as bad dreams, but as the raw material for genuine growth? Is the real me in touch with the scene? Will the real me please stand up?

These are the questions implicitly formulated at least in the orientation-disorientation-reorientation process. However, they reach clearer formulation in the transformation process which is the Book of Job. Unlike the psalms and passages from Second Isaiah, the Book of Job develops the entire process at length. It complements these psalms and prophetic passages by enfleshing their intent in the person of Job. Response to the Word of God in community dare not decline the invitation to Job.

BACKGROUND

It is generally agreed that the Book of Job is a literary masterpiece. Hence it would be useful to know something of the author and his background. Unfortunately there are only a few hints which pique our curiosity but do not satisfy it.

The role of the prosecuting attorney—the śāṭān—in Jb 1:6-2:7 is the same as the one in Zec 3:1-2, a prophetic work dated around 520 B.C. In both instances we are dealing with a prosecutor who, as a member of God's court, performs the task of accusing various individuals (in Zec 3:1-2 it is Joshua the high priest). He is not, therefore, the individual named "Satan" but simply the prosecuting attorney who carries out the divine will (contrast 1 Chr 1:21 with 2 Sm 24:1). In addition to this observation A. Hurvitz has collected other linguistic evidence regarding the prose folk tale that suggests the exilic or early postexilic period. A date around 500 B.C. would not be too far from the mark.

The whole question of the exile and the less than grandiose restoration (despite the exalted poetry of Second Isaiah!) posed significant problems for Israel's thinkers. This setting evoked inquiries into God's dealings with Israel. As we shall see, it was more than the perennial problem of evil. It was basically one of relationship. The author of the Book of Job most likely undertook his literary effort in this setting. However, even if this background should prove to be wrong, the work would still remain a masterpiece since it is a unique perception of the timeless question of the divine-human drama.

JOB THE PATIENT (JP)

Job the Patient (JP) is the admirable individual who is the subject of the prose folk tale contained in Jb 1:1-2:13; 42:7-17. This is the Job who is the paragon of virtue and the epitome of total acceptance.

This is clearly the Job we all admire. Such a Job was also well known in antiquity. In proclaiming the doctrine of personal responsibility, the prophet Ezekiel recalled the venerable tradition about certain exemplars of integrity: ". . . and even if these three men were in it (a land), Noah, Daniel, and Job, they could save only themselves by their virtue, says the Lord God" (Ez 14:14; see also 14:20). The Book of Job opens, therefore, with a figure already well known and revered.

The folk tale begins with the scene in the heavenly court. Yahweh, the divine council, and the prosecuting attorney (1:6). Yahweh's initial question sums up the image of JP: "'Have you noticed my servant Job, and that there is no one on earth like him, blameless and upright, fearing God and avoiding evil?'" (1:8). The prosecutor's reply is to note Job's incredible wealth—he is an extremely rich patriarch of the ancient Near East who has enjoyed nothing but divine beneficence. After obtaining Yahweh's permission, the prosecutor sets out to introduce Job to an appreciation of human misery and frustration. The hero's devastation is both sudden and total. However, the outcome (42:7-17) is even more amazing than the beginning. Job is restored; in fact he is more than amply compensated for the miseries he has so virtuously endured.

JOB THE IMPATIENT (JIP)

Job the Impatient (JIP) is the protagonist of the poetic dialogues in chaps. 3-27 and the poetic summation in chaps. 29-31 (chaps. 28, 32-37 are later additions). This is the Job unknown from antiquity and hardly the exemplar of unquestionable virtue. The author of JIP took over the traditional image of JP in the prose folk tale but then proceeded to reduce the hero to common clay, especially in the three poetic dialogues: chaps. 3-14, 15-21, and 22-27 (the arrangement of chaps. 22-27 is disputed). Actually these chapters are not dialogues since they do not proceed by the making of points. Nevertheless the speeches do refer to what has gone before. Here the author introduces three sages from the ancient Near East (Eliphaz of Teman, Bildad of Shuh, and Zophar of Naamath) who attempt to resolve the hero's misfortune.

H. L. Ginsberg (responsible for the sigla JP and JIP) has persuasively noted that it is relatively easy to interpret JP but exceedingly difficult to exegete JIP. He contends that the genuis of the author of JIP consists in reversing roles. Thus JIP now speaks out against the traditional doctrine of retribution. In the other direction the three friends become the voice of orthodoxy, a position formerly held by JP. JIP's argument is that because of his experience God really makes no distinction between the good and the bad. The friends' argument is that the wicked encounter catastrophe at an early age and do not recover from it—the righteous, of course, are different.

JIP'S REVELATION

In H. L. Ginsberg's view suffering, although it plays a key role in the book, is actually only one dimension of the real problem. That problem is the relationship between God and humans. The suffering serves as the setting for developing that relationship. Who is this God who permits JIP to undergo such catastrophe? Who is this human who must endure the catastrophe and at the same time make some effort to understand its place in his life? What is the relationship between God and JIP? As H. L. Ginsberg observes, the author of the poetic dialogues struggles with this theme in a way yet to be surpassed.

In H. L. Ginsberg's analysis the basis of Job's anxiety is a revelation he has received from a heavenly being. There has been a communications leak from on high to which JIP has been privy. It proves to be a nightmare since its content is that there is no such category as "righteous"—consequently Job has been living in a fool's paradise. This revelation is found in 3:25; 4:12-15; 9:11; 4:16-20. Although 4:12-20 are attributed to Eliphaz, H. L. Ginsberg holds that they are really part of JIP's speech since elsewhere the friends refer specifically to this revelation (see, e.g., 5:1).

JIP describes the fear that this revelation brought in its wake: "For a word was stealthily brought to me, and my ear caught a whisper of it . . . Fear came upon me, and shuddering that terrified me to the bones. Then a spirit passed before me, and the hair of my flesh stood up" (4:12, 14-15). JIP then shares the incredible secret of this terrifying revelation: ". . . and I heard a still voice: 'Can a man be righteous as against God? Can a mortal be blameless against his Maker? Lo, he puts no trust in his servants, and with his angels he can find fault. How much more with those that dwell in houses of clay, whose foundation is in the dust, and who are crushed more easily than the moth!'" (4:16-19). With this divine disclosure JIP must conclude that his life-style has been a colossal failure, since his righteousness is no guarantee against unexpected and unforeseen recrimination from on high. For JIP God is no longer the equitable partner in the game of retribution.

ELIPHAZ AND JOB (JIP)

In 4:1-11; 5:1-5; 4:21; 5:6-27 Eliphaz reacts to Job's blasphemous theology, playing the part of spokesperson for orthodoxy. He begins by observing Job's known piety: "Behold, you have instructed many, and have made firm their feeble hands. Your words have upheld the stumbler" (4:3-4). According to Eliphaz this former piety should prove to be a source of confidence (4:6). He now plainly states the case for orthodoxy: "Reflect now, what innocent man perishes? Since when are the upright destroyed?" (4:7). Instead of invoking another communication from on high (5:11), JIP would do well to recall the traditional doctrine of disciplinary suffering: "Happy is the man whom God reproves! The Almighty's chastening do not reject. For he wounds, but he binds up; he smites, but his hands give healing" (5:17-18). For Eliphaz it is only too obvious that JIP has committed some wrong. However, confession is good for the soul. This follows from tried and true teaching: "Lo, this we have searched out; so it is! This we have heard, and you should know" (5:27).

JIP responds to the arguments of the three friends by observing that they are not the only intelligent people around: "No doubt you are the intelligent folk, and with you wisdom shall die!" (12:2). After citing their pious platitudes (see, e.g., 12:4), he accuses them of speaking falsely for God: "You are glossing over falsehoods and offering vain remedies, every one of you! . . . Is it for God that you speak falsehood? Is it for him that you utter deceit?" (13:4, 7). Experience and revelation, i.e., JIP's distress and the private communication, clearly demonstrate that the position of the three friends is utterly untenable. For JIP their theology is mere fabrication; he longs to be left alone: "Your reminders are ashy maxims, your fabrications are mounds of clay. Be silent, let me alone! that I may speak and give vent to my feelings" (13:12-13).

JIP'S SUMMATION

Chaps. 29-31 sum up JIP's dilemma. They are a review of the glorious past that is now painfully absent. They are an evaluation of the present that is all too agonizingly evident. They are a judgment on God's lack of concern and a final protestation of innocence. They conclude with a plea for a fair hearing.

JIP begins by recalling the halcyon days of yore: "Oh, that I were as in the months past! as in the days when God watched over me . . . when my footsteps were bathed in milk, and the rock flowed with streams of oil" (29:2, 6). Those were the times when he received due honors at the city gate (29:7-10, 21-25) and when the poor, the orphans, and the outcasts blessed him (29:11-13). Those were the days when he was eyes to the blind and feet to the lame (29:11-13). Those were the occasions that led him to believe that he would enjoy a comfortable old age: "Then I said: 'In my own nest I shall grow old; I shall multiply years like the phoenix'" (29:18).

Chap. 30, however, introduces the precise opposite of his anticipations: "But now they hold me in derision who are younger in years than I . . ." (30:1). Whereas formerly his name was a blessing, it is now a mockery and a byword (30:9). Human taunts would be enough.

167

But injury is now added to insult when JIP's God joins the ranks of his enemies: "I cry to you, but you do not answer me . . . Then you turn upon me without mercy, and with your strong hand you buffet me" (30:20, 21). JIP's God refuses to become involved with the former paragon of virtue.

In a final gesture of anguish, JIP proclaims his total innocence. He does this by uttering a conditional curse on himself (see Ex 22:9-10; 1 Kgs 8:30-32): "If my heart has been enticed toward a woman, and I have lain in wait at my neighbor's door; then may my wife grind for another, and may others cohabit with her!" (31:9-10). He solemnly protests that he did not rejoice at the destruction of his enemy (31:29), that he provided hospitality for all strangers (31:32), that he did not suffer from a guilty conscience (31:33-34). His final request is to have the charges against him drawn up so that, when he is judged innocent, he may wear the indictment for all to see (31:35-36). He concludes: "This is my final plea; let the Almighty answer me!" (31:37).

GOD'S REPLY

A reply from God is clearly necessary. JIP requested an answer not only at the end of his speeches but even earlier (see 13:22-24; 16:19-21). Perhaps a stronger reason for some explanation of God's seemingly bizarre way of acting is the attitude of the reader. The author has presented his principal character in disputation with the three friends. He has set forth their claims: for Job the divine disclaiming of the category of righteous, for the friends the divine doctrine of retribution. Not to introduce God would be to frustrate the interest of the reader. Chaps. 38-41, therefore, form the author's reply to his audience. (Some consider 39:13-18; 40:1, 3-7; 40:15-41: 26 additions by a later author.)

Yahweh now speaks out of the storm: a theophany is the author's manner of divine presentation. The very first line spoken by Yahweh is indicative of the approach taken by the author: "Who is this that obscures divine plans with words of ignorance?" (39:2). As R. A. F. MacKenzie has shown, the approach is one of irony. The Job of the poetic dialogues and monologue has not allowed for any degree of divine mystery (neither have his friends!). Thus JIP has dared to speak of matters beyond his ken. However, the irony never descends to sarcasm. This is a God who loves JIP yet does not hesitate to expose his shortcomings.

The divine answer focuses on the world of nature and the animal world. These worlds contain marvels over which JIP has absolutely no control or say. They emphasize the role of mystery. God provides for these worlds in a way that should move the beholder to stand back and acknowledge God's care and providence. Making use of the triple-decker view of Semitic cosmogony, the author has Yahweh lecture Job, first of all, on the creation of the world: "Where were you when I founded the earth? Tell me, if you have understanding. Who determined its size; do you know?" (38:4-5). To all such queries Job must shake his head in ignorance and, at the same time, be astonished at the divine plan. The series of questions (perhaps based on Egyptian models) is staggering: "Have you ever in your lifetime commanded the morning . . . Have you entered into the sources of the sea . . . Have the gates of death been shown to you . . . Have you comprehended the breadth of the earth?" (38:12, 16, 17, 18).

The questions from the animal world are no less instructive. "Do you know about the birth of the mountain goats . . . Who has given the wild ass his freedom . . . Will the wild ox consent to serve you . . . Do you give the horse his strength?" (39:1, 5, 9, 19). Once again Job must betray his ignorance. It is all too evident that the Almighty is involved here; it is equally evident that JIP is unaware of the manner of that involvement. Hence we are not surprised when JIP owns up to his ignorance: "I have dealt with great things that I do not understand; things too wonderful for me, which I cannot know" (42:3).

As R. A. F. MacKenzie has emphasized, this parade of miracles from both the world of nature and the animal world is not simply an exercise in eliciting ignorance from the hero. These chapters indicate God's providence but also imply something greater. If God takes such great interest in these worlds, will that God take less interest in JIP's world? Will the Almighty labor over the creation of the world and the creation of the animals but then manifest less concern for JIP's predicament? The author implies all this; he lets his audience draw the logical conclusion that the Creator is also the God of JIP and his world of ills.

It is significant that the author has Yahweh ignoring JIP's question. There is no reference to the issues discussed at length by JIP and the friends. For the author these questions are simply the wrong questions. The right question must deal with the element of paradox. Hence God is able to afflict one who is righteous simply because he is righteous. The author is suggesting that JIP—and hence his audience—must learn to cultivate a sense of mystery. They must allow for a God of love and compassion who, bypassing the retribution equation of the friends, deals with humans in a concerned yet paradoxical manner. This God is not the cold impersonal celestial administrator. This God is a God of fidelity who refuses to be manipulated by all too neat human equations. And—in answer to JIP's communications leak from on high—this God does distinguish between the good and the bad, although the manner of distinction is also part of the realm of mystery. God loves JIP but it is a love that does not provide answers to the wrong questions.

THE HUMANIZING PROCESS

R. A. F. MacKenzie has suggested that the humanizing process or the transformation process in Job consists of three steps. First, there is a superman who exists in a never-never world. He is a person whom we can admire but dare not imitate. Such a person is impervious to the shocks and upsets that afflict normal humans. Secondly, the superman is reduced to the level of the ordinary human. He thus experiences inferiority. He learns to appreciate frustration and pain. He can now identify with the plight of ordinary mortals—something impossible in the first stage. Thirdly, the superman is reinstated. God intervenes and gives a new and unexpected direction to the life of the superman. He has regained the status of stage number one, although there is a decisive difference.

Samson is a good example of this transformation process. He is an amoral giant of superhuman strength. At this stage he cannot appreciate the weakness of ordinary mortals. However, he is reduced to that level of weakness when Delilah has his seven locks of hair shaved off (see Jgs 16:19). Preparation for the third stage begins when the author notes: "But the hair of his head began to grow as soon as it was shaved off" (Jgs 16:22). Samson regains his strength and topples the Philistine temple. However, Samson has also been profoundly changed.

Both in Job and the Samson episode the final state of the heroes is not the same as the first. To be sure, both Job and Samson are reinstated but at the same time they are changed men. They have now entered a new level of existence. In stage number one both Job and Samson were totally ignorant of the weaknesses and inferiority of ordinary mortals. In stage number three, however, both Job and Samson are transformed. Although they have regained their former status, they have now experienced the human condition as it really is. At the end of the story of Job we can not only admire the hero but also imitate him. He has become one of us.

THE HUMANIZING PROCESS IN HEBREWS

Hebrews is either a homily or a collection of homilies by a Hellenistic Jewish Christian. His audience is made up of Jewish Christians who are tempted to apostasy, i.e., to return to their former Jewish allegiance. The author in answer to this need shows how the Christ Event has superseded the old covenant. What is particularly striking about Hebrews is that, while it clearly attests Christ's divinity, it also highlights his humanity, and indeed a weak humanity.

In becoming human, Jesus is made a little lower than the angels.

However, according to Heb 2:10 it was altogether fitting that Jesus, the leader, should be exalted through suffering. Heb 2:17 insists that Jesus had to become like his brothers and sisters in every way. Indeed, "since he was himself tested through what he suffered, he is able to help those who are tempted" (Heb 2:18). Jesus is a high priest who can appreciate the weakness of his people. He was often tempted and, as a result, appreciates the problems of the human condition (see Heb 4:15). According to Heb 5:7 Jesus prayed the prayer of lament to the Father, especially at the passion, and received the appropriate answer in his exaltation. Such pain taught Jesus obedience: "Son though he was, he learned obedience from what he suffered" (Heb 5:8).

Prior to the incarnation the Second Person knows of human pain and frustration but not in a human way. At this phase the Word is in stage number one. With the incarnation, however, there is the personal experience of the total human condition, stage number two. God is thus reduced to the level of ordinary mortals and acquainted firsthand with human problems. The exaltation is stage number three. At this point the Word is reinstated, regaining all the glory withheld at the time of the incarnation. At the same time, however, there is a change. The Word as a result of stage number two has been transformed. Jesus' exaltation is the sacrament of divine involvement and understanding. We must not only admire Jesus, we must also imitate Jesus. The incarnation, therefore, is a gain for God. However, it also remains a gain for humans. Response to the Word of God in community cannot overlook this transformation process.

THE MEANING OF FRIENDSHIP IN JOB

N. C. Habel has written powerfully on friendship in Job. He speaks of this friendship as a radical relationship and an ultimate loyalty. He maintains that we truly discover our friends when we lose our God. He speaks of friendship as a ministry. Unlike Job's friends, we are not judged to be friends simply because we are able to explain the situation or able to defend God's teaching in this particular case. The friendship revealed in the Book of Job is one that transcends counseling. It is a friendship whereby one individual stands by another and continues to believe in that person in the face of all alienating forces.

Response to the Word of God in community must reflect on the demands of real friendship. Job thereby presents a challenge that few of us may realize. At that same time we are reminded that we may not cease responding to that challenge. The covenant relationship is ultimately a totally engaging enterprise. To love our covenant

God means to support our covenant friends, especially when they seem to have fallen out of covenant.

BIBLIOGRAPHICAL SUGGESTIONS

Barr, James. "The Book of Job and Its Modern Interpreters," *BJRL* 54 (1971–1972) 28–46.

Collins, John J. "Job and His Friends: God as a Pastoral Problem," *Chicago Studies* 14 (1975) 97–109.

Cox, Dermot. *The Triumph of Impotence: Job and the Tradition of the Absurd.* Rome: Gregorian University Press, 1978.

Dhorme, Édouard P. *A Commentary on the Book of Job.* London: Nelson, 1967.

Ginsberg, Harold L. "Job the Patient and Job the Impatient," *VTS* 17 (1969) 88–111.

Gordis, Robert. *The Book of God and Man: A Study of Job.* Chicago: Chicago University Press, 1965.

_____ . *The Book of Job. Commentary, New Translation and Special Studies.* New York: Jewish Theological Seminary of America, 1978.

Habel, Norman C. "Appeal to Ancient Tradition as a Literary Form," *ZAW* 88 (1976) 253–272.

_____ . "'Only the Jackal Is My Friend.' On Friends and Redeemers in Job," *Int* 31 (1977) 227–236.

Hurvitz, Avi. "The Date of the Prose-Tale of Job Linguistically Reconsidered," *HTR* 67 (1974) 17–34.

Kissane, Edward J. *The Book of Job.* Dublin: Browne & Nolan, 1939.

MacKenzie, Roderick A. F. "The Purpose of the Yahweh Speeches in the Book of Job," *Bib* 40 (1959) 435–445.

_____ . "The Transformation of Job," *BTB* 9 (1979) 51–57.

Pope, Marvin H. *Job.* AB. Garden City: Doubleday, 1965.

Rad, Gerhard von. "Job XXXVIII and Ancient Egyptian Wisdom," *The Problem of the Hexateuch and Other Essays.* New York: McGraw-Hill, 1966, 281–291.

Rowley, Harold H. "The Book of Job and Its Meaning," *BJRL* 41 (1958–1959) 167–207 = *From Moses to Qumran.* New York: Association Press, 1963, 141–183.

Snaith, Norman H. *The Book of Job. Its Origin and Purpose.* SBT. Naperville: Allenson, 1968.

Terrien, Samuel. "The Book of Job, Introduction and Exegesis," *IB* 3. New York: Abingdon, 1954, 875–1198.

_____ . *Job: Poet of Existence.* Indianapolis: Bobbs-Merrill, 1958.

Tsevat, Matitiahu. "The Meaning of the Book of Job," *HUCA* 37 (1966) 73–106 = *Studies in Ancient Israelite Wisdom,* 341–374.

Vogels, Walter. "The Spiritual Growth of Job: A Psychological Approach to the Book of Job," *BTB* 11 (1981) 77–80.

Westermann, Claus. *The Structure of the Book of Job. A Form-Critical Analysis.* Philadelphia: Fortress, 1981.

Williams, James G. "'You Have Not Spoken Truth of Me' - Mystery and Irony in Job," *ZAW* 83 (1971) 231–255.

Zerafa, Peter P. *The Wisdom of God in the Book of Job.* Studia Universitatis S. Thomae in Urbe. Rome: Herder, 1978.

CHAPTER 17

The Invitation to Qoheleth

Biblical passages to be read: the Book of Qoheleth.

SOCIETY'S COMPLACENCY

We all suffer from the conflict between experience and doctrine. Belief very often is a listing of the tenets or principles that members of the community are to accept. Experience is not infrequently the unmasking of the contradictions between the tenets or principles and real life. We suffer from broken symbols. Our American flag expresses the belief in liberty and justice for all. Yet prejudice raises doubts as to our intentions. Our Eucharist expresses the belief in mutual support and understanding. Yet in-fighting casts doubts as to our genuineness.

No difficulties, no problems, no inconsistencies. These are the slogans of the bureaucrat and the party liner. To admit difficulties suggests that all is not perfect, to discover problems implies that something is wrong, to detect inconsistencies insinuates that something is not in tune. We less than perfect humans like to start the rumor that our plans and programs are airtight and foolproof.

In the face of such complacency we may hesitate to speak out, maintaining that silence is golden. We may prefer not to make waves and so try to live with the unlivable. We may choose to perpetuate the error by telling others that everything is not really the way it appears. Even though the king is totally naked, we would have him masquerade in his new clothes. After all, masquerading is better than the naked truth. The world of belief has suddenly become make-believe.

Response to the Word of God in community must always be an

175

honest reply, based on reality as we see it, not as we would like to see it. Such response is the sworn enemy of complacency that is in effect no response. The Word of God—both ancient and ongoing—challenges us to resist masquerading, to admit the brokenness of our symbols, to confess the wide chasm between doctrine and experience. In this setting we are invited to read, better, to live the Book of Qoheleth. It is the biblical book that calls a spade a spade.

THE BACKGROUND OF QOHELETH

The title of this strange book in Hebrew is Qoheleth, a name that suggests some community function (Hebrew *qāhāl* means "assembly"). Its Greek title—Ecclesiastes—means "leader of the assembly." Hence Luther speaks of "the Preacher." What is clear, however, is that the author was a wisdom teacher. The epilogue of the book notes in the third person: "Besides being wise, Qoheleth taught the people knowledge, and weighed, scrutinized and arranged many proverbs" (12:9). It is also likely that he was a member of the upper class both by birth and position. The poem on youth and old age (11: 7-12:8) may imply that the author has already passed from youth to a more mature middle age.

It is likely, though by no means certain, that Qoheleth flourished in the third century B.C. Hence he could have been exposed to the inroads of Greek thought which reached the ancient Near East with the arrival of Alexander the Great. The evidence of the book, however, is that he belonged to the mainstream of Near Eastern wisdom literature. Although some have labelled him an iconoclast, it is more accurate to say that he was a faithful member of the people of God who believed that honesty was the only policy. His great claim to fame is that he denounced the shallowness of current Jewish thought and insisted on a return to reality. His attitude toward such shallowness has earned him a unique place in the canon of Scripture.

THE BOOK AND ITS STRUCTURE

The book immediately strikes the reader as being somewhat erratic and disorganized. One way of resolving the difficulty has been to posit one author and a variety of editors and glossators. This presupposes that the inconsistencies cannot be the work of one author. Another approach has been to regard the book as a collection of independent pieces totally unrelated to each other. When pressed to provide a structure for the book, the first view maintains that there is no structure at all, while the second view is content to proffer an outline of the contents of the individual pieces.

In an original study A. G. Wright has insisted that in working out structures, the critic should concentrate on the book itself and hence work with the linguistic evidence provided by the text. For the first half of the book (1:12-6:9) the structural element is the phrase "vanity (in Hebrew *hebel*) and a chase after wind." For the second half (6:10-11:6) the structural elements are found in the introduction in 6:10-12, viz., (1) one does not/cannot find out what is good to do (developed in 7:1-8:17); and (2) one does not know/ has no knowledge (developed in 9:1-11:6). Wright concludes that the theme of the book is the impossibility of understanding what God has done and that this theme is built on the "vanity" motif in the first half.

The implications of this structure are far-reaching. Instead of citing his favorite proverbs, as some authors contend, Qoheleth is lining up the traditional wisdom and passing judgment on its inadequacies. For example, in 7:12-24 he considers the problem of retribution: a just man perishes in his justice while a wicked man survives in his wickedness (v 15). He then cites the traditional wisdom in vv 16-18, recalling the advice about not being just to excess and not being wicked to excess and noting "he who fears God will win through at all events" (v 18). In vv 19-22 he adds three more sayings of contemporary thought to the effect that wisdom is something valuable, "yet there is no man on earth so just as to do good and never sin" (v 20). In v 23 he discloses his pursuit of wisdom. Yet, when he considers the reality of the equation "justice = life, wickedness = death," he must honestly conclude that the equation does not work. "What exists is far-reaching; it is deep, very deep; who *can find* it *out?*" (v 24).

Imbalance reigns in life. According to 9:11 the swift do not necessarily win the race nor do the valiant necessarily win the battle. Wisdom does not necessarily lead to livelihood nor shrewdness to riches. The reason for this state of affairs is that misfortune strikes everyone. In 9:12 he states that humans are no better off than fish in the net or birds in the snare: "Man *no* more *knows* his own time . . ."

Allow for mystery and venture forth in spite of uncertainty. This is the gist of 11:3-6. In v 3 Qoheleth observes that what is going to happen will happen: "when the clouds are full, they pour out rain upon the earth." But too much caution leads to inactivity: "and one who watches the clouds will never reap" (v 4). Just as humans do *not know* God's marvellous work with the child in the womb, "so you *know not* the work of God which he is accomplishing in the universe" (v 5). Therefore, humans should proceed with their efforts and not cop out: "for you *know not* which of the two will be successful, or whether both alike will turn out well" (v 6).

Building upon the study of E. M. Good, T. Polk has demonstrated how creatively Qoheleth uses the Hebrew word *hebel* (usually translated "vanity") in his approach to the reality of life. In Is 30:7 the prophet proclaims that seeking Egyptian aid against the neo-Assyrians is doomed to failure because Egypt is *hebel* and empty. In an attack on false idols Jer 10:5 maintains that these idols are *hebel*, a ridiculous work—they lack the breath of life. In a description of the human condition Ps 144:4 notes that humans are like *hebel*, their days like a passing shadow. For both Good and Polk *hebel* has to do with irony, i.e., the perception of the distance between pretense and reality, between what is and what should be. *Hebel* is, therefore, an apt term for destroying the illusions under which people labor by exposing the incongruity of their actions.

In 2:18-26 Qoheleth discusses the futility of life wherein one leaves the fruit of one's labor to another. One does not know if that person will be wise or foolish. Yet such a person will have control of the acquired goods. For Qoheleth this is *hebel*—it is an ironic/incongruous situation (v 19). So too the worker must leave his property to a non-worker. This too, says Qoheleth, is ironic/incongruous.

In his discussion of the right time in 3:1-4:6 Qoheleth teaches that death is the great equalizer. If one maintains there is a difference between humans and beasts, then it is not evident at the time of death. "For the lot of man and of beast is one lot; the one dies as well as the other. Both have the same life-breath, and man has no advantage over the beast" (3:19). Death, therefore, is the ironic eraser of any distinction between the two.

In 8:1-17 Qoheleth critiques the traditional wisdom on the sage and the king. In vv 12b-13 he repeats the cliché regarding retribution: ". . . I know that it shall be well with those who fear God, for their reverence toward him; and that it shall not be well with the wicked man . . ." But clichés must cede to fact, formulas must yield to experience. For Qoheleth the fact is that "there are just men treated as though they had done evil and wicked men treated as though they had done justly" (v 14). The author's conclusion (v 14) is that these reverses are ironic/incongruous.

GOD'S LIBERTY RESTORED

According to Qoheleth Israel's sages expounded all too neat, facile equations for what he judged to be complex situations. In reacting to these oversimplified versions of human life, Qoheleth implies that these sages are unfaithful to the tradition. They are destroying God's freedom by making the Creator conform to their own prefabricated theological systems. They bind God within the parameters of their school of thought. Although he does not state it explicitly, his thought may be paraphrased this way: how ironic/ incongruous it is that creatures should set limits to the Creator.

As W. Zimmerli has noted, Qoheleth discovers the reality of the Creator more clearly than any other Israelite sage before him. He proclaims this reality by insisting on the dimension of mystery. Hence humans do not/cannot find out what is good to do and they do not know/have knowledge. He also expounds this reality by observing that so many human situations are ironic/incongruous and a chase after wind. However, Qoheleth also suggests a more positive approach, viz., God always acts in freedom.

W. Zimmerli also observes that Qoheleth underlines God's absolute freedom by his use of the verb "to give" (in Hebrew *nātan*). He remarks that Qoheleth employs this verb twelve out of twenty-five times with God as the subject. In 1:13 Qoheleth communicates his mission, viz., to question reality with the help of wisdom. For Qoheleth this is clearly a demanding task, yet God is free to command it: "A thankless task God has appointed (literally 'given') for men to be busied about." On the positive side God is the one who *gives* a limited number of days for humans to enjoy the good things of life (5:17). God is also the one who *gives* humans the breath of life: "and the life breath returns to God who *gave* it" (12:7).

It is no small accomplishment to strike a blow for God's freedom. To insist on God's liberty to give is to insist on God's sovereignty. While the book may create a picture of iconoclasm for some, it is fruitful to reflect on the fact that humans for Qoheleth are in God's image, God is not in humans' image. Qoheleth thereby maintains that the sovereignty of the act of creation—God's demonstration of the ability to give—must be revered and respected in the ongoing-ness of creation. Unlike his opponents, Qoheleth seeks to free God so that the Creator may continue to be God, the giver par excellence.

DIMENSIONS OF HAPPINESS

Qoheleth does not offer any systematic treatment of "the way to happiness." However, throughout his work he suggests different dimensions of life which flow from God's capacity to give. Happiness consists in acknowledging such gifts and living them to the full.

Qoheleth urges a non-manipulative stance towards the good-ness that God provides. It is a question, therefore, of seeing and appreciating. "For every man, moreover, to eat and drink and enjoy the fruit of all his labor (literally: 'to see the good in all his labor') is a gift of God" (3:13). He also connects this advice with the mention of God's freedom: "Here is what I recognize (literally: "see") as good; it is well for a man to eat and drink and enjoy all the fruits of his labor (literally: "to see the good in all his labor") during the limited days of the life which God *gives* him; for this is his lot" (5:17).

Qoheleth also recommends being content and rejoicing. Life is not simply a stiff upper lip test of endurance. "Any man to whom God *gives* riches and property, and grants power to partake of them, so that he receives his lot and finds joy in the fruits of his toil, has a *gift* of God" (5:18). Although there is a great injustice whereby the good are treated as evil and vice versa (see 8:14), still this state of affairs should not restrain the believer from seeking happiness. He must conclude: "Therefore I commend mirth . . ." (8:15).

Part of Qoheleth's recommendations is the awareness that God approves the work of humans. It is one thing to eat and drink, it is another to do so with the realization that God commends human activity: "Go, eat your bread with joy and drink your wine with a merry heart, because it is now that God favors your works" (9:7).

Community is another category that Qoheleth includes in his dimensions of happiness. In a world full of tragedies and disappointments humans should recognize that married love can be a sustaining force. Such love is obviously a gift. "Enjoy life with the woman you love, all the days of the fleeting life that is granted you under the sun" (9:9).

A final aspect of happiness is the ability to cope. It is the recognition that life has both its ups and its downs. To relish the good and sustain the evil is the mark of a believer. It cannot be a question of "I wish it were different!" but "Well, that's the way it is!" Hence Qoheleth advises: "On a good day enjoy good things, and on an evil day consider: Both the one and the other God has made, so that man *cannot find* fault with him in anything" (7:14).

QOHELETH AND THE THEOLOGICAL ADVANTAGES OF THE WISDOM STANCE

Chapter 15 dealt in part with the theological advantages of the wisdom stance. It is perhaps rewarding at this point to assess Qoheleth in that framework. Hopefully response to the Word of God in community can profit from this assessment.

The goal and meaning of life is healthy community life; it is not a matter of surviving but living. For Qoheleth this certainly includes the community of married love (9:9). But it also entails the willingness to contribute one's talents and observations to the community. Authority for life flows from our experience. Qoheleth's use of the ironic/incongruous indicates that experience can be ignored only to one's disadvantage. Humans are responsible for their world. Qoheleth speaks of a world where God's gift-giving and human effort go hand in hand. He endorses not a retreat from reality but the embrace of reality in community. Life is for enjoyment and appreciation.

For Qoheleth eating, drinking, and seeing the good in one's work are the sacraments of divine presence. For Qoheleth these are religious acts which give meaning to the rhythm of life. Finally humans are celebrated as the kings/queens of creation. Although Qoheleth allots the same fate to both humans and beasts (see 3:19), he nonetheless addresses the challenge of creation only to humans. He assumes that only humans can make a difference in providing a more human world.

OVERTURNING COMPLACENCY

The community is not intended to be a gathering of claques who applaud policies and statements merely because authority has endorsed them. Such applause is dehumanizing since it considers authority a fast doctrine dispenser servicing an anonymous public. The community must have its intellectuals and thinkers who seek to serve the common good by acknowledging constructive policies but also by unmasking false clichés. This service is in the tradition of Qoheleth, a tradition that encourages us to label as *hebel* what does not advance healthy community life. At the same time, however, this service is not limited to only intellectuals and thinkers. The entire community should react to policies, principles, doctrines, etc. The development of doctrine implies that the community is more than a spoon-fed entity. In discharging this aspect of criticizing, such members of the community demonstrate their loyalty to the community.

If death is the great equalizer for Qoheleth, then history must be the great equalizer for us. Devotion to the community demands that we know our community's history—not only the glossy pictures in the family album and the beautifully written entries in the family Bible but also the skeletons in the family closet. Knowing that we are the refuge of sinners as well as a holy nation should help in recalling those times when allegiance to the party line meant disaster for many. We must remember the times when the slogans for peace meant only the proliferation of military might and interest in the poor meant only the abolition of needed programs. Ultimately we must be willing to remember the *hebel* of the past and have it bear on the *hebel* of the present.

In the tradition of Qoheleth we are urged to cultivate a genuine taste for the simple yet invaluable dimensions of our living. Thus eating and drinking must be more than the nourishment of our bodies; they must become the art of cultivating community, especially in the family circle. Married love must also be prized for what it is, viz., the response to the Creator for the goodness of another and the recognition of that value in daily living. Working, holding a job must be more than the acquisition of so much money. It must

181

also be the acceptance of meeting the needs of others. People-oriented jobs alone satisfy.

The tradition of Qoheleth points in the direction of gift-giving. That tradition demands that we view eating/drinking, marriage, work, etc., as gifts from the Creator. It further entails that we see the gift-giving of the Creator in other people. To recognize a gift as a gift is to continue the chorus of Genesis: "It is good, very good!" Gratitude is still our most important product.

The world of Qoheleth must impinge on our celebration of Eucharist. Here we eat and drink and retell the story of God's greatest gift, viz., the giving of his Son in death. In this setting we hear the Word that rejects all *hebel*. In this setting we also identify ourselves and others as members of the community who are called upon to put aside all pretense and to address reality. The viability of our sign of peace is demonstrated outside the Church where we seek to relate to others as gifts from our God and people deserving of honesty and sincerity. Eucharist is the sign of the leveling of all *hebel*; it is the symbol of the end of all chases after wind.

BIBLIOGRAPHICAL SUGGESTIONS

Bickerman, Elias. *Four Strange Books of the Bible.* New York: Schocken, 1962, 139-167.

Crenshaw, James L. "Popular Questioning of the Justice of God in Ancient Israel," *ZAW* 82 (1970) 380-395 = *Studies in Ancient Israelite Wisdom,* 289-304.

—————— . "The Eternal Gospel (Eccl. 3:11)," *Essays in Old Testament Ethics.* Edited by J. L. Crenshaw & J. T. Willis. New York: Ktav, 1974, 25-55.

Good, Edwin M. "Qoheleth: The Limits of Wisdom," *Irony in the Old Testament.* Philadelphia: Westminster, 1965, 168-195.

Gordis, Robert. *Koheleth—The Man and His World.* New York: Schocken, 1967.

Johnston, Robert K. "Confessions of a Workaholic: A Reappraisal of Qoheleth," *CBQ* 38 (1976) 14-28.

Murphy, Roland E. *Seven Books of Wisdom.* Milwaukee: Bruce, 1960, 87-103.

Polk, Timothy. "The Wisdom of Irony: A Study of *Hebel* and Its Relation to Joy and the Fear of God in Ecclesiastes," *Studia Biblica et Theologica* 6, #1 (March, 1976) 3-17.

Priest, John F. "Humanism, Skepticism, and Pessimism in Israel," *JAAR* 36 (1968) 311-326.

—————— . "Ecclesiastes," *IDBSup,* 249-250.

Rad, Gerhard von. *Wisdom in Israel.* New York: Abingdon, 1972, 226-239.

Scott, Robert B. Y. *Proverbs and Ecclesiastes.* AB. Garden City: Doubleday, 1965, 189-257.

Sheppard, Gerald T. "The Epilogue to Qoheleth as Theological Commentary," *CBQ* 39 (1977) 182-187.

Whitley, Charles F. *Koheleth*. BZAW. New York: de Gruyter, 1979.

Whybray, Roger N. "Qoheleth the Immoralist?" *Israelite Wisdom: Theological and Literary Essays in Honor of Samuel Terrien*. Edited by J. G. Gammie et al. New York: Union Theological Seminary, 1978, 191-204.

Williams, James G. "'What Does It Profit a Man?' The Wisdom of Koheleth," *Judaism* 20 (1971) 179-193 = *Studies in Ancient Israelite Wisdom*, 375-389.

Wright, Addison G. "The Riddle of the Sphinx: The Structure of the Book of Qoheleth," *CBQ* 30 (1968) 313-334 = *Studies in Ancient Israelite Wisdom*, 245-266.

_____ . "The Riddle of the Sphinx Revisited: Numerical Patterns in the Book of Qoheleth," *CBQ* 42 (1980) 38-51.

Zimmerli, Walther. "The Place and Limit of the Wisdom in the Framework of the Old Testament," *Scottish Journal of Theology* 17 (1964) 146-158, esp. 155-158 = *Studies in Ancient Israelite Wisdom*, 314-326, esp. 323-326.

Zimmermann, Frank. *The Inner World of Qohelet*. New York: Ktav, 1973.

CHAPTER 18

The Invitation to Jonah

Biblical passages to be read: the Book of Jonah.

STORY OF A WHALE OR WHALE OF A STORY?

We may be prone to laughter when we read the Book of Jonah where idiosyncrasies abound. The three-day and three-night hostel is indeed an odd place. A sea monster swallows the prophet alive and then regurgitates him safe and sound. The prophet himself is no less of a curiosity. Whereas in the other books of the minor prophets the emphasis is on the prophet's words and not his life (Am 7:10-17 is an exception), the Book of Jonah has only one small prophetic saying (3:4) and is otherwise an account of the prophet's adventures. While we realize that prophets may be somewhat reluctant to accept their calling, e.g., Jeremiah (see Jer 1:6), only Jonah goes to the greatest lengths to evade the all-present God of Israel. We feel assured that this book is a quaint addition to an otherwise balanced selection of biblical literature.

However, if we limit our questioning to the story of a whale or a whale of a story, we actually avoid the message of the author. The right question is really: do we recognize ourselves in Jonah? are we after all a latter-day version of the prophet who copped out? Response to the Word of God in community obliges us to examine our consciences and inquire if we determine precisely how our God should act. Do we curtail the biblical message to cater to our own theological constructs? Do we make our God in Jonah's image, i.e., a God who is programmed to respond with maximum efficiency and, at the same time, maximum intolerance? Is our God the object of intractable theological equations who cannot break through our inhuman impositions to exercise the prerogative of grace? Is there always just one way to go with ourselves as the divinely appointed guardians of the travel conditions? Are we more Jonah and less Yahweh? A sound spirituality of the Old Testament invites us to a more serious reading of this intriguing yet demanding book.

BACKGROUND

The author takes his principal character from 2 Kgs 14:25. In that passage Jonah is the son of Amittai from Gath-hepher in Galilee who preached a message of hope during the prosperous days of Jeroboam II. His contemporary was Amos, who proclaimed the destruction of the northern kingdom—a proclamation vindicated by the overthrow of Samaria by the neo-Assyrians in 722 B.C. By making "Jonah" the name of the principal character, the author forces his audience to think of the eighth century B.C. prophet. The message is now one of hope and forgiveness for the city of Nineveh, the neo-Assyrian capital from the beginning of the eighth century B.C. Since the neo-Assyrians were the quintessence of brutality and oppression to God's people, Jonah's mission is tantamount to folly, if not contradiction (see Zep 2:13-15; Jdt 1:1 as well as the Book of Nahum). By choosing Nineveh, the author has deliberately opted to focus on the worst form of pagan life.

The idiosyncrasies already mentioned are enough to indicate that the author does not intend to write sober history. The question of the literary genre of the book has evoked a variety of answers: allegory, parable, satire, short story, short story in the form of a parable, satirical/didactic short story. The patterns demanded by an allegory for uncovering the hidden or figurative meanings of the account are not evident. While Jonah is didactic after the manner of a parable, it differs from a parable by focusing on an "historical" personage. The most balanced approach is to label Jonah a short story. It is a short story that combines satire and also intends to teach, especially through the questions (see 1:6, 8, 10, 11; 4:4, 9, 11). The author also borrows from the figure of the prophet Elijah who also fled and sought to end his life (see 1 Kgs 19:4). Rather than a quaint short story appended to the more serious pieces in the biblical collection, the Jonah short story is a significant theological contribution.

In writing about Jonah, the author is writing about his audience. Like Jonah, that audience is copping out, refusing to cope with reality. As T. E. Fretheim puts it, the audience is given over to self-pity and indulges in anger. Such a description has led not a few exegetes to regard the book as a statement of universalism, especially in the light of the narrow nationalism sponsored by Ezra and Nehemiah. Thus

Israel excludes no one from God's concern, not even the hated Nine-vites. Others see the book as an endorsement of the doctrine of repentance as expounded by, e.g., Jer 18:1-10 and Ez 18:21. Hence if people will change, God in turn will change.

By making Nineveh the object of God's concern and forgiveness, the author seems to be treating a much more radical problem, viz., God's absolute right to give. Jonah is, therefore, the short story form of Qoheleth's wisdom. It seeks to vindicate God's freedom and sovereignty, especially when these prerogatives are endangered by a theology of rigid conformity. As T. E. Fretheim has observed, Jonah is a parade example of God's freedom to be compassionate. The hated Ninevites, the acme of inhumanity, can also be recipients of God's boundless giftedness, a giftedness not to be measured by human restrictions.

Those who see Jonah as a response to the nationalistic policies of Ezra and Nehemiah (cir. 450-400 B.C.), place the work in the late fifth or early fourth century B.C. Those who link the book to the doctrine of repentance associated with Jeremiah and Ezekiel opt for a date in the postexilic period of the late sixth century B.C. However, if one accepts the description of the audience as angry and self-pitying as well as reluctant to accept the implications of divine liberty, then a date around 475-450 B.C. is tenable. Such a date would make the author of Jonah a contemporary of the prophet Malachi. The questions raised by Malachi's audience (see Mal 1:2-5; 2:17; 3:14-15) are not unlike those posed by Jonah's audience.

GO EAST, YOUNG MAN, GO EAST

God instructs Jonah to proceed east to Nineveh and preach against it (1:2). Instead, the prophet proceeds to Joppa, the modern Jaffa, and there boards a ship going west to Tarshish (1:3), located on the southwestern coast of Spain and reputed to be a place of luxury and security (see Is 66:19; Ez 27:12). The geography articulates the attitude of Jonah. Rather than preach God's Word to the hated Ninevites, he chooses to evade his mission by seeking the relative security of Tarshish. The flight is a flight from God, a violent reaction to a theology of divine freedom, as chap. 4 indicates.

The structure of chap. 1 is significant since the author will employ the same in chap. 2. The first element is a crisis, here in the form of a storm (1:4). The second element is the response to the crisis, here the sailors' prayer: "'We beseech you, O Lord, let us not perish for taking this man's life . . .'" (1:14). The third element is God's reaction, viz., the cessation of the storm (1:15). The fourth and final element is the recognition of Yahweh's intervention, here the vows and sacrifices of the sailors (1:16).

In this chapter the author uses fear to great advantage. In 1:5 the sailors experience fear because of the violent storm. When they discover that Jonah has occasioned the storm, they interrogate him (1:8). The prophet's answer is to recite his Israelite faith: "'I worship ("fear" in Hebrew) the Lord, the God of heaven, who made the sea and the dry land'" (1:9). In 1:10 the sailors manifest great fear since they connect the storm with Jonah's dereliction of duty. Finally in 1:16 this great fear moves them to offer sacrifices and make vows at the abating of the storm. In this scene the pagan sailors advance in faith, i.e., they realize Yahweh's involvement in the storm and acknowledge it by prayer and sacrifice. Only the prophet has refused to change his attitude. The pagans are more believers, God-fearers, than Jonah.

In this chapter the author capitalizes on the verb "to throw." In 1:4 Yahweh throws a violent wind upon the sea. This, in turn, forces the sailors to throw their cargo into the sea in order to lighten their vessel (1:5). Realizing that his own conduct has brought on the storm, the prophet urges in 1:12: "'Pick me up and throw me into the sea, that it may quiet down for you . . .'" After their prayer the sailors take Jonah's suggestion seriously and throw him into the sea. The result is that the storm abates (1:15). Throwing captures the author's theological stance. It is an action that symbolizes God's determination to provide a preacher for the Ninevites. At the same time the action also demonstrates God's need of Jonah.

Irony is also in evidence in this chapter. There is, first of all, the prophet's sleep in the midst of a violent storm. Jonah's slumber demonstrates his complete rejection of the divine plan and mission. Secondly, there is the contrast between the actions of the pagans and the Israelite prophet. While the pagans are planning a prayer service because of the storm, Jonah refuses to become involved in their efforts at placating the author of the storm. While the pagans exemplify piety, the prophet manifests only indifference.

In Jonah's actions the author reflects the attitude of his audience. Jonah does not object to the pagan sailors' efforts to obtain divine mercy and compassion. However, he does object—and with the greatest violence—to Yahweh's efforts to show divine mercy and compassion to the hated Ninevites. Jonah, and hence the audience, would have God consult the record book and determine the enormity of Nineveh's sin. This determination should then check Yahweh's forgiveness. Jonah's God must make the punishment fit the crime at all costs. The author's God must make humans release their strangle hold on divine operations.

In chap. 2 the author employs the same structure as in chap. 1. The prophet experiences a crisis, viz., the threat of death (2:3). He responds to this crisis like the pagan sailors: "From the belly of the fish Jonah said this prayer to the Lord, his God . . ." (2:2). The Lord then reacts to Jonah's prayer by delivering him from this mortal danger (2:7). Finally Jonah recognizes the Lord's intervention by sacrifices and vows (2:10).

Yahweh is the giver of gifts. While the great fish captures the reader's imagination, it should also provoke the reader's understanding. The great fish is the instrument of divine freedom. The author expresses this by using a verb that will later appear in chap. 4, i.e., the verb "to appoint": "But the Lord appointed (rather than NAB's "sent") a large fish, that swallowed Jonah . . ." (2:1). Yahweh chooses to appoint a large fish simply because Yahweh is Yahweh.

The psalm in 2:3-10 contrasts with the prose of the rest of the account. Several authors suggest that the psalm is a work of a later author. They urge that prayer is not in keeping with Jonah's character—here Jonah is too much a man of faith. Moreover the vocabulary and style are significantly different from the prose sections. In response to these objections G. M. Landes has shown how the structure of the psalm fits the structure of chap. 1. Jonah's prayer in this instance is in keeping with his character since it is a prayer for himself, not others. It is quite likely that the author of Jonah made use of a pre-existing psalm and worked it into his narrative. Such a procedure would account for the differences in vocabulary and style. Ultimately this means that Jonah praying in the belly of the fish is really the author's audience adjudicating the cases of divine deliverance. While Jonah and the audience are sincere believers, they are violent believers.

The psalm is a psalm of declarative praise that celebrates newness, viz., God's intervention on behalf of the psalmist. As such, it is an ironic type of prayer. The psalm of declarative praise proclaims God's radical capacity to give; it is a newness that does not flow from ordinary cause and effect. The author captures this in 2:10 when the prophet is made to sing: "deliverance is from the Lord." Although lacking all claims on God's compassion in this predicament, Jonah experiences compassion. This is precisely the experience he will deny to the Ninevites. It is one thing for Jonah to know such compassion personally, it is another thing for Yahweh to extend such compassion to the sinful Ninevites. Jonah has created a false image: Yahweh is in his image.

The author has adjusted the psalm to meet the needs of his story. In 2:4 the psalm speaks of drowning: "For you cast me into the deep, into the heart of the sea, and the flood enveloped me; all your breakers and your billows passed over me." For the original psalmist this drowning could have symbolized sickness, enemies, frustration, etc. However, the author of Jonah has taken it literally in order to make it fit the plight of the prophet. As a result, he has implicated the pagan sailors in a possible drowning death. At the same time he has also involved Jonah in a prayerful reaction that clashes with his effort to elude Yahweh. The prophet who seeks to flee *from* the presence of the Lord directs his prayer *to* the temple presence of the Lord: "When my soul fainted within me, I remembered the Lord; my prayer reached you in your holy temple" (2:9). Distress is the great leveller of many theological positions.

In 2:11-3:3a there is compliance at last. The great fish spews Jonah up on the shore (2:11) and the prophet receives the command to proceed to Nineveh for a second time (3:2) There follows the laconic statement: "So Jonah made ready and went to Nineveh, according to the Lord's bidding" (3:3). The author, however, leaves his audience with a number of questions. Has the experience at sea really changed the prophet? Because of his own deliverance is the prophet now prepared to accept the deliverance of the Ninevites? Will the prophet who energetically besought the Lord for his own needs (2:3) beseech the Lord as energetically for the needs of the city of Nineveh? Has there really been a change in Jonah?

THE SUCCESS OF THE WORD

The author's structural elements in 3:3b-10 (which will reappear in chap. 4) are similar to those in chaps. 1 and 2. In 3:4 there is a crisis situation, viz., the threatened destruction of Nineveh (3:4). The Ninevites respond to this crisis by a dramatic conversion (3:5-8). In turn Yahweh reacts to this conversion by cancelling his plans to destroy the city: "When God saw by their actions how they turned from their evil way, he repented of the evil that he had threatened to do to them; he did not carry it out" (3:10).

The author indulges in some exaggeration in order to dramatize the success of the proclamation. A three-day walk through Nineveh (3:3) would involve something like fifty miles. In the Nineveh of Sennacherib's time (704-681 B.C.) a one-day walk would have put Jonah well beyond the center of the city. The element of exaggeration, however, is not limited to the prophet's trek. It includes the terseness of the message: "'Forty days more and Nineveh shall be destroyed'" (3:4). Using only five Hebrew words, the author captures the heinousness of the populace and yet their total change of heart.

190

The verb translated "destroyed" in the NAB is the verb "to over-throw," the classical expression for the annihilation of the cities of Sodom and Gomorrah (see Gn 19:21, 25, 29). However, the same verb can also mean a change of heart, as when Saul was changed into another man in 1 Sm 10:6, 9.

The response of the populace is overwhelming. Although he covered only one third of the city, Jonah experiences a massive con-version. The brief message moves not only the commoners but also the king himself. In fact, the practice of penance extends to the animals. According to the king's command "'neither man nor beast, neither cattle nor sheep, shall taste anything; they shall not eat, nor shall they drink water'" (3:7). Like the sailors of chap. 1, the Nine-vites are models of repentance. And to think that all this occurred because Jonah reluctantly carried out his mission!

God's reaction is a study in divine freedom. Faced with the re-sponse of the city, God decides upon compassion rather than anni-hilation. Such compassion is not an expression of love which is due to the Ninevites. As the king remarks in 3:9, "'who knows, God may relent and forgive . . .'" Deliverance is the result of divine free-dom, not human cause and effect. This is an object lesson that the unyielding prophet has yet to learn.

JONAH VERSUS YAHWEH

The structure of chap. 4 matches that of 3:3b-10. There is the crisis situation resulting from the saving of Nineveh. Jonah responds to this situation by becoming angry: "But this was greatly displeasing to Jonah and he became angry" (4:1). The Lord finally reacts to Jonah's anger by attempting to budge him from his entrenched theological position. Although the pagan Ninevites manifest a total change of heart, the believing Israelite is reluctant to show even a partial change of heart.

What Jonah feared all along has transpired. According to 4:2 the flight to Tarshish in chap. 1 was not the prophet's first attempt to escape the precariousness of divine freedom. He readily recites Israel's faith: "'a gracious and merciful God, slow to anger, rich in clemency, loathe to punish'" (4:3; see also Ex 34:6; Nm 14:18-19). However, Jonah cannot bring himself to see such compassion demon-strated in favor of the Ninevites. According to the prophet one must set reasonable limits to the display of mercy. Otherwise, he fears, there is no effective control. The averting of destruction is, for the prophet, an instructive example of lack of control. The God made in Jonah's image must practice restraint.

Whereas Jonah responded to his deliverance from the belly of the fish with sacrifices and vows (2:10), he cannot countenance any expression of rejoicing now. In fact, he seeks death: "'And now, Lord, please take my life from me, for it is better for me to die than to live'" (4:3; see 1 Kgs 19:4). Whereas all the pagans—captain, sailors, king, and Ninevites—sought life in the face of death, this believer seeks death in the face of life. Jonah's warped theological values do not permit him to rejoice with those who rejoice.

Yahweh's question in 4:4 ("'Have you reason to be angry?'") is an assault on Jonah's flimsy theology. The question assumes that Jonah's anger is a prejudging of divine compassion. The question also presupposes that Jonah's thought process is as follows: if God has overstepped the bounds of decorum and propriety by such a precarious show of mercy, then Jonah will adjust such irrational behavior by making the punishment fit the crime. In Jonah's view and hence in the audience's view Yahweh must exercise greater restraint. Otherwise the whole theological system is endangered.

Jonah refuses to give up. He moves farther east and builds a hut to provide shade from the sun. He hopes that he will yet see the end of the city from this vantage point. However, Yahweh also refuses to give up, devising a plan not simply to undo the prophet's hut but to tear down his prefabricated theology. The plan focuses on the gourd plant, i.e., a wide-leaved plant belonging to either the cucumber or castor-bean species.

The author captures the essence of divine freedom by dwelling on the verb "to appoint" (translated "to provide" in 4:6 and "to send" in 4:7, 8 of the NAB). In 4:6 Yahweh appoints a gourd plant and elicits a reaction of joy from the prophet. In 4:7 Yahweh appoints a worm to attack the plant and in 4:8 appoints a burning east wind to let the hot wind come pouring through the opening in Jonah's hut. By these actions Yahweh now elicits a reaction of anger from the prophet, an anger that only death can placate (4:9). God's question is once again a blow for divine freedom: "'Have you reason to be angry over the plant?'" (4:9). The question implies that Jonah has absolutely no right to foist his theological presuppositions on Yahweh.

In 4:10-11 the author discusses his view of divine gift-giving. The gourd plant symbolizes Yahweh's radical ability to give; it is something to which the prophet can advance no claim. Yet Jonah would place the loss of the plant on the same level as the loss of the city of Nineveh. "Then the Lord said, 'You are concerned over the plant which cost you no labor and which you did not raise; it came up in one night and in one night it perished. And should I not be concerned over Nineveh ... ?'" (4:10-11). While some commentators interpret the 120,000 of 4:11 as children, both the text ("persons") and context suggest referring the number to the adult population of the city who, like children, are unable to make their own judgments. Hence the pitiable situation of the Ninevites is all the more reason to prefer the city to the plant.

MODERN JONAHS

Are we the measuring stick of divine freedom? Are we the line of demarcation of divine gift-giving? Response to the Word of God in community cannot evade such questions. These questions presume a latent human tendency to play God and determine the rules of the game. The questions further presume the devious human quality to take a shallow look at ourselves and make our own shallowness the norm of divine generosity. Jonah is indeed alive and well in our midst.

The Book of Jonah is the death of such statements as "Well, it simply can't be done!" It is the biblical book that decries slogans such as "Well, there's just one way to go!" More fundamentally, it is the inspired work that must force us to take a long, hard look at our God and only then at ourselves. We are challenged not only to recite with Jonah: "'. . . you are a gracious and merciful God, slow to anger, rich in clemency, loathe to punish'" (4:2). We are also challenged to live out the implications of this statement in community living. The God of the author of the book is a most ecumenical God transcending the barriers erected by humans to manipulate divine love and mercy.

The sign of Jonah means the death of human prejudice and the resurrection of divine grace. It finds its clearest expression in the experience of Jesus. The death-resurrection of Jesus is the most profound symbol of divine gift-giving. The Risen Lord is the assurance that there can be no limitations placed on the Father's generosity. The empty tomb represents the plenitude of divine freedom.

BIBLIOGRAPHICAL SUGGESTIONS

Ackerman, James S. "Satire and Symbolism in the Song of Jonah," *Traditions in Transformation. Turning Points in Biblical Faith*. Edited by B. Halpern & J. D. Levenson. Winona Lake: Eisenbrauns, 1981, 213-246.

Bickerman, Elias. *Four Strange Books of the Bible*. New York: Schocken, 1962, 1-49.

Burrows, Millar. "The Literary Category of the Book of Jonah," *Translating and Understanding the Old Testament*. Edited by H. T. Frank and W. O. Reed. New York: Abingdon, 1970, 80-107.

Clements, Ronald E. "The Purpose of the Book of Jonah," *VTS* 28 (1975) 16-28.

Craghan, John F. *Esther, Judith, Tobit, Jonah, Ruth*. Old Testament Message. Wilmington: Michael Glazier, 1982, 163-193.

Fretheim, Terence E. *The Message of Jonah. A Theological Commentary*. Minneapolis: Augsburg, 1977.

Fretheim, Terence E. "Jonah and Theodicy," *ZAW* 90 (1978) 227-237.

Gaster, Theodor H. *Myth, Legend, and Custom in the Old Testament.* New York: Harper & Row, 1969, 652-656, 724-725.

Good, Edwin M. "Jonah: The Absurdity of God," *Irony in the Old Testament.* Philadelphia: Westminster, 1965, 39-55.

Landes, George M. "The Kerygma of the Book of Jonah," *Int* 21 (1967) 3-31.

_____ . "Three Days and Three Nights Motif in Jonah 2:1," *JBL* 86 (1967) 446-450.

_____ . "Jonah, Book of," *IDBSup,* 488-491.

_____ . "Jonah: A *Māšāl?*" *Israelite Wisdom: Theological and Literary Essays in Honor of Samuel Terrien.* Edited by J. G. Gammie et al. New York: Union Theological Seminary, 1978, 137-158.

Miles, John A., Jr. "Laughing at the Bible," *Jewish Quarterly Review* 65 (1974-1975) 168-181.

Pelli, Moshe. "The Literary Art of Jonah," *Hebrew Studies* 20/21 (1979-1980) 18-28.

Stek, John H. "Message of the Book of Jonah," *Calvin Theological Journal* 4 (1969) 23-50.

Warshaw, Thayer S. "The Book of Jonah," *Literary Interpretations of Biblical Narratives.* Edited by K. R. R. Gros Louis et al. New York: Abingdon, 1974, 191-207.

Wolff, Hans W. *Jonah: Church in Revolt.* St. Louis: Clayton, 1979.

CHAPTER 19

The Invitation to Esther, Judith and Ruth

Biblical passages to be read: the Book of Ruth; Jdt 8-16; the Book of Esther with the exclusion of the deuterocanonical additions.

BIBLICAL WOMEN AND PARADIGMS FOR HUMAN LIBERATION

In the canon there are only three books that bear the name of a woman as their title, viz., Esther, Judith, and Ruth. At the same time the thrust of these books and hence of these women is liberation of one type or another. Against the background of the "new hermeneutic" the following questions may be raised: with whom should we identify? what does the text mean now? what is the world in which we are invited to be not spectators but participants? In his study of Isaiah 53, D. J. A. Clines suggests that there is a multiplicity of interpretations because the text is open-ended. Thus the reader is able to enter the world of the poem and identify with the "personae" of the poem, i.e., by assuming one of the several roles presented.

We are challenged to reflect on the qualities of human liberation as they are found in the figures of Esther, Judith, Ruth, and, to a certain extent, Naomi. These figures serve as our paradigms, i.e., according to G. Lindbeck they increase rather than limit our ability to deal with our world. They are patterns from the past that offer present hope in coping with future problems. Response to the Word of God in community demands that we reassess these patterns in order to address our task of human liberation.

THE SETTING OF LIBERATION

A politics of oppression and exploitation calls for liberation. This implies the challenge: is it possible to set up a genuine alternative community? The task of the liberator is to strike a blow for God's freedom, even when the name of God is not even mentioned as in Hebrew Esther. (This study of Esther will not include the so-called deuterocanonical additions, i.e., six passages in Greek which, for example, attribute prayers to Esther and Mordecai and cite documents to increase the historical stature of the account.)

In Esther oppression and exploitation find expression in the notion of irrevocable decrees. According to 1:19 the laws of the Medes and the Persians (see Dn 6:9, 13, 16) cannot be undone. The first decree in Esther concerns the demise of Vashti (1:19). The reason for the decree is given in 1:18: "'This very day the Persian and Median ladies who hear of the queen's conduct will rebel against all the royal officials, with corresponding disdain and rancor.'" In 1:20 the Persian official is confident that the decree will make wives honor their husbands.

The court intrigue between Haman and Mordecai has links with the Joseph Story and Daniel 2-6. In Esther the biblical basis of the antagonism is the ongoing feud between Mordecai the Benjaminite and Haman the Amalekite. Exploitation demands not simply the death of Mordecai but of all the Jews (3:6). Accordingly an irrevocable decree is drawn up that guarantees the slaughter of all the Jews in the Persian Empire (3:9, 13). Ironically the fate of the Jews is determined on the day before Passover (3:12).

The irrevocable decree is also present in the prohibition under penalty of death to appear before the king unsummoned (4:8, 11). Esther, who has not been summoned to the king in thirty days (4:11), chooses to disobey and thus run the risk of death. In Esther liberation means bravado and the understanding that laws can be legitimately challenged. The object of liberation is not the undoing of the vacillating Ahasuerus but a frontal attack on such legislation, although that necessarily entails the demise of Haman.

Finally the Jews gain the upper hand. By reverse logic Mordecai becomes one of the untouchables. As Zeresh and the advisers inform Haman, "'If Mordecai . . . is of the Jewish race, you will not prevail against him, but will surely be defeated by him'" (6:13). In order to undo the decree ordering the annihilation, Ahasuerus permits Esther and Mordecai to write a letter in his name, noting, "'For whatever is written in the name of the king and sealed with the royal signet cannot be revoked'" (8:8). Liberation calls for undoing the irrevocable by a counter irrevocable.

The setting of liberation in Judith entails a study of the literary genre. E. Haag has suggested a phenomenological study of the figure of Nebuchadnezzar. In the light of such texts as Ex 5:1-2; Is 10:7-11, 32-33; 47:10-11, etc., Nebuchadnezzar and the Assyrians have a suprahistorical character. In Jdt 3:8; 6:2 Nebuchadnezzar lays claim to the same prerogatives as Yahweh: no other deity may be tolerated. Nebuchadnezzar is thereby the quintessence of opposition to Yahweh. For Haag, Judith is a free parabolic presentation of history, dealing with the ideal characterization of Israel's resistance to the anti-Yahweh.

E. Zenger has developed Haag's approach. He connects the deliverance from Sennacherib and the neo-Assyrians in 701 B.C. (see 2 Kgs 18-19; Is 36-37; and especially 2 Chr 32:1-23) with Yahweh's action against Egypt in the Exodus. The fight between Holofernes and Judith is really between Pharaoh and Yahweh.

Judith's task is to strike a blow for God's liberty: "'For if he does not wish to come to our aid within the five days, he has it equally within his power to protect us . . . or to destroy us'" (8:15). As P. Skehan perceived, Judith's hand is really Yahweh's hand in the Exodus experience. The canticle in Jdt 16:1-12 is the new Song of the Sea in Ex 15:1-18. The divine Nebuchadnezzar like Pharaoh can be matched and defeated. Indeed, according to Jdt 9:7, 11, powerlessness is the most potent weapon against the Assyrian war machine, for Yahweh is the helper of the oppressed and the supporter of the weak. Liberation in Judith means the dedeification of Pharaoh/Nebuchadnezzar, not the revoking of the irrevocable decrees of the Medes and the Persians as in Esther.

While Esther deals with a pogrom and Judith proves the metahistorical, typical stance against all oppression, Ruth has to do with the seemingly trivial occurrences of a family: famine, bereavement, gleaning, the search for a husband, the desire for a family, the birth of a child, etc. However, the setting of liberation is nonetheless real. The male dominated society makes the lives of women, especially widows, and more especially childless widows, most precarious. This is demonstrated by the unnamed redeemer's reluctance in 4:5-6 to take Ruth as his wife because of fear of depreciating his estate. The setting of liberation is ultimately Ruth's resolution to cling to Naomi and not abandon her. More specifically, the setting of liberation is the determination of the women to have the prayers of covenant support and fidelity (Hebrew *ḥesed*) reduced to reality, e.g., Boaz's prayer in 2:12 that Ruth receive a full reward from Yahweh. The setting of liberation in Ruth is the quest for the *gō'ēl*.

LAMENTATION

The public expression of hurt is the first step in the effort to overcome the irrevocability of decrees, a suprahistorical war machine, or the lack of a husband or *gō'ēl*. Given Israel's history, we are not surprised to see it interpreted as an experience of cry and rescue. Although the Exodus pattern does not fit all the material contained in these books, it is obvious that Israel's self-understanding is rooted in the experience of oppression and exploitation in thirteenth century B.C. Egypt.

Upon learning of the decree, Mordecai does both the expected and the unexpected. Rending one's clothes, putting on sackcloth, and sprinkling ashes were traditional ways of giving expression to pain and frustration (see Gn 37:34; 2 Kgs 18:37). According to Hebrew Esther, he cries out but not to Yahweh (4:1-2). Similarly in the provinces the Jews undertake a fast, but not unto the Lord (4:3). The author's intent is to underline the part to be played by God's people, especially Esther. In order to overcome exploitation and oppression there must be a public outcry to which humans are invited to interact. In Esther, lamentation means provoking human response.

Esther and her maids also express their pain in fasting (4:16). However, their fast contains a glimmer of hope and hence of Esther's success in approaching the king. Whereas the fast in the provinces (4:3) is resignation, Esther's fast is a certain confidence that human response will be forthcoming.

In Judith the Judeans become greatly alarmed at Holofernes' retaliation against the insubordinate nations: "They were in extreme dread of him, and greatly alarmed for Jerusalem and the temple of the Lord, their God" (4:2). When the Assyrian forces encamp outside Bethulia, God's people are in great dismay (7:4). Realizing that they are surrounded, they cry out to the Lord (7:19; see 6:18-19). In her prayer in chap. 9 Judith culminates the anguish of her people. In her lament she presupposes that Israel's problem has now become God's problem. At the same time liberation demands that Bethulia's problem is also her own problem. Lamentation in Judith, therefore, has greater insistence than in Esther on the need for divine help.

In the Book of Ruth, Naomi vents her emotions against the Lord. The Lord has turned against her and thereby ruled out all possible avenues of her regaining any identity (1:11-13). In recommending the change of name from Naomi ("pleasant") to Mara ("bitter"), she charges the Lord with infidelity to the terms of the covenant: "'Why should you call me Naomi, since the Lord has pronounced against me and the Almighty (Shaddai) has brought evil upon me?'" (1:21). The punishment meted out by Shaddai is by definition unjust. While the grief in Ruth is not the result of a forthcoming pogrom or the imminence of military attack, it is nonetheless real. Since the lamentation is directed to Yahweh in Ruth, it is, therefore, close to that in Judith, although the setting is less dramatic.

In all three books lamentation is calculated to expose the human predicament and hence human weakness. The question it spontaneously suggests is: who will emerge as leader?

THE EMERGENCE OF THE LEADER

In 2:7 Esther is introduced for the first time. Her credentials are not imposing: she is an orphan and ward of cousin Mordecai. She takes no initiative since her cousin makes all the decisions, including telling her to conceal her Jewish ancestry. During the course of the beauty contest Mordecai constantly seeks information about her progress (2:11). The author notes in 2:9 that Esther pleased Hegai, the custodian of the women. The Hebrew text may imply that Esther actively provoked Hegai's favor.

When the plot against the king is discovered in chap. 2, Esther merely serves as the go-between for Mordecai and Ahasuerus: "she informed the king for Mordecai" (2:22). In 4:16 Esther begins to emerge as a leader. Instead of taking orders, she gives orders to Mordecai to assemble all the Jews in Susa. Instead of being the pliable, obliging Hadassah, the queen is now in charge. The author clearly indicates this new relationship in 4:17 when he notes that Mordecai did everything as Esther had ordered him.

Her leadership qualities are evident in chap. 5 when she chooses to disregard the law about appearing before the king unsummoned. It seems more the self-assurance of the queen rather than the generosity of the king that effects the touch of the golden scepter. Only the queen is now capable of defusing the explosive situation.

In 7:7 Esther refuses Haman's request for leniency. Here she appears not so much ruthless as determined, not so much pitiless as inflexible. Although Haman is conniving and Ahasuerus vacillating, Esther follows the inexorable course dictated by the common good. She is not only a queen but an admirable leader.

In chap. 8 Esther controls the destiny of her cousin and former guardian. She hands over to Mordecai the property that once belonged to Haman. In the same chapter she uses all of her feminine charm to undo the irrevocable decree. Finally in 9:11-14 she obtains two more favors from the king: (1) she has the defensive war extended for one day in Susa; and (2) she wins the king's permission to have Haman's ten sons hanged. At this time it is only too clear that Esther is more than the winner of a beauty contest. She is the incontestable leader of her people. In Esther, therefore, the emergence of the leader is a gradual but rewarding process.

At first glance Judith's credentials are not imposing. She is a widow, although a wealthy one. However, any doubt about her leadership qualities is soon dispelled when she sends her maid in 8:10 to summon Uzziah and the two elders and then proceeds to lecture

199

them. In 8:29 Uzziah remarks that this is but another display of her wisdom—a wisdom long recognized by the people. As L. Alonso Schökel has pointed out, the author reverses the foolish woman/wise old man motif, viz., that the foolish woman has clearly outwitted the wise old man.

The beauty process in 10:2-4 is really a disguise. In R. B. Coote's view Judith is actually a female warrior who has mapped out her military strategy and concealed her weapon, viz., her beauty. Thus the female sets out to rescue the male, using the most effective weapon —beauty. In the person of Judith a female warrior will invade the camp of the world's greatest male warrior.

In her first speech with Holofernes in 11:5-19 Judith assures him that the Jews will not repel him but that death will overtake them (11:11). At this point the challenged one has become the challenger, the timid one, an object of fear. Similarly in the death scene (13:7, 9) Judith strikes twice—hardly what one would expect of a weak woman. In taking the canopy from its supports, Judith reverses roles. At their first meeting (10:21) Holofernes was lying under the canopy. Now Judith tumbles his body off the bed and pulls down the canopy. In 14:1-4 Judith assumes control of the army and begins to deploy her troops. Like Deborah, however, she does not take part in the actual military effort. In the same chapter she has Achior summoned. Though the wise man par excellence, Achior did not succeed in convincing Holofernes. Where Achior failed, Judith succeeded. Again the foolish woman/wise old man motif emerges. The canticle (16:5) summarizes the hand motif developed by P. Skehan: "'. . . by a woman's hand she confounded them.'" Or more simply in the words of Bagoas: "'A single Hebrew woman has brought disgrace on the house of King Nebuchadnezzar'" (14:18).

In Judith, therefore, the part played by the leading character is not as gradual as in Esther. According to 8:29 Judith was long recognized for her wisdom.

In the Book of Ruth, Naomi shares the leadership role with her daughter-in-law, although Ruth eventually is center stage, especially in chap. 3. In 1:6-22 it is apparent that the women are now in charge. For example, as P. Trible has noted, Naomi is no longer identified in terms of her husband and sons but in her own right. She is now the subject of a sentence and the initiator of action.

P. Trible observes Ruth's emergence in Boaz's two questions. In 2:5 he asks the overseer of the harvesters: "'Whose girl is this?'" However, in 3:9 on the occasion of the nocturnal encounter at the threshing floor, he asks: "'Who are you?'" Ruth has her own identity.

The structure of chaps. 2 and 3 indicates that the women continue to initiate the actions. Thus Boaz, when he does intervene, is responding to their initiatives. In 2:1-2 and 3:1-5 Naomi and Ruth plan the day's activities. At the end in 2:18-22 and 3:16-18 the two women discuss the results of their plan. In between (2:3-17 and 3:6-15) Ruth executes the plan. The central action is framed by the opening and closing conversation of the women.

The women are the catalysts for divine intervention. Reacting to the limitations of patriarchal society, they shock, provoke, and intimidate. In 2:2 Ruth announces her intention to go gleaning in a field belonging to a person in whose eyes she can find favor. 2:10 reports that she has accomplished just that. Indeed, her ingenuity triggers Boaz's recognition of her qualities, i.e., her devotion to her mother-in-law (2:11).

Ruth challenges Boaz to make good his blessing. In 2:12 he prayed that Ruth might receive a full reward from Yahweh under whose wings (*kᵉnāpaim*) she sought refuge. In the nocturnal encounter in 3:9 Ruth asks Boaz to spread his wing (*kānāp*), i.e., the corner of his cloak, over her. Boaz is thereby challenged to make good his prayer by marrying her.

In 3:4 Naomi assures Ruth that Boaz will tell her what to do at the threshing floor. In 3:16 Ruth reports to Naomi all that Boaz has done for her. Ironically it is Ruth who has done everything for Boaz. Ruth is clearly in charge.

In the litigation at the city gate in 4:1-12 males determine the fates of females, although females have been the catalyst throughout. In 4:10 Boaz takes Ruth as his wife with the intention of raising up a family for Mahlon. In the prayer of the elders in 4:11 ("'May the Lord make this wife come into your house like Rachel and Leah . . .'") the task of the women is to provide children for the men.

In P. Trible's study, however, the women's celebration at the birth of Obed is a corrective and an indication that the women are the leaders, not the men. In 4:17 the women maintain that a son has been born to Naomi, not Mahlon. In their opinion Obed restores life to an old but courageous woman rather than a name to her deceased. As for Ruth, the women announce that for Naomi she is worth more than seven sons. In the birth of the child the women of Bethlehem offer the needed corrective to the decidedly male proceedings.

In Ruth the emergence of the leader(s) is initially gradual, as in Esther. The women take over only at the death of the men and then provoke the other men to react. Such a manner of leadership is much more subtle than that used in Judith.

BANQUETING AND EMPOWERING/DISEMPOWERING

S. B. Berg has pointed out the centrality of banqueting and empowering/disempowering in the Book of Esther. Banquets become the setting for the rise and fall of the principal characters. To sit down to eat and drink is to put oneself in the occasion of promotion or demise.

The Book of Esther opens with Ahasuerus' two banquets: the first for his officials which lasts no less than 180 days (1:3-4), the second for all the people in Susa which lasts seven days (1:5). The text also mentions that Vashti hosts a separate banquet for the women (1:9).

The disempowering takes place when Vashti refuses to appear and be a sex object, although presumably asked to appear in full regal attire (1:12). It is not without significance that Ahasuerus was feeling merry when he issued the command (1:10). Vashti's demise thus prepares the way for Esther's climb to fame and fortune. When Esther wins the beauty contest (2:16-17), the king reacts by hosting a great banquet in honor of Esther. Thus Vashti's refusal anticipated Esther's success. Whereas Vashti declined to wear the royal crown at the banquet (1:12), Esther complies (2:17). In C. A. Moore's translation the king grants a holiday on this occasion and also gives gifts. Liberation is synonymous with holidays and gift-giving.

Banqueting is also a fitting way to celebrate the annihilation of a people. According to 3:15 both Ahasuerus and Haman feast on the occasion of the decision to exterminate the Jews. While the leading politicos celebrate, Susa is thrown into confusion.

In chaps. 5 and 6 Esther matches Ahasuerus' two banquets. For the first Ahasuerus is asked to bring Haman along (5:4-6). For the second both Ahasuerus and Haman come as somewhat coequal guests. The enjoyable atmosphere of the first banquet dissipates as the showdown between Esther and Haman approaches at the second. Just as the king's second banquet proved to be the undoing of Vashti, so Esther's second banquet proves to be the undoing of Haman. Liberation begins with the disempowering of Haman. It should be noted that in both the deposing of Vashti (2:1) and the deposing of Haman (7:10) the king's anger abated. Esther, therefore, provides liberation by playing the part of the hostess. In this way she can offset the machinations of her guest Haman.

The Book of Judith also employs the banqueting motif. In 1:16 Nebuchadnezzar and his army rest and feast for 120 days after the death of Arphaxad and the fall of Ecbatana. In 6:21 Uzziah treated the Ammonite Achior and the elders to a banquet. However, the joy of the celebration was interrupted by the presence of the Assyrian threat. Holofernes' banquet on the fourth day (12:10) is also concerned with empowering/disempowering.

The banquet is intended to be a victory celebration, viz., Holofernes' conquest of Judith. However, just as the banquets in Esther led to the demise of Vashti and Haman, so too the banquet in Judith results in the demise of Holofernes and the Assyrians. The banquet is a life and death struggle. It connotes life for Judith/Israel but death for Holofernes/Assyria. T. Craven notes Judith's ironic remark to Holofernes: "'I will gladly drink, my lord, for at no time since I was born have I ever enjoyed life as much as I do today'" (12:18). Not unlike Ahasuerus, Holofernes is in his cups. Indeed this was the greatest quantity of wine he had ever drunk on a single day in his life (12:20).

Judith provokes liberation by playing the part of the guest. In this way she can undo the evil planned by Holofernes. As compared with Esther, Judith is a much more violent character. Though both Esther and Judith betray feminine delicacy, Judith manifests a decidedly different brand of such delicacy.

Although less exuberant than the Books of Esther and Judith, the Book of Ruth also develops eating and drinking and empowering/ disempowering. 3:2 notes that Boaz will be winnowing at the threshing floor and 3:3 adds that he will be eating and drinking. Only after Boaz has eaten and drunk and his heart is merry (3:7), is Ruth to approach Boaz and thus prepare to disempower him. The conquest of the future husband takes place in the aftermath of celebration. The feast thus empowers Ruth and to that extent disempowers Boaz. Unlike the Books of Esther and Judith, the Book of Ruth does not envision the death of the guest/host. Liberation consists in fostering life but life wherein the obligations of covenant must be carried out. Although neither hostess nor guest, Ruth employs the disempowering dimension of celebrations to advantage. In this way she resembles her two sisters.

THE SEXUAL ELEMENT

The sexual element is not in and for itself. Rather, it is subsumed under the larger category of the liberation in question. It serves in different ways to help resolve the problems faced by the women.

In introducing Esther for the first time, the author states that she is both beautifully formed and lovely to behold (2:7). It is significant that only Esther and Vashti are described as beautiful. All the other maidens are simply pleasant to look at. The author also indicates that the wait was worth it. According to 1:3 and 2:16 the process of testing virgins took four years. In order to cater to the sexual preferences of Ahasuerus, a twelve-month beauty treatment is required: six months with oil of myrrh and another six months with balsalm and other cosmetics (2:12). To be sure, the entire process betrays an exotic atmosphere. For example, in the Song of Songs

1:13 the beloved wears a pouch of myrrh while the lover rests between her breasts. In Prv 7:17 the adulteress sprinkles her bed with myrrh and other spices.

The popular etymology of Esther may also be significant here. As C. A. Moore suggests, for the audience her name may have suggested the goddess Ishtar. Hence she would be seen as a counterpart to her cousin Marduk/Mordecai. In any event, one is not surprised when in 2:17 Esther has won the heart of the king.

At the conclusion of Esther's second banquet Ahasuerus concludes that Haman's intentions toward his queen are less than honorable. Haman's position on Esther's couch is in the judgment of Ahasuerus an attempt to violate Esther (8:8). However, the position is more indicative of his dire request for leniency, since only Esther could save him.

In Esther, therefore, the sexual element is concentrated on the period of harem preparation where Esther enjoys the expertise of the officials of the harem. This sexual dimension thus prepares for her position as queen. After that the beauty of the queen is not emphasized in the task of empowering Mordecai and disempowering Haman. The sexual element is the catalyst for achieving political power which in turn enhances the good both of Jews and of the Persian Empire.

The sexual element is most pronounced in the Book of Judith. Like Esther, Judith is beautifully formed and lovely to behold (8:7). In 8:4 the author states that her mourning for Manasseh lasted forty months. While this underlines Judith's piety, it also suggests in W. Shumaker's view that a longer period of time might diminish her beauty and make her less appealing to Holofernes.

In her prayer in chap. 9 Judith cites the rape of Dinah in Genesis 34. In 9:8 she adds that the Assyrians are now bent upon defiling the sanctuary and polluting the tabernacle. Just as Shechem raped a virgin, Assyria now threatens a widow, Israel/Judith. In the same prayer the words "sword" (9:2) and "bed" (9:3) anticipate chap. 13 where Judith will use Holofernes' sword against him as he lies in a drunken stupor in his bed. The possible attack on Judith symbolizes the possible attack on Israel.

In 10:3-4 there is the move from the prayer room to the beauty parlor. The scene relates the following activities: undressing, a beauty bath, perfumes, hair styling, a new hat, a dress from her married days (see 16:8), attractive footwear (see 16:9), as well as jewelry for ankles, arms, fingers, and ears. It is indeed something of an understatement when the author records rather naively in 10:4: "Thus she made herself very beautiful."

Both L. Alonso Schökel and W. H. Peterson have commented

that the trek from Bethulia to the Assyrian camp is nothing less than a beauty pageant. In 10:4 the author observes that Judith's rediscovered beauty is designed to entice the eyes of the men. When Uzziah and the two elders meet the transformed widow in 10:7, they are utterly astounded. In 10:14 the Assyrian sentries are also overtaken by her beauty and no less than a hundred of them provide an escort and conduct her to Holofernes' tent (10:17). Judith's arrival is nothing less than the breakdown of military discipline in the Assyrian camp (10:18-19). Finally in 10:23 Holofernes and his servants also marvel at the beauty of her face. There is no doubt that Judith's beauty, *the* weapon of the female warrior, will undo the world's greatest army.

According to A. Dundes there may be sexual imagery in the description of the entrance to Bethulia. According to 4:7 this entrance is narrow, yet Holofernes is bent upon penetrating the city. In turn, Judith's whole strategy is to ward off such penetration. Ultimately Judith's sexual appeal will overcome her opponent so that, when he does try to penetrate, he will be killed in the process.

In chap. 12 Judith manages to restrain the sexually aroused Holofernes for three days. Obviously her ploy is to make him more vulnerable. Earlier in 2:21 there was also mention of three days. Prior to devastating and plundering, there was a three-day march. I. Kikawada thinks the author is perhaps suggesting that Judith may be able to counteract Holofernes' devastation and plundering on the fourth day.

In preparation for the banquet the female warrior resorts to her arsenal: a party dress and cosmetics. At this point the author combines food, furniture, and violation (see 2 Sm 13:7-14). There is mention of the soft fleece on which Judith reclines while eating. The author next mentions that Holofernes is passionate; in fact he has merely been biding his time until the right moment for seduction arrives (12:16). With regard to the furniture, Judith receives all of it as war trophies from the plundering Israelites (15:11). In 16:19 she dedicates the canopy from Holofernes' bedroom to the Lord in Jerusalem. The setting of violation eventually becomes an ornament for the Lord.

In Judith the sexual element is so pronounced that it is *the* military weapon. Whereas Esther's beauty leads to her position as queen, Judith's beauty leads to her position as the seemingly vulnerable guest of the sexually aroused Holofernes.

In the Book of Ruth, Naomi's ploy in matchmaking also involves a sexual element. To capture Boaz, she recommends: grooming, perfumes, and wardrobe (3:3). Naomi further suggests that Ruth uncover his legs (3:4). E. Campbell raises the question whether the storyteller means to be ambiguous and hence provocative. He concludes that he does. The ambiguity of "legs" makes the reader wonder just how much of the legs.

E. Campbell points out other double meanings in the situation at the threshing floor. In 3:9 Ruth instructs Boaz to spread his *kānāp*, i.e., cloak, over her. A comparison with Ez 16:8, where Yahweh spreads his *kānāp* over Jerusalem to cover her nakedness and then marries her, more than suggests that Ruth is proposing marriage. The use of the verb "to lie down" (*šākab*) no less than eight times (3:4, 7, 8, 13, 14) contributes to the sexual atmosphere. While the verb "to know" (*yāda'*) has a considerably wide range including covenantal knowledge (2:1; 3:2), ordinary observation (3:4, 11), and awareness (3:18), the author may be hinting at its sexual connotation. Thus in 3:3 Naomi instructs Ruth not to make herself known until the proper time and in 3:14 it is not to become public knowledge that a woman came to the threshing floor at night.

Finally in 4:13 the women's tactics achieve success. The encounter at the threshing floor has led to marriage and marriage has led to almost immediate conception. Here the author remarks: "The Lord enabled her to conceive."

In Ruth the sexual element is more spontaneous than in Esther. However, it is not as pronounced or as flaunted as in Judith. In Ruth the sexual element is calculated to achieve recognition of the obligations of covenant.

COMMUNAL CONCERN

In the Book of Esther the author raises the question: what does it mean to be Jewish? In answer to that question S. B. Berg notes that the author suggests avoiding two extremes: (1) concern for the state but without Jewish solidarity; and (2) Jewish solidarity but without concern for the state. Esther and Mordecai become his models of communal concern.

Mordecai's initial advice to his cousin is to have her conceal her Jewish identity (2:10). However, with the promulgation of the decree against the Jews Esther is now bidden to intercede on behalf of her people (4:8). Mordecai also adds that her presence in the palace will afford her no special protection (4:13). However, he coyly implies that Esther has come to the throne at precisely this moment to provide for the needs of her people. According to 4:16 Esther like Mordecai is willing to accept the consequences of her action. The author implies that civil disobedience (appearing before the king unsummoned) is now in keeping with Jewish solidarity. However, though this solidarity comes first, it also fulfills the best interests of the Persian Empire.

In chap. 7 Esther intercedes on behalf of the Jews at the second banquet. She points out that the destruction of the Jews is diametrically opposed to the best interests of the state (7:4). At the same time she identifies her personal fate with that of her people: "'. . . I ask that my life be spared, and I beg that you spare the lives of my people. For my people and I have been delivered to destruction . . .'" (7:3-4).

Esther's success is measured not only by the execution of Haman (7:10) but also by the recognition that Haman, the enemy of the Jews, is also the enemy of the state (8:7). In undoing the decree against the Jews, Esther again identifies in terms of her people: "'For how can I witness the evil that is to befall my people, and how can I behold the destruction of my race?'" (8:6). After writing the second decree, Esther continues her efforts on behalf of her people. In 9:13 she pleads for the extension of the defensive war in Susa and is once again successful. All of these feats demonstrate not only her leadership ability but also her sense of communal commitment. In the task of liberation she is dedicated to her people's cause yet in such a way that the good of the Persian Empire is promoted.

Against the background of the Maccabean wars (second century B.C.) one does not expect the audience of Judith to support and promote Assyria. Indeed Judith stresses the uniqueness of the Jews (see the false charge in Est 3:8). The Gentiles are willing to renounce their gods, accepting Nebuchadnezzar in their place, and to send their forces to fight with Holofernes (2:28-3:8). Only the Jews are different by opposing the Assyrian war machine (4:1-13). Thus Bethulia is the symbol of resistance to the coalition of pagan nations under Holofernes.

The author establishes Judith's dedication to the common cause by rooting her in Israel's history. Judith has the longest genealogy of any woman in the Bible (8:1). In her meeting with Uzziah and the two elders she emphasizes that nothing less than the honor of the country is at stake (8:21-23). She goes on to suggest resistance that will surely serve as an example for fellow Jews. Judith is the embodiment of Israel.

While praying prior to the decapitation of Holofernes, she sees her action as bound up with the cause of her people: "'. . . now is the time for aiding *your* heritage and for carrying out *my* design to shatter the enemies who have risen against us'" (13:5). Judith's blow is Israel's blow.

In chap. 15 the Jewish success is a national effort (see 15:3-7). The distances mentioned in 15:5 support this contention. Hence Bethulia has not won a great victory, Israel has. Fittingly in the same chapter Judith is not respected as merely the leading widow in Bethulia. Rather, she is Jerusalem's exaltation, Israel's glory, and the nation's pride (15:9).

In the canticle of chap. 16 "'a song to *my* God'" (16:1) is a song to Israel's God. When "'he snatched me from the hands of my persecutors,'" (16:2) he snatched Israel. Judith's feat is the nation's accomplishment. The conclusion of the book anchors Judith in Israel's history. According to 16:25 no one dared to disturb the Israelites for a long time. Judith continued to live because Israel continued to live.

In the task of liberation Judith envisions the annihilation of the enemy. Unlike Esther, she cannot envision a dual nationalism. In Judith to opt for Yahweh is to destroy the enemy.

Whereas both Esther and Judith clearly identify in terms of the common good, one hesitates to say the same about Ruth. In Ruth the apparently "small" events of family life do not have the epic character of Esther and Judith. However, because of the obvious covenantal concern of Ruth the liberation undertaken by the two women may be more revolutionary than the liberation achieved by Esther and Judith. Ruth and her mother-in-law are catalysts for instigating covenantal responsibility. In their patriarchal society they are concerned with provoking Boaz to live out the consequences of covenant. Ruth demonstrates the revolutionary meaning of covenant. Israel's covenant relationship with Yahweh is only viable when the disenfranchised are provided for. The honor of the nation is reflected in honoring the legally helpless. To disregard the implications of covenant implies a greater threat than a Persian pogrom or an Assyrian attack.

The later hand responsible for appending the genealogy in 4:18-22 may have thought along the same lines. Though the story comes to its natural conclusion in 4:17 and hence makes the genealogy appear anticlimactic, larger concerns seem to have predominated. While this later hand anchors David more securely in the history of his people, he may also suggest the implications of covenantal living. If Ruth and Naomi had not cajoled Boaz into making good his prayer for Ruth's welfare (2:12), then David would never have been born. The seemingly individual concern of Ruth and Naomi is, after all, a communal concern.

THE CHALLENGE OF PARADIGM/PARADIGMS

With whom shall we identify? The answer obviously depends on a variety of circumstances. There is no one paradigm for all times. What are the possibilities or what are the paradigms? This biblical reflection suggests that there are at least three significantly different paradigms for the tedious task of human liberation.

In Esther exploitation appears in the form of laws that cannot be changed. Hand in hand with such irrevocability goes the abuse of power and authority. In such circumstances civil disobedience is the only proper response. The lament shows that humans must assume positions of leadership. There can be no retreat to the sanctuary since humans can and must determine their own world. In terms of the necessary leadership one need not look for already proven leaders. In the given situation awareness can bring about the gradual awakening of assuming key positions in the community. Sexual gifts, while they can be the occasion for obtaining a key position, need not be used in the actual accomplishment of one's role. Finally allegiance need not be split. Awareness of the religious community comes first but need not exclude concern for the civil community. It is possible to have dual citizenship. Delicacy, not annihilation, is the modus agendi.

In Judith exploitation takes the form of a new deity or idol. The anti-Yahweh must be overcome. In this task one cannot determine parameters for God to act. Counteracting exploitation must leave room for God's freedom. God must respond to the public outcry. The people's problem must become God's problem. At the same time certain individuals must assume responsibility together with God. In this undertaking born leaders, those already tried and tested, must come forward. Lack of credentials is no handicap. Powerlessness is God's most potent weapon. Warriors can come forward from the most unassuming quarters. However, no half-hearted efforts can be tolerated: there must be total destruction of the enemy. Even as a guest, one can be and is expected to employ violence. In terms of sexual qualities they must be exploited to the full since they are the weapons par excellence. This follows from total dedication to the cause. Capitulation of any kind is impossible.

In Ruth exploitation/oppression occurs in the seemingly trivial events of everyday life. One must have the ability to cling and not give up. Lack of covenant response must be seen as the greatest evil. Public outcry exposes such an evil. However, without disparaging God, humans must make every effort themselves to attack the problem. If the usual leaders in society are non-existent or not functioning, other leaders must be found. Such leaders must initiate the required action and be catalysts for human responsibility. They must shock, provoke, intimidate in order to make covenantal promises covenantal realities. In the very midst of celebration or in its aftermath they must seek to disempower. As for sexual qualities, these may be employed to bring about a world of covenantal awareness. While not *the* weapon, they are significant. The society these leaders seek to create is one of covenant living. Concern, even when it seems to be individual, must have communal contours. Even the most private actions have public and hence communal impact.

Response to the Word of God in community demands that Esther, Judith, and Ruth be read in a fresh way in the modern community. Which paradigm to choose is an understandable question. But not to choose any paradigm or combination of paradigms is unforgivable. To be human means to be engaged in human liberation, and to be engaged in human liberation is to have a paradigm or paradigms.

BIBLIOGRAPHICAL SUGGESTIONS

Alonso Schökel, Luis. "Narrative Structures in the Book of Judith," *Protocol Series of the Colloquies of the Center for Hermeneutical Studies in Hellenistic and Modern Culture* 11 (1975) 1-20. This volume also contains the responses and reactions to this paper in the presentations of R. B. Coote, A. Dundes, I. Kikawada, W. H. Peterson, and W. Shumaker.

Anderson, Bernhard W. "The Place of the Book of Esther in the Christian Bible," *Journal of Religion* 30 (1950) 32-43.

Berg, Sandra B. *The Book of Esther: Motifs, Themes, and Structures.* SBLDS. Missoula: Scholars Press, 1979.

Campbell, Edward F., Jr. "The Hebrew Short Story: A Study of Ruth," *A Light unto My Path. Old Testament Studies in Honor of Jacob M. Myers.* Gettysburg Theological Studies. Edited by H. N. Bream et al. Philadelphia: Temple University Press, 1974, 83-101.

_____ . *Ruth.* AB. Garden City: Doubleday, 1976.

Clines, David J. A. *I, He, We, and They. A Literary Approach to Isaiah 53.* JSOT Supplement Series. Sheffield: University of Sheffield Press, 1976.

Craghan, John F. *Esther, Judith, Tobit, Jonah, Ruth.* Old Testament Message. Wilmington: Michael Glazier, 1982, 3-126, 197-226.

Craven, Toni. "Artistry and Faith in the Book of Judith," *Semeia* 8 (1977) 75-101.

Daube, David. *The Exodus Pattern in the Bible.* All Souls Studies. London: Faber & Faber, 1963.

Gordis, Robert. "Love, Marriage, and Business in the Book of Ruth: A Chapter in Hebrew Customary Law," *A Light unto My Path,* 241-264.

_____ . "Studies in the Esther Narrative," *JBL* 95 (1976) 43-58.

Haag, Ernst. "Die besondere literarische Art des Buches Judith und seine theologische Bedeutung," *Trierer Theologische Zeitschrift* 71 (1962) 288-301.

_____ . *Studien zum Buche Judith.* Trierer Theologische Studien. Trier: Paulinus, 1963.

Hals, Ronald M. *The Theology of the Book of Ruth.* Facet Books—Biblical Series. Philadelphia: Fortress, 1969.

Humphreys, W. Lee. "A Life-Style for Diaspora: A Study of the Tales of Esther and Daniel," *JBL* 92 (1973) 211-223.

Jones, B. W. "Two Misconceptions about the Book of Esther," *CBQ* 39 (1977) 171-181.

Lindbeck, George A. "Theological Revolutions and the Present Crisis," *TD* 23 (1975) 308-319.

Moore, Carey A. *Esther*. AB. Garden City: Doubleday, 1971.

_____ . "Archaeology and the Book of Esther," *BA* 38 (1975) 62-79.

Rowley, Harold H. "The Marriage of Ruth," *The Servant of the Lord and Other Essays*. 2nd edition. Oxford: Blackwell, 1965, 171-194.

Sasson, Jack M. *Ruth. A New Translation with a Philological Commentary and a Formalist-Folklorist Interpretation*. Baltimore: The Johns Hopkins University Press, 1979.

Sheehan, John F. X. "The Word of God as Myth: The Book of Ruth," *The Word in the World. Essays in Honor of Frederick L. Moriarty, S.J.* Edited by R. J. Clifford & G. W. MacRae. Cambridge: Weston College Press, 1973, 35-46.

Skehan, Patrick. "The Hand of Judith," *CBQ* 25 (1963) 94-109.

Talmon, S. "'Wisdom' in the Book of Esther," *VT* 13 (1963) 419-455.

Trible, Phyllis, "Two Women in a Man's World: A Reading of the Book of Ruth," *Soundings* 59 (1976) 251-279.

_____ . "A Human Comedy," *God and the Rhetoric of Sexuality*. Overtures to Biblical Theology. Philadelphia: Fortress, 1978, 166-199.

Zenger, Erich. "Der Juditroman als Traditionsmodell des Jahweglaubens," *Trierer Theologische Zeitschrift* 83 (1974) 65-80.

CHAPTER 20

The Invitation to
The Song of Songs

Biblical passages to be read: the Song of Songs.

SEXUAL EXPERIENCE AND THEOLOGY

Theology and sex are not odd bedfellows. Theology does not focus on souls but on persons and indeed in a given time and place. Theology seeks to interpret persons and their experiences in a covenant setting: God, the community, and the individual. Theology does not discount any realm of human experience. Theology demands that we regard our total person and our total experience as worthy of the human-divine dialogue known as covenant.

In the area of sexuality, however, border theology was rampant to a large extent. Such theology determined with the most meticulous precision that point where the covenant relationship would be jeopardized. Too often it concentrated on acts and not the human qualities involved in those acts. It was too negative. It stressed what was not to be done. It did not emphasize sufficiently what was to be done. In his study on Christian tradition and human sexuality, J. Blenkinsopp suggests that a positive interpretation of sexual experience is essential. Such a positive interpretation is to provide answers to these questions: (1) can the Christian accept his or her sexuality openly and without guilt or fear? and (2) can the Christian integrate his or her sexuality into a total vision of faith?

This positive interpretation must deal with the meaning of love. Since the word "eros" is wanting in both the New Testament and the Greek translation of the Old Testament, it has become commonplace to insist that Christian love must be "agape"—it must be divorced from longing and desire. However, in ancient Greek thought

213

eros did not necessarily mean passionate sexual love violating the limits of reason. As J. Blenkinsopp points out, for the ancient Greeks eros was also the impulse that moves one to go beyond oneself. For Plato it is the search for wholeness that unites both reason and passion. In P. Tillich's view human sexuality can be a powerful form of creative eros—an eros that impels one away from isolationism and non-identity into a world of union with another, not pleasure acquired through another.

The Song of Songs (a Hebrew way of saying the greatest song) is that biblical book which presents eros as a positive dimension in the covenant relationship. In this book eros becomes a transforming power that looks to loving and, therefore, to living. Response to the Word of God in community must come to grips with the Song if it is going to provide a positive interpretation of human sexuality. The Song challenges us to appreciate human sexuality as another gift from the Creator, a gift that necessarily evokes the chant of Genesis 1: "It is good, very good!"

THE HISTORY OF INTERPRETATION

If the Song of Songs (also called the Canticle of Canticles) were not part of the Bible, there would be no hesitation to label it love poetry. A glance at the history of interpretation, especially the allegorical school, indicates a certain reluctance to accept human love as a fit candidate for inclusion in the Bible. It is an instructive example of a negative response to the Word of God in community.

According to the *allegorical* school (supported by both the Jewish and Christian communities) the Song is an extended metaphor of the relationship between Yahweh and Israel or Christ and the church. Thus "I sought him but did not find him" (3:1) refers to the wilderness experience of the Israelites. "His left hand is under my head and his right arm embraces me" (2:6) meant for the third century scholar Origen the Church's desire for Christ. The difficulty with the allegorical school is that the text does not provide the necessary clues for identifying scenes and characters and then foisting a new interpretation on them. For some members of this school human sexual erotic love must be expurgated to give way to a non-physical divine love.

According to the *cultic* school the Song represents the myth of the dying and rising god. The profusion of allusions to flowers and spices, the erotic images, and the hide-and-seek game are alleged to support this position. However, the Song never mentions the divine name. The allusions, erotic images, and hide-and-seek game find an easier explanation in love poetry.

According to the *dramatic* school the Song is a play with plot and characters: either two principals (Solomon and a rustic maiden) or three principals (addition of the maiden's country lover). However, in the Song there is no evidence of plot development. The division of scenes is, moreover, too subjective.

According to the *literal* school the Song is a collection of love lyrics expressing the joy, ecstasy, and frustration of human love. J. B. White has shown that the most striking extrabiblical parallels come from Egypt of 1350-1150 B.C., a period associated with a new sense of freedom. This Egyptian love poetry uses "sister" for the beloved and "brother" for the lover. It also delights in the world of make-believe, exotic gardens, and intimacy—a world akin to that of the Song. It is this love poetry interpretation that is the most plausible approach to the Song. It provides elements for a positive interpretation of human sexuality.

BODINESS

Both 4:1-7 and 7:2-7 are descriptive songs, i.e., they extol the physical beauty of either the beloved or the lover. In 4:1-7 the lover looks directly at the beloved and observes her physical attributes in a descending order, viz., from her eyes to her breasts. Her streaming hair is jet black like the goats of Palestine: "Your hair is like a flock of goats streaming down the mountains of Gilead" (4:1). Her teeth are white and her lips bright like scarlet (4:2-3). Her breasts resemble two fawns—they are youthful and symmetrical (4:5). The lover proposes to go to the mountain of myrrh and the hill of incense (4:6) —embracing the beloved is tantamount to entering the wonderland of aromatic spices. The concluding verse is almost anticlimactic: "You are all-beautiful, my beloved, and there is no blemish in you" (4:7).

The most sensuous descriptive song is clearly 7:2-7. The lover's accolades proceed in an ascending order, viz., from her feet to her hair. She is an agile and skillful dancer (see 7:1): "How beautiful are your feet in sandals . . . your rounded thighs are like jewels . . ." (7:2). Her vulva ("navel") is a round bowl which is not wanting the mixed wine connected with love-making (7:3; see 5:1). Her neck is elegant and stately: "Your neck is like a tower of ivory" (7:5) while her eyes reveal the sparkle of pools of water: "Your eyes are like the pools in Heshbon . . ." (7:5). The lover, described as a king, is infatuated by her hair: "a king is held captive in its tresses" (7:6). This descriptive song concludes, as it began (7:2), with the accent on the beauty of the beloved: "How beautiful you are, how pleasing, my love, my delight!" (7:7).

In the admiration song of 5:10-16 it is the beloved's turn to laud the lover. An admiration song often concentrates on the apparel and adornments of the one admired but always expresses the effect on the viewer. Here the beloved announces that her lover is radiant and ruddy, standing out among thousands (5:10). Many of his attributes are like the statue seen by Nebuchadnezzar in Dn 2:32-33: a head of pure gold (5:11), arms of rods of gold (5:14), loins ("body") of ivory (5:14), legs of marble columns resting on gold bases (5:15). He grooms his beard properly with oil: "His cheeks are like beds of spice with ripening aromatic herbs" (5:13). The beloved also observes the effects of the sense of smell: "His lips are red blossoms; they drip choice myrrh" (5:13). The beloved's concluding remark is an apt answer to the daughters' (the third party in the Song who develop the action by raising questions and making objections) question about the uniqueness of the lover (5:9). "Such is my lover, and such my friend, O daughters of Jerusalem" (5:16).

SPONTANEITY

Love must follow its own schedule; it cannot be constrained to react automatically. This characteristic of human love is not unlike the statement in Qoh 3:5: "a time to embrace, and a time to be far from embraces." Human love is thus a spontaneous response, not a mechanically induced condition in optimum circumstances.

In 2:4-5 the beloved sings of her yearning for the lover. In 2:6-7 she gives expression to the realization of that yearning: "His left hand is under my head and his right arm embraces me" (2:6). She next feels compelled to make the daughters swear an oath, an oath that smacks of the world of nature (by gazelles and hinds of the field). The matter of the oath is the timetable of love, a timetable dictated by nature, not provoked by mechanical means: "Do not arouse, do not stir up love before its own time" (2:7). The significance of such spontaneity is enhanced by the repetition of this phrase in the Song (see 3:5; 8:4). Love that is genuinely human is genuinely spontaneous.

LONGING

Hide-and-seek is a typically human expression of the longing experienced by lovers. In the poem of 3:1-4 the verb "to seek" is used four times while the verb "to find" is likewise employed four times (see 1:7-8). "On my bed at night I sought him" (3:1) gives the impression of a dream with its concomitant anxieties and frustrations. In this dream the beloved searches frantically in the city for her lover. She approaches the watchmen or police as they carry out their traditional office of safeguarding the city (see Ps 127:1; Is 21:11-12): "The watchmen came upon me, as they made their rounds of the city: Have you seen him whom my heart loves?" The fourfold use of "him whom my heart loves" in the poem underlines the beloved's frustration and subsequent release of tension. This release of tension occurs almost immediately after her conversation with the police: "I had hardly left them when I found him whom my heart loves" (3:4). At this point the beloved refuses to let her lover go. She is intent upon bringing him to a place of security, viz., her mother's home (3:4; see 8:2).

In 5:2-6a the beloved relates what appears to be another dream. She is asleep but hears a knocking at the door. It is her lover who is soaked to the skin and asks to be let in: "'Open to me, my sister, my beloved, my dove, my perfect one!'" (5:2). She teases him by remarking that she has taken off her robe and bathed her feet (5:3). M. Pope observes that this is an example of the locked out lover, an experience that lives on in such songs as "Who's that knocking at my door?" The scene has sexual overtones. "To bathe one's feet" is a euphemism for sexual intercourse (see 2 Sm 11:8-11) and "hand" is also a euphemism for the phallus (see Is 57:8). "My lover put his hand through the opening; my heart (i.e., the insides) trembled within me . . . I rose to open to my lover, with my hands dripping myrrh . . ." (5:4-5).

Continuing her dream in 5:6b-7, she recounts that she no sooner opened up to him than he vanished as quickly as he arrived. In her dismay she calls to him but he does not reply. Once again she encounters the police but this time they assault her, possibly thinking that she is a prostitute. She next has recourse to the daughters, earnestly beseeching them to communicate this message to the lover, if they find him: "What shall you tell him?—that I am faint with love" (5:8). It is obvious that only one thing will relieve her anxiety, viz., the presence of her lover.

FIDELITY

The poem in 1:5-6 is a self-description, i.e., a poem emphasizing one's charms and qualities in the event of a challenge or boast. Here the daughters criticize her for her dark complexion. She replies that she is admittedly dark, as dark as the goat-hair used by the Bedouin for their tents: "I am as dark—but lovely, O daughters of Jerusalem—as the tents of Kedar, as the curtains of Salma" (1:5). She protests, however, that her brothers are the cause, viz., they have made her the caretaker in the vineyards and thus exposed her to the sun. Since "vineyard, field," etc., are often sexual symbols, the beloved's statement in 1:6 ("my own vineyard I have not cared for") may imply that she has not protected her chastity.

The development in 6:1-3, however, supports the exclusiveness of the couple's love. In reply to the daughters' question about the whereabouts of the lover (6:1), the beloved responds that he has come down to his garden, i.e., herself (see 4:12, 16; 5:1) and is gathering lilies. Awareness of the lover's whereabouts then prompts this expression of mutual fidelity: "My beloved belongs to me and I to him . . ." (6:3). To limit their affection to each other is to solidify their love. But to admit a third party would only lead to a weakening of that mutual bond (see Prv 5:15-20).

The expression of faithfulness in 7:11 is particularly significant in view of the garden account in Genesis 3. In 7:11 the beloved proclaims: "I belong to my lover and for me he yearns." In Gn 3:16 the woman receives the following as part of her punishment: "'Yet your urge (= "yearning" in the Song) shall be for your husband and he shall be your master.'" The woman of Genesis 3 will not possess her husband, rather she will be possessed (see Gn 4:7). Thus the covenant bond of husband and wife in Gn 2:20b, 23a, 24 has been attacked since the woman is no longer the complementary-supplementary partner to her husband. In the Song, however, harmony has been restored. The lover's yearning/urge for the beloved is balanced by the beloved's statement: "I belong to my lover" (7:11).

The classical expression of fidelity is 8:6-7. In this song of yearning the beloved asks the lover: "Set me as a seal on your heart, as a seal on your arm . . ." (8:6). In the ancient Near East the seal was considered one of a person's most highly prized possessions since it served as a signature or form of identification. A person could wear the cylinder seal on a chain or cord and hence close to the heart (see Gn 38:18). One could also wear the seal as a ring, the so-called signet ring (see Gn 41:42). Some prophetic texts show that the king's signet ring connoted importance and election (see Jer 22:24; Hg 2:23).

The beloved then compares love to Sheol, the nether world: "For strong as death is love, relentless as the nether world is devotion . . ." (8:6). The nether world was reputed to have a violent hold on people (see Hos 13:14). It was a place that used cords and snares (see Ps 116:3) as well as bars (see Jon 2:7) to exercise its violent rule over all its inhabitants. Human love/passion (rather than NAB's "devotion"—see Prv 14:30; Ez 5:13) is made of such tenacity.

The beloved next speaks of fire and water: "its flames are a blazing fire. Deep waters cannot quench love, nor floods sweep it away" (8:6-7). Since it is possible to translate the first phrase as "its flames are darts of fire," there may be a reference here to Cupid's arrows. The word translated "dart" is the Canaanite god Reshep who is associated with destruction (war, pestilence, death) and love/fertility. Love/passion is, therefore, a power that exerts an enormous claim on the couple. The other image—deep water and floods—is also applied to Sheol. It is the deep par excellence (see 2 Sm 22:6, 16a,

218

17 = Ps 18:6, 16a, 17). However, not even the mighty waters of the underworld can extinguish true love and sweep it away.

The remainder of 8:7 is probably a prose addition to the Song: "Were one to offer all he owns to purchase love, he would be roundly mocked." Love is not a commodity to be bought and sold in the marketplace. Genuine human love cannot be manipulated and so reduced to the category of thing. Such love is always a deeply personal exchange which demands generous self-giving partners.

UNION

In 2:4-5, a song of yearning, the lover brings his beloved to "the house of wine" ("banquet hall" in NAB) for purposes of love making. The scene is similar to 1:4 where the beloved is anxious to enter the lover's chambers. In 2:5, however, the beloved cries out that she needs proper nourishment for this scene: "Strengthen me with raisin cakes, refresh me with apples, for I am faint with love." Prophetic texts connect raisin cakes with the Canaanite fertility rite (see Jer 7:18; Hos 3:1). The Book of Jeremiah adds that these cakes were actually shaped in the form of the goddess, the Queen of heaven (see Jer 44:19). The appropriate cure for the beloved's lovesickness is threefold: the house of wine, the lover's intentions, and the nourishment afforded by raisin cakes and apples. The last named are, therefore, stimulants that will help the beloved in her forthcoming intimacies. Such intimacies find expression in 2:6: "His left hand is under my head and his right arm embraces me." The lovesickness has been cured!

In 7:8-10a the lover employs an admiration song that expresses his deep desire for physical union with the beloved. He compares her figure to a palm tree, alluding to the date palm which flourishes in the Near East (see Dt 34:3; Jgs 3:13). Her breasts are like two clusters of dates on the tree: "Your very figure is like a palm tree, your breasts are like clusters" (7:8). He then vents his yearning for union: "I said, I will climb the palm tree, I will take hold of its branches" (7:9). He picks out three areas of her body, anticipating reactions that will correspond to the texture, scent, and taste of apples and grapes: "Now let your breasts be like clusters of the vine and the fragrance of your breath like apples, and your mouth like excellent wine . . ." (7:9-10). Only union will satisfy the passionate longing of the lover.

JOY AND THE BEAUTY OF NATURE

In 2:8-10 the couple prepares for a tryst in the spring. In 2:9 the lover invites his beloved to come away. He observes that death has given way to life, that winter has now ceded to spring. The heavy seasonal rains which last from December to March are at an end:

219

"For see, the winter is past, the rains are over and gone" (2:11). However, the lover is not content with such a lapidary statement. He goes on to note five changes in the world of nature that capture the atmosphere of joy and satisfaction. With the passing of the rains there is a profusion of flowers: "The flowers appear on the earth" (2:12). There is also pruning time (see Is 18:5): "the time of pruning the vines has come" (2:12). The turtledove has returned and has resumed its cooing: "and the song of the dove is heard in our land" (2:12). The fig tree commences its budding: "The fig tree puts forth its figs" (2:13). And finally the vine exudes its fragrance: "and the vines, in bloom, give forth fragrance" (2:13). It is only fitting that, given this lush spring scene, the lover will repeat his request to his beloved: "Arise, my beloved, my beautiful one, and come!" (2:13).

In 4:9-10a the lover chants an admiration song that announces the effect the beloved has on him. The Hebrew text of 4:13 suggests that the beloved is a conduit supplying water (see Neh 3:15) and thus providing pomegranates and choice fruits. In 4:14 there is a profusion of condiments (saffron), aromatic spices (nard cane ["calamus" in NAB], cinnamon, myrrh, aloes) and frankincense. According to Prv 7:17 the adulterous woman sprinkles her bed with myrrh, aloes, and cinnamon. In 4:16a the lover completes his admiration song with the request that the north wind and the south wind waft the fragrance of such a garden: "Arise, north wind! Come, south wind! blow upon my garden that its perfumes may spread abroad."

THE THEOLOGY OF THE SONG

The Song endorses the acceptance of human sexuality openly and without fear or guilt. At the same time the Song insists on the integration of human sexuality into a total vision of faith. It is a vision of faith that demands the following acknowledgements: God is the author of human love, of human sexual love, of human sexual erotic love. In this regard it is useful to observe that the Song never mentions the divine name (8:6 is debatable). However, the God of Israel permeates the entire piece. Unlike her neighbors, Israel did not believe in a god or goddess of love. Instead, Israel saw herself as part of the plan of creation wherein the human couple is the paradigm of human sexual erotic love.

The Song teaches that human sexuality is part of ongoing creation. Genuine human love is a powerful symbol of the Creator's ongoing concern and presence. This love moves people to flee from themselves and their ego-oriented world to the community of persons where eros is union with another, not pleasure dispensed by another. It is the community that continues to sing the refrain of Genesis 1: "It is good, very good!"

The Song urges a return to the world of Genesis 2 where the woman is the man's complement-supplement, not the world of Genesis 3 where the woman is possessed by the man. The Song reiterates the exclamation of Gn 2:23: "'This one, at last, is bone of my bones and flesh of my flesh . . .'" The Song speaks of a covenant relationship, i.e., a union of persons relating to each other as persons. Although other biblical passages laud the charms of women because they meet the needs of the men (see Prv 5:18-19; 31:10-31; Sir 26:1-18; 36:21-27), the Song refuses to accept such a limited view. Instead, the Song extols the beloved as an individual while not disparaging her value as a partner.

The Song calls for a return to a solid biblical anthropology. In such an anthropology humans are never compartmentalized into two distinctive parts, viz., body and soul. Humans are never merely the sum of their parts. On the contrary, the Song insists that the Creator's spirit affects the entire human person. The human sexuality of the Song reflects an anthropology where the entire person responds to the Creator not only with the ardor of passion but also with the vivacity of faith.

Although the Song is not an allegory, it witnesses to a distinctive aspect of human love, viz., its ability to reflect divine love. Genuine human love is always a movement outward, a movement towards meeting the needs of another. Genuine human love is thus covenantal and consequently a reflection of Israel's God. We humans begin to glimpse the deep love of our God for us when we experience the deep love of another person. To know human love is to begin to appreciate divine love. Response to the Word of God in community must see the powerful drive of human love as a reflection of the insatiable urge of divine love.

BIBLIOGRAPHICAL SUGGESTIONS

Blenkinsopp, Joseph. *Sexuality and the Christian Tradition.* Dayton: Pflaum, 1969.

Craghan, John F. *The Song of Songs and the Book of Wisdom.* Old Testament Reading Guide. Collegeville: The Liturgical Press, 1979, 3-41.

Exum, J. Cheryl. "A Literary and Structural Analysis of the Song of Songs," *ZAW* 85 (1973) 47-79.

Gollwitzer, Helmut. *Song of Love. A Biblical Understanding of Sex.* Philadelphia: Fortress, 1979.

Gordis, Robert. *The Song of Songs and Lamentations.* Revised and augmented edition. New York: Ktav, 1974.

Landy, Francis. "The Song of Songs and the Garden of Eden," *JBL* 98 (1979) 513-528.

——————. "Beauty and the Enigma: An Inquiry into Some Interrelated Episodes of the Song of Songs," *JSOT* 17 (June, 1980) 55-106.

Murphy, Roland E. "Form-Critical Studies in the Song of Songs," *Int* 27 (1973) 413–422.

_____ . "Song of Songs," *IDBSup*, 836–839.

_____ . "Towards a Commentary on the Song of Songs," *CBQ* 39 (1977) 482–496.

_____ . "Interpreting the Song of Songs," *BTB* 9 (1979) 99–105.

_____ . "A Biblical Model of Human Intimacy: The Song of Songs," *Concilium* 121 (1979) 61–66.

_____ . "The Unity of the Song of Songs," *VT* 29 (1979) 436–443.

Phipps, William E. "The Sensuousness of Agape," *TToday* 29 (1972-1973) 370–379.

_____ . "The Plight of the Song of Songs," *JAAR* 42 (1974) 82–100.

Pope, Marvin H. *Song of Songs*. AB. Garden City: Doubleday, 1977.

Rylaarsdam, J. Coert. "Song of Songs and Biblical Faith," *Biblical Research* 10 (1965) 7–18.

Sasson, Jack M. "On M. H. Pope's *Song of Songs* (AB 7c)," *Maarav* 1/2 (1978-1979) 177–196.

Schonfield, Hugh J. *The Song of Songs*. New York: New American Library, 1959.

Soulen, Richard N. "The *Wasfs* of the Song of Songs and Hermeneutic," *JBL* 86 (1967) 183–190.

Tillich, Paul. *Love, Power, and Justice. Ontological Analyses and Ethical Applications*. New York: Oxford University Press, 1960.

Trible, Phyllis. "Depatriarchalizing in Biblical Interpretation," *JAAR* 41 (1973) 30–48.

_____ . "Love's Lyrics Redeemed," *God and the Rhetoric of Sexuality*. Overtures to Biblical Theology. Philadelphia: Fortress, 1978, 144–166.

White, John B. *A Study of the Language of Love in the Song of Songs and Ancient Egyptian Poetry*. SBLDS. Missoula: Scholars Press, 1978.

INDEX OF BIBLICAL PASSAGES

224

226

INDEX OF AUTHORS